TERRI LYNE CARRINGTON
LEAH CHASE
KATHLEEN COLLINS
DOROTHY HEIGHT
ANITA HILL
CELIA CRUZ
bell hooks
JUDITH JAMISON
CHARLES DAWSON
DIANE NASH
HANNAH CRAFTS
ROY
DOROTHY DANDRIDGE
IVAN HERNÁNDEZ
ALTHEA GIBSON
DECARAVA
FANNIE LOU HAMER
LENA HORNE
BETHANN HARDISON
BASS REEVES
JACOB LAWRENCE
CANNON
DICK GREGORY
GRACE JONES
AUDRE LORDE
KWAME TURE
BILL T. JONES
JOHN LEWIS
DEE REES
FAITH RINGGOLD
PENNIMAN
EVA JEFFERSON PATERSON
HARRIET POWERS
MINNIE RIPERTON
IDA B. WELLS
ANDRE LEON TALLEY
MARIE
ROBESON
PATRICE RUSHEN
MARY CHURCH TERRELL
SISTER ROSETTA
NINA SIMONE
CARRIE MAE WEEMS
MAURICE WHITE
GEORGE WASHINGTON WILLIAMS
REVERE
CHARLES WHITE
RAVEN WILKINSON
WILLIAMS
BRADFORD YOUNG

ILLUSTRATED BLACK HISTORY

HONORING THE ICONIC AND THE UNSEEN

George McCalman

with April Reynolds

HarperOne
An Imprint of HarperCollins*Publishers*

HarperCollins books may be purchased for educational, business, or sales promotional use. For information, please email the Special Markets Department at SPsales@harpercollins.com.

FIRST EDITION

Designed by George McCalman with Aliena Cameron

Library of Congress Cataloging-in-Publication Data has been applied for.

ISBN 978-0-06-291323-4

22 23 24 25 26   TC   10 9 8 7 6 5 4 3 2 1

To my father, my first soul mate.

To my grandmother, my second.

*To Catherine Janice Holder,
who witnessed it all, lived fully on
her terms, and died in peace.*

I love you, Mom.

TABLE OF CONTENTS

An illustrated guide to our Black history pioneers

TABLE OF CONTENTS

TABLE OF CONTENTS

TABLE OF CONTENTS

TABLE OF CONTENTS

TABLE OF CONTENTS

TABLE OF CONTENTS

TABLE OF CONTENTS

TABLE OF CONTENTS

TABLE OF CONTENTS

TABLE OF CONTENTS

TABLE OF CONTENTS

TABLE OF CONTENTS

ESSAYISTS

ACKNOWLEDGMENTS

This book would not exist without my internal compass: my curiosity, pride, insecurity, spirituality, and doubt. I'm grateful for each of those aspects of my soul. In the external world, I'm grateful to my father for making me who I am. I am devoted to my grandmother Lyris Holder, who taught me everything that is good in me, and made me the storyteller that I am. I love you madly, Grannie. I'm indebted to my mother for giving me the family who taught me everything else about the world. Mom, I'm glad we found each other again. I love you.

I'm grateful to my friends who are my family. My community who has bolstered and supported and loved and grounded and taught and challenged and defined who I am. Thank you.

Thank you to Marian and Llane for being the church that feeds my soul. Let us pray. To Leonard, for being my first husband. To Kari, for being the priestess. To Rachel, for keeping our marriage strong. To Moira, for coming and going and coming back. To Pookie, for being there when you were there. To Kelly, for just being there. To Georgia, for sharing so much of this experience with me. To Brodie, for being my soul mate. To Memsor, for being my brother. To James and Roderick, for everything.

Thank you to Miriam Allen and Jen Hewett for illuminating my path.

Gracias to La Norma for ushering us into the universe of Mexico City. You have no idea.

Thank you to Hagwa for just knowing.

Thank you to Aunt Jeanette, Uncle Errington, and cousin Christine for their unconditional love.

ACKNOWLEDGMENTS

A special thank-you to my incredible cousins Fayola, Nigel, Terel, Adanna, Nyasha, Lee, and Malacai for their love and for welcoming me home.

Thank you to Aunt Elsa and Uncle Terrence for creating a home to lay down my burdens. I am so grateful.

Thank you to Aunt Fay. You are incredible.

A deep thank-you to Nancy for seeing the ephemeral truth in between life and death.

A note of gratitude to Leigh, Isaak, Daniel, and Maurice for facilitating my somatic evolution. Thank you to David for the lessons.

I'm grateful to Peter for reminding me of my worth.

I'm grateful to John for being my dedicated family. I love you.

I'm grateful to Nathaniel for just loving me.

A special and personal and eternal thank-you to Rose Wanjugu. You saw this before I did.

My deepest love and appreciation to the Black Brunch Club. The pioneering people who have kept me in San Francisco. This human resource has grounded me and given me wings. Thank you, Zana.

Thank you to the East Bay Ladies, my literary wives: Jan, Lisa, and Rachel. Thank you for always keeping it real.

Thank you to the Dinner Club, in all of its joyful incarnations. Thank you to Christo and Brenda for being my family.

Thank you to my IBH Board of Directors: Shakirah, Oriana, Sean, June, Rose, Melonie, Melorra, Kim, Jen, George.

Thank you to my IBH White Board: Brodie, Georgia, and Rachel.

To Aliena, for being my hands and being so curious about the world.

To April, for being a true collaborator in all forms.

To Kate, for being my unwavering advocate.

To the power, force, fury, grace, and history of being Black.

INTRODUCTION

I had a curiosity. This project was born out of an interest in a series of separate things that overlapped. The past and the present. My internal and external self. My understanding of my soul through a connection with my community. I was curious about knowing Black history better than I already did, and I was also curious to see if I was an artist.

I had never allowed myself to explore two things in counterpoise like that, and I reached a juncture in my life to inquire: If not now, when? I had the novel idea of doing a daily challenge and painting a Black history pioneer every day for a month, choosing the shortest month of the year. A simple yet ambitious idea, which bloomed out of my professional experience as an art director tethered to my personal interest in identity. I had assigned lots of art to many artists over many years, and I knew that people worked well within parameters. So I gave myself some terms. I decided I was going to research, write, and paint one pioneer a day. It seemed achievable, it seemed attainable, it was just brazen enough, and it also gave me some room to observe my own process and work out my nerves.

I limited the framework of the original series to black-and-white portraits. I knew that my inclination to think expansively about color would paralyze my momentum (so many colors!) and sabotage my enthusiasm. That limitation forced me to see beyond the words of my research and focus on intangibles like line quality, composition, emotion, and the personality of the person I was rendering. I needed to meet my subjects where they were. To see the hardships and sacrifices, but also hear the laughter, feel the inner definition of self-reliance. I spent a lot of time communing with the people I was researching, so by the time my paintbrush hit the paper for each one, I had a lived-in sense of who this person might have been as an individual. And I trusted my perceptions.

I found I was approaching each portrait differently, requiring a variety of tools. Sometimes I used acrylics, sometimes watercolors. Sometimes pen and ink, sometimes colored pencil. Along the way, I got to know the body language of Edna Lewis, the matriarch of southern American cuisine. The quiet resolve of revolutionary activist Amy Ashwood Garvey. The searching, curious eyes of Alain LeRoy Locke, progenitor of the Harlem Renaissance. I was basically starting from scratch each day. That realization was an epiphany. And parallel to that enlightenment, I recognized that that was how I was going to approach Black history. That is how I was going to climb that mountain. From the beginning again. This giant, impenetrable thing. I had to tease, massage, and release my unformed notions and become a student. Throw down my defenses and learn. Yet as I started doing more portraits, I began to be more afraid, not less. I was terrified the first week, and then the second, and then I was terrified the third week, and I didn't stop being terrified until I had finished twenty-nine portraits, twenty-nine days later. (It was a leap year.)

I need to be awkwardly honest: there was no historical anchoring in my initial exercise. There was no organized rigor. At first. I just went by feeling. I was looking around on the internet, inside various digital cubbyholes of information. When I did a search for, say, James

Baldwin, Langston Hughes would pop up. That would lead to another person, and perhaps to another hidden accomplishment, which in turn led to pockets of history that I had never realized or recognized. It felt as if I were in truly uncharted territory, had reached the edge of space and found out that there was a whole other universe beyond that. And it made me hungry to discover more. Because I didn't know enough to structure my approach from a historical lens, that approach was too intimidating. But that is also not who I am. I would have found that way impenetrable. I just wanted to give in: I wanted to trust my feelings, wanted to find the luminaries who wanted me to find them.

"Black history" tends to mean the ten people who are lauded during every Black History Month of every Black History Year. I absorbed some of those individual histories in elementary school, some of them in college. I didn't go to a historically Black university; I attended a liberal arts institution (which is an oxymoron, yes?). When I thought of it occasionally, I was embarrassed to admit that I didn't know enough American history. And I always *did* see it as American history. I never saw it as just Black history. I saw it that way because I am an immigrant. I exist outside the *outside* of Black and American history. I am a voyeur. I see the intersections and the wide-open spaces. It always incensed me that the Black community wasn't seen as part of American history, not in a meaningful way. Meaningful to *us*, sure. And yet that dichotomy was also exactly what the country was about. That's what America was: separate. Two halves of a whole. And with every person I found and researched, I was angered as to how this country could fail to celebrate the bounty these pioneers had brought to everyone's life. A whole in two halves.

I thought of the movements they had started, the techniques they had invented, the culture they had defined, the science they had created, the policies they had imbued. And then I began to get intimidated, again, because all that accomplishment *is* intimidating. At that point, I was thinking of doing a book on Black history. Illustrated Black history. I thought, "Who am I to be shepherding this idea?" Who am I? I knew I was not the first Black human to consider this. A contemporary book that was beautiful and accessible and a gift that anyone could buy for anyone else, a volume that wasn't layered in all the history of an academic book, yet not just a children's book either. Something to share. A simple and ambitious idea.

The process of making this book has scared me because it invites a critique of how I view people who are both well and not well known: the pillars of our community. This book is presented entirely through my perspective; it is very internal and very personal. And yet I'm creating it in a *communal* way for my community. I'm saying, "Here's a way for you, the reader, to engage in your relationship with Black history too." I'm suggesting that you can also get to know our pioneers. And it doesn't have to be intimidating. And it doesn't have to be just heavy. Because the history is daunting, is intense, is haunted. But you know, one of the things that I also learned in doing this project is that there's a false perception that we don't know our own history—we as Black people. I have always rejected that. We have our ways of carrying history. We carry it in our bodies—we carry that trauma, we carry that collective ideal. We carry the language of dance and culture and human expression. We've passed it down effortlessly to each other, attached to our DNA. We know pain. We know hardship. We know

resistance. We know all these things that are active with words in our culture today. We've carried our history the whole time. We know how hard it's been. And while we Black people may not always know the dates, the times, or who said what to whom, such details aren't the only way to learn history. In *carrying* history, we have internalized it, learned from it. We live our history on a daily basis. We've learned a lot of lessons that we couldn't have learned from history books. So while something like this book in your hands is a glorious thing, I don't want to minimize how intuitive we are, as a Black community, and how attentive we are to our own history.

For a year I toiled with a feeling of guilt that I was getting an opportunity that other people had been denied. A rolling internal dialogue ensued. I was told repeatedly by people who loved me that it was my responsibility to get my head out of my ass; I just had to get going and *do* the book. It was more important that I do it, even in an imperfect way, they said, than that I get it exactly right. Isn't that the definition of pioneering? What I was doing was long past due, I was told, but when you're a pioneer, as all these titans were and are, there's no road map. There's no architecture. There's no railroad. They made it up. Many of them sacrificed their lives or livelihoods or forfeited their homes and sanctuaries. Like them, I just had to do it; I had a *requirement* to do it. That message began shifting my relationship with this book and my relationship with Black history yet again. It made me curious, and a little less prideful at wanting to get it "right"; I concluded that it was more important for me to place my full heart and soul into this project and simply focus on honoring the people who had defined American history. We are the bedrock of this country. And so, just accepting my own entitlement feels good. It is an entitlement that feels earned.

I started illustrating as a boy to understand the world. I make art as an adult to understand human identity. I try to understand my surroundings; I try to understand my community by documenting what I see. I document body language, I document exuberance, I document pain. I draw like a reporter because I *am* a reporter. I've always been. I study and I reflect and I take information, try to understand it, and then reflect it back out. I'm always curious about humans. I don't have a utopian view of humanity. But I'm not cynical about it either. I think there's a real beauty and a real uniqueness about us as humans. Our ability to convey our feelings to each other is what separates us from every other creature on the planet. We are different and distinct from the rest of the natural world in that way. And our ability to share how we make each other feel and how we impact each other is what has created our entire human existence. As a result of those feelings and impacts, and their communication, we rise and we fall, and we rise and we fall. Then again. And that is what continues. We have language with which we can communicate—words, yes, but also silence language, and body language, and sexual language, and imagery. And all of it contributes. And that feels like alchemy.

It seems to me that artists are the magicians of our planet. We make somethings out of nothings. Making this book has reignited my joy in the deeper discovery of the hope in Black history. I'm grateful that I get to make things out of my emotional awareness tethered to the stories of our complicated and divine history. If that isn't magic, I don't know what is.

KAREEM ABDUL-JABBAR

(1947–PRESENT)

"One man can be a crucial ingredient on a team, but one man cannot make a team."

During his esteemed basketball career, Kareem Abdul-Jabbar became an all-time lead scorer on the Los Angeles Lakers' 1980s team as its star seven-foot-two center. But his greatness isn't articulated solely by his winning Rookie of the Year, being a six-time Most Valuable Player, making All-Star nineteen times, playing on six championship teams, and boasting eight playoff records. In 1989, when Abdul-Jabbar retired at forty-two years of age, no other NBA player had scored more, blocked more, won more MVP awards, played in more All-Star games, or logged more seasons. His athleticism is undisputed, but it's his character off court that truly defines his contributions.

From his earliest days as a student athlete at UCLA, Abdul-Jabbar has taken great pride in consistently using his position as a platform to speak up about social justice issues. For him, the game was a job—one he was exceptional at, certainly. But the real work of being someone who looks out for others demanded more of him. And he has taken that task seriously.

After Martin Luther King Jr. was assassinated in 1968, Abdul-Jabbar joined protests at UCLA; he had been recruited to play ball there in 1965 for legendary coach John Wooden. (He played then under his given name, Lewis Alcindor Jr. It was not until 1971 that he converted to Islam and changed his name.) Abdul-Jabbar dismissed advice that he should avoid political matters to ensure a profitable career in the NBA. "To me there was no correlation," he said decades later in an interview with NPR. "Somebody needed to speak out about what had happened."

Growing up in Harlem, Abdul-Jabbar had worked as a novice journalist in connection with the Harlem Youth Action Project, where he encountered King at a news conference in 1964 and was inspired by the leader's commitment to nonviolent protest. A few years later, he watched his friend Muhammad Ali refuse induction into the US army as a conscientious objector to the war in Vietnam, which resulted in his being blocked from boxing competition in the prime of his career. From that example, Abdul-Jabbar understood that his life as an athlete put him in a unique position. He had won a public platform and needed to use it.

Throughout his adult life, Abdul-Jabbar has stood up for his Muslim faith, courageously denouncing acts of violence made in the name of Islam while refusing to overlook commentary that conflates the religion and the violence. He continues to write opinion pieces and essays placing current events in the context of civil rights struggles.

In addition to publishing his autobiography in 1983, he has written over a dozen books, including several that focus on the achievements of Black Americans—among them, *On the Shoulders of Giants: My Journey Through the Harlem Renaissance* and *Black Profiles in Courage: A Legacy of African-American Achievement* (with Alan Steinberg)—and a mystery series, *Mycroft Holmes*, centered on Sherlock Holmes's older brother (with Anna Waterhouse). In 2016, Barack Obama awarded Abdul-Jabbar the highest civilian honor, the Presidential Medal of Freedom, in recognition of his positive impact on society.

CATO ALEXANDER

(1780–1858)

"Who has not heard of Cato Alexander!? Not to know Cato's is not to know the world."

—William Dunlap, from "A Scene at Cato's" by playwright, author, and actor William Dunlap (1766–1839)

In the early nineteenth century, the hottest place to get a drink in New York City was Cato's Tavern, run by a South Carolina transplant, Cato Alexander. His watering hole, founded in 1810, was on the road leading into the municipal center, around what is now Fifty-Fourth Street and Second Avenue. Alexander was famous for making boozy mint juleps and punches—*so* famous that he even received mention in the news media and a midcentury play. He also invented the word *cocktail*.

Alexander's early days are unclear, but it appears he was one of many Black people to gain freedom as a result of New York State's 1799 Act for the Gradual Abolition of Slavery. Known for his culinary skills and beverage service, Alexander offered patrons okra soup, terrapin stew, curried oysters, roasted game, and beverages such as milk punch, eggnog, and brandy cocktails. He managed to stay in business for forty-eight years.

He lost his business for dramatic and tragic reasons. Alexander was apparently known to make loans to patrons that went unrepaid. It's hard to imagine how, if asked for an extension by a white man, an amiable Black host and restaurateur like Alexander could repeatedly say no and not worry about the implications. Those implications caught up with him one night. In January 1831, two broth-

ers, George and Andrew Luke, led an angry mob to Cato's Tavern. They enlisted the help of a woman who pretended to be sick at Alexander's door. When she "fainted," Alexander let her inside and locked the door behind her, since he was shutting down for the night. But the woman rose from her pretend stupor, unlocked the door, and let the mob in. Alexander and his pregnant wife were attacked. White men armed with chains and homemade weapons tore the tavern apart.

In the months ahead, Alexander put the place back together, but it wasn't quite the same. And once again, his very elite clientele eventually began asking for money. Many of these loans too were never repaid. Life must have been very difficult for him.

Cato Alexander was arguably the first mixologist. He was a superb chef. But in the face of unrelenting racism and the constant threat of violence, this creative mixologist wasn't allowed to thrive. He died broke in 1858. This pioneer did leave a legacy, however. Future generations of mixologists would learn his story, along with those of Tom Bullock and Louis Deal, Jim Cook and Washington Woods—Black bartenders who created the proverbial witch's brew for America's rich and powerful.

Best of all, Cato Alexander is remembered here, and that makes me want to raise a glass.

JOURDON ANDERSON

(1825–1907)

"If you fail to pay us for faithful labours in the past, we can have little faith in your promises in the future."

The circumstances under which a former white slave owner, Colonel P. H. Anderson, wrote a letter to a freed man asking him to return to the Tennessee farm where he'd once been enslaved aren't clear. But when Jourdon Anderson received word of this request in 1865, he responded. His letter's authenticity has been questioned, but historians seem to agree at least that Anderson was a real person. He writes:

Sir:
I got your letter, and was glad to find that you had not forgotten Jourdon, and that you wanted me to come back and live with you again, promising to do better for me than anybody else can. I have often felt uneasy about you. I thought the Yankees would have hung you long before this, for harboring rebs they found at your house. I suppose they never heard about your going to Colonel Martin's to kill the union soldier that was left by his company in their stable. Although you shot at me twice before I left you, I did not want to hear of your being hurt, and am glad you are still living. It would do me good to go back to the dear old home again, and see Miss Mary and Miss Martha and Allen, Esther, Green, and Lee. Give my love to them all, and tell them I hope we will meet in the better world, if not in this. I would have gone back to see you all when I was working in the Nashville hospital, but one of the neighbors told me that Henry intended to shoot me if he ever got a chance. . . .

As to my freedom, which you say I can have, there is nothing to be gained on that score, as I got my free papers in 1864 from the Provost-Marshal-General of the Department of Nashville. . . . We have concluded to test your sincerity by asking you to send us our wages for the time we served you. This will make us forget and forgive old scores, and rely on your justice and friendship in the future. I served you faithfully for thirty-two years, and Mandy twenty years. At twenty-five dollars a month for me, and two dollars a week for Mandy, our earnings would amount to eleven thousand six hundred and eighty dollars. Add to this the interest for the time our wages have been kept back, and deduct what you paid for our clothing, and three doctor's visits to me, and pulling a tooth for Mandy, and the balance will show what we are in justice entitled to. Please send the money by Adams's Express. . . . If you fail to pay us for faithful labours in the past, we can have little faith in your promises in the future. We trust the good Maker has opened your eyes to the wrongs which you and your fathers have done to me and my fathers, in making us toil for you for generations without recompense. . . .

Say howdy to George Carter, and thank him for taking the pistol from you when you were shooting at me.

From your old servant,
Jourdon Anderson

MADELINE ANDERSON

(1923–PRESENT)

"I wanted to . . . teach African Americans what their history was . . . to inspire pride in who we were and are."

"Ever since I was a little girl," says the Black narrator of the 1970 documentary *I Am Somebody*, "I could remember that the tourists would come to Charleston. . . . They would come to see Fort Sumter, where the first shot of the Civil War was fired. And they would come to see our stately, beautiful mansions. And they would come to see all the lovely gardens. But those who came in the spring of 1969 saw Charleston as it really was if you were poor and Black." So begins Madeline Anderson's account of the Black hospital workers' strike that involved four hundred strikers—all but twelve women.

This documentary plainly and poignantly addresses the circumstances of the workers and their fight for fair treatment and equitable pay, citing outright verbal abuse toward Black employees. Anderson shows women dressed in hospital uniforms of the day—white blouses, white skirts, sensible shoes—who, unarmed and quietly picketing, were viciously handled by police. More than one thousand strikers and supporters were jailed. But their efforts were not in vain. Supported by appearances and organizational aid from the Reverend Ralph Abernathy, the civil rights leader and friend of Martin Luther King Jr., and King's widow, Coretta Scott King, the union ultimately won.

Anderson realized that these Black women were confronting the constraints of gender and race that she herself had experienced. She was just the second Black student ever admitted to Millersville State Teacher's College in Pennsylvania, and she was the only Black student there at the time of her attendance. The racism and harassment were so constant that she dropped out after a year. But eventually, she received a partial scholarship at NYU, where she earned a bachelor's degree in psychology. She found work as a freelance editor while trying to break into the film industry. She was faced with a strange catch-22: to get into the industry, she had to be part of a union, but to become part of a union, she had to have a job. Most of the unions were white father-son alliances, leaving no place for a creative Black woman to fit in. This pioneer finally got into New York's editors' union, Local 771. She had threatened to sue the editors' union before they allowed her admittance.

This experience underscored for Anderson that such obstacles are everywhere, and she didn't want to shy away from them. She also sought to show that Black people have always spoken up for themselves.

Anderson is the first Black woman to produce and direct a televised documentary film, *Integration Report 1* (1960), and the first to produce and direct a syndicated series, *Infinity Factory*. She was also the first Black employee at WNET, the public access channel in New York. For a time she produced and directed *Sesame Street*, which inclusively mirrored (and continues to mirror) the lives of children of color. Anderson also helped found the country's first Black-owned public television station, at Howard University.

MAYA ANGELOU

(1928–2014)

"I think we all have empathy. We may not have enough courage to display it."

They say you've lived a good life if you're around long enough to smell the flowers. We all know Maya Angelou. She's a poet. An icon. An auntie. We speak her words without attribution because we speak her poetry when we believe we are grown-ups. "I know why the caged bird sings" is not rarefied speech closeted in her books; it is the shout given in church, or between girlfriends who don't know what else to say. "When people show you who they are, believe them" is a direction on how to survive. In her lifetime, which was decorated with awards and acclaim, this St. Louis–born girl named Marguerite Johnson would be a dancer, actress, composer, film director, playwright, civil rights activist, editor, and professor. But her greatest feat was that she managed to do what most Black folks could not: Maya Angelou got to sit down and survey the world she shaped; she got to smell the flowers. With breathtaking consistency, in book after book, poem after poem, speech after speech, Angelou found ways to resuscitate the heartbeat of language. Her tongue is Black, feminine, American. Her poetry is aspirational, inspirational. Black or white, if you are of a certain age, you remember when you first heard Maya Angelou's poetry. For me, it was during Clinton's inauguration. My eleventh-grade teacher rolled out the television. In the middle of a winter day, there was Maya Angelou. Her words sang hope and caution. All these years later, Black folk know we say her words whenever we want to be wise.

The facing illustrated portrait captures this Black poet at the tail end of her life—the Oprah years. Oprah told the world what some of us already knew: Maya Angelou was brilliant. And Angelou was probably startled to hear that, because she was used to people not recognizing her beauty, her grace, her strength. Her words carried her singular style, clear and alive with imagery, physicality, and a deep love of sound. This seminal woman knew herself, knew the world, and broke conventions left, right, and center. She lived a lifetime of exhausting change. But in that moment when I captured her image, she was getting to relax just a little bit. Her gaze was settled on other Black artists confirming their brilliance. That is the ultimate fruit of Angelou's labor: by the time she passed away, she knew she was not alone. Her poetry had inspired and fed generations. Oprah lavished praise, and it was deserved. Maya Angelou got to hear the world's applause. She knew that at every Juneteenth and Fourth of July, and at some point during Black History Month, some young child dressed in Sunday's best would stand before grandmothers and uncles who looked on with clasped hands. There's that young child, brave and trembling, reciting Angelou's words as if they were his or her own, because they are.

AMY ASHWOOD GARVEY

(1897–1969)

"A nation without great women is a nation frolicking in peril. Let us go forward and lift the degradations which rest on the Negro woman."

What it means to be Black has inspired exploration and activism for hundreds of years. During the nineteenth and early twentieth centuries, Black-led movements were driven by figures such as W. E. B. Du Bois, who founded the NAACP in 1909; Martin Delany, co-publisher with Frederick Douglass of the *North Star*, an antislavery newspaper; and Alexander Crummell, founder of the American Negro Academy, an organization of Black intellectuals.

Women have not often been credited for their efforts in the founding of these historic movements. The first Pan-African Conference, held in London in 1900, featured only six women from the United States and Europe. There should have been more. Women's voices shaped these institutions. Marcus Garvey is credited as the founder of the Universal Negro Improvement Association (UNIA), which grew to become the preeminent Pan-Africanist organization of the twentieth century, mobilizing Black people from its home base in Harlem, New York. But Amy Ashwood Garvey, later to become Garvey's wife in 1919, described herself as a co-founder when the organization launched in 1914 in their native Jamaica.

The UNIA, inspired in part by Booker T. Washington's notions of self-reliance, focused on Black-owned businesses. Its members included everyday people throughout the United States, the Caribbean, and other countries. It featured dedicated groups for women, including the Black Cross Nurses, largely credited to Ashwood Garvey, who founded UNIA's international newspaper, *Negro World*. Bonded by their shared political beliefs, the Garveys married in 1919, but the relationship is believed to have been brief; Garvey sought an annulment soon after. (Historians sometimes refer to Amy Ashwood as "the first Mrs. Garvey," because Marcus later married Amy Jacques.)

Ashwood Garvey's activism continued. She helped found the Nigerian Progress Union in the 1920s and helped establish the African Service Bureau in the 1930s. She traveled widely. A collection of her photography, taken between the 1930s and the 1950s in West Africa, is housed at Duke University. The pictures feature political figures and academics, including one of Liberian president William Tubman, with whom she had a relationship.

Ashwood Garvey used her platform to champion decolonization and Black women's unity. In an address at the fifth Pan-African Congress in 1945, she said: "Very much has been written and spoken on the Negro, but for some reason very little has been said about the Black woman. She has been shunted to the background to be a child-bearer." Ashwood Garvey tirelessly advocated for Black women. As a result, Black women the world over now demand the right to contribute to their nations' political discourse.

AUGUSTA BRAXTON BAKER

(1911–1998)

"Folklore makes one aware of the brotherhood of man."

Augusta Braxton Baker understood the power of children's books, which stoke the imagination and help shape the emotional intelligence and critical thinking of young readers. When Baker began her role as a New York Public Library (NYPL) children's librarian in 1937 and observed the absence of books on the shelves that accurately reflected the lives of Black children, she made it her mission to correct the insufficient narrative.

Not only did Baker source books that conveyed positive role models for Black children, she also removed books that depicted harmful images and story lines—stories that spoke of Black people as uneducated and lazy and images that portrayed offensive physical distortions, playing off centuries-old stereotypes rooted in the dehumanizing of Africans in order to justify slavery. She was based at the NYPL's 135th Street Harlem Branch—today named the Countee Cullen Branch.

A Baltimore native, Baker earned her bachelor's degree in education from New York College for Teachers (now SUNY Albany) in 1933. She remained there and received her bachelor's in library science in 1934, the first Black person to earn that degree. As she continued her career with the NYPL, she worked as an assistant coordinator and storytelling specialist. In 1961 Baker became the NYPL's children's services coordinator, which required that she oversee all branches of the city's children's library system (more than eighty locations), but she never lost her love of connecting to children's stories and the kids themselves. The 1946 book *My Dog Rinty* is a sweet story of a Harlem boy and his dog. In the book, the boy hears a story by the storyteller librarian in his neighborhood—that woman is actually Baker. She retired from the NYPL in 1974, after thirty-seven years.

Baker went on to consult for *Sesame Street*, the inclusive public access children's TV show. She later became the University of South Carolina's storyteller-in-residence at the College of Library and Information Science in Columbia. In 1986, the college helped to form an annual storytelling celebration in her honor. Baker gifted to the university her fifteen-hundred-volume collection of children's books, one of the most diverse groupings of children's books of the mid-twentieth century.

Though she died in 1998, her work inspired a young girl decades later. In 2015, at the age of ten, Marley Dias noticed that the books in her fifth-grade class were mostly about white boys and their pets. She began an initiative to collect a thousand books in which Black girls were the main characters. She soon got up to twelve thousand and inspired thousands of kids and their families to pursue the reading, buying, and sharing of diverse children's literature. In an interview with CBS, a young Dias cited Baker as an unsung hero of the literary world: "I wasn't alive when she was alive, but I know I follow in her footsteps."

JAMES BALDWIN

(1924–1987)

"Great art can only be created out of love."

James Baldwin was an accomplished writer, lecturer, and activist. But he was also a gay man. That fact isn't shocking, but I've been thinking about it a lot lately. How that shaped his personal and professional life, and how my homosexuality shapes my own life. One of the reasons why Baldwin is my hero is that he placed himself inside experiences he was not asked to join. I admire that, I love that, because that's a really hard thing to do. Most people aren't brave enough to attempt such a thing. He was a person who loved his people while fully aware of their bias against homosexuality. In Black communities, we tsk tsk and suck teeth about homosexuality. To this day, the Black community still doesn't talk about Baldwin's gayness; we talk about how brilliant he was, how brave. But by not talking about his homosexuality, we neuter this pioneer. That is an uncomfortable truth. And Baldwin knew more than a thing or two about uncomfortable truths.

But you know, I've always felt that James Baldwin's gayness was his superpower. It allowed him to frequently shatter his community's discomfort with a single glance and verbally tie in knots racist blowhards like William F. Buckley without breaking a sweat. Being gay was one of the reasons James Baldwin could look at the world with such piercing insight. He knew what he was talking about because he belonged to both communities, while simultaneously belonging to neither. He was an outlier. Baldwin was intimately aware of his people's discomfort about his homosexuality, but he also knew the intricacies of their generosity and their longing for justice. Toward

the end of his life, Baldwin was interviewed by Ken Burns, the legendary documentarian, about the Statue of Liberty. Few knew that originally the Statue of Liberty was built to celebrate Black people's liberation from enslavement. Baldwin was asked a philosophical question: "What is liberty?" His answer—musing, brief, and devastating—is filled with weariness. Your heart clinches when you listen to his critique of America and its dreaming, of Black folk's pursuit of happiness—it is a bitter joke for us. That deep knowledge was part of his gay superpower, comforting the discomforted while still pursuing the truth.

Like all superpowers, Baldwin's gayness came at a cost. There was a deep sadness in James Baldwin, a rarely mentioned loneliness. But his answer to the question "What is liberty?" tells the tale. How many times can you be asked to remind the world of its better self? Baldwin verbally leaped tall buildings with a single bound, but toward the end of his life, you could hear his voice giving out. Throughout his lifetime, Baldwin not only brilliantly told the woes of racism and how it affects and infects our society; he patiently gave his readers and audiences the road map for how to walk out of that darkness. It is little wonder how tired Baldwin seemed in his interview with Ken Burns. He kept telling all of us what we had done and what we could do about it. Most of us failed to listen. I wonder if Baldwin asked himself how often he could love a place, a person, a community with all his heart, only to be by turn blatantly or subtly cast aside. At the end of your life, do you still wear the cape announcing your superpower? Do you still want to? As a gay man, I know what that feeling is. It's often said that Black creativity is birthed from a place of lack. The scraps of this, the edges of that, the denial of entry, the lack of money and means—these are the starting places of most Black artistry. Think of soul food or jazz. Baldwin embraced the pointed expulsion of what it means to be a Black gay man, and with sass and charm, by leaps and bounds, he entered rooms, salons, assemblies that very much wanted to deny him entry.

Celebrating Baldwin and the other pioneers in this book shouldn't be just a reverence fest, and yet I can't contain my praise. This man, who managed to make himself comfortable in a world that was inclined to chafe at his gay presence, stood up and spoke out and gave advice to Malcolm and Martin and all the giants. Marvel at that. Please. That's why Baldwin is one of my heroes. My load is lighter as an out Black gay man because he charted a path for me. When you're an outsider everywhere, it gives you a unique perspective. You're *in* the world but not allowed to be *of* the world, and this isolation gave Baldwin's thoughts and words clarity. One thing that people always say about Baldwin is that he was one of the most lucid speakers on race of anyone from that period. There's a reason for that. He wore the skin of a Black man, but he was also outside of that experience because he was a gay man. Baldwin's life gives us a fascinating look into a certain kind of intersectionality. Baldwin knew the church; he was an active participant in civil rights. But he was also a man on the run, and thus different from a gay icon like Bayard Rustin, who was in the same relationship for thirty-odd years. Baldwin had a series of failed relationships. He even had relationships with white men who didn't understand him, while he was fighting white people and their racism.

In 2020 I spoke on a panel at the Swiss Consulate in San Francisco about the screening of *I Am Not Your Negro*, a documentary that does a really great job of distilling how James Baldwin became who he was by leaving the United States. His travels gave him some room and space to grow creatively; he discovered European racism and saw how different it was from American racism. One of the Swiss historians who was a participant on that panel was talking about a town in Switzerland where Baldwin and his boyfriend had spent some time. The historian delightfully recounted the numerous occasions when Baldwin had found himself surrounded by townspeople who peppered him with questions about race and being Black. And I listened on, thinking, "That man must have been exhausted!" I imagined him being bone-tired of having to live with that all the time. And on top of all that, he was also openly gay? I can't imagine the burden on this generous man.

And all the while, he charmed. We should never forget that. He charmed the upper echelon of the Black civil rights movement. That's not something a person can pull off any old Tuesday. That's some *Ocean's Eleven* finesse.

Another thing I love about James Baldwin is that he totally debunked academic superiority. People don't tend to highlight the fact that Baldwin didn't attend Harvard or Yale or any Ivy League school; he wasn't a professor either. He couldn't throw those accolades around, but nonetheless he was in the intellectual stratosphere. He made sense of the Black experience in a way that few have managed. He refused to shy away from all our mess, hatred, selfishness. Rather, he peered analytically into all our problems. He told us the truth even when we didn't want to hear it. Up, up in the sky is James Baldwin, leaping over towering lies in a single bound. For Black gay men like me, he showed us how to stitch our own capes.

EDWARD BANNISTER

(1828–1901)

"Whatever may be my success as an artist is due more to inherited potential than to instruction."

Nearly ten million visitors trekked to the Centennial Exhibition in Philadelphia in 1876, marking the one-hundredth anniversary of American independence. The international gathering featured vendors from more than thirty countries, who came to sell both luxury and everyday goods. The scope of the event, which took place at Fairmount Park on almost three hundred acres in two hundred buildings from May to November that year, was massive. President Ulysses Grant was among the attendees, who were introduced to new foods, inventions, performances, and art.

One painting in particular received great attention: *Under the Oaks*, a landscape piece created by the artist Edward Bannister, originally from New Brunswick, Canada, who had launched his painting career in Boston. The painting was awarded the first-prize medal. Upon realizing that Bannister was a Black man, the white judges unsuccessfully sought to reconsider their decision. It's believed that other white competitors supported the judges' initial vote. Still, the painting seems to have disappeared.

Bannister was born to a Barbadian father in Canada. His mother's racial identity is not documented, but she reportedly supported her son's early interest in the arts. After both his parents died, he was taken in by a white family before he took jobs on ships, working as a cook and porter. Upon his return to North America around 1848, he settled in Boston, where he was able to enroll in art classes at the Lowell Institute and painted at the Boston Studio Building. This startlingly intelligent artist was inspired by authors such as Spenser, Virgil, Ruskin, and Tennyson. He later moved to Providence, Rhode Island, with his wife, Christiana, of the Narragansett nation. In 1867 he saw an article in the *New York Herald* claiming that, although Negroes had an appreciation of art, they were "manifestly unable to produce it." Historians believe this slight provoked Bannister to disprove the racist critics.

After receiving the 1876 Centennial prize, he won ongoing commissions that enabled him to paint full-time. To prepare for his oil paintings, he sketched in pencil or watercolors. Bannister was known for his landscapes and seascapes, but he also painted portraits. Using biblical and mythological narratives as inspiration, Bannister created pastoral, peaceful scenes. He created dreamy skies, thick woods, still waters, and tree-lined coasts. One can see his contrast of darks and lights, his delicate use of color to depict shadow and atmosphere, his loose brushwork. Rare for a Black man of the period, he achieved widespread acclaim. He became a founding board member of the Rhode Island School of Design.

JEAN-MICHEL BASQUIAT

(1960–1988)

"I don't listen to what art critics say. I don't know anybody who needs a critic to find out what art is."

By the age of four, Jean-Michel Basquiat had already shown an affinity for drawing. His father, Gérard, a Haitian immigrant from Port-au-Prince, would bring blank paper home from his job at an accounting firm for his son to use for sketching. His mother, Matilde Andrades, a Brooklyn native of Puerto Rican heritage, had an interest in fashion and often drew alongside her son. Matilde took the child to the Brooklyn Museum, the Metropolitan Museum of Art, and the Museum of Modern Art, but he also took inspiration from less exalted sources: he was known to recreate cartoonish images of scenes from his favorite television shows. As a teen, Basquiat landed in Lower Manhattan after a brief stint in Puerto Rico with his father, following his parents' separation. Known for his rebellious spirit, Basquiat would run away for weeks at a time and hang out in the Village dropping acid. As part of a drama theater group, he created a fictional character called SAMO, or "Same Old Shit."

In the 1970s, Basquiat and his partner Al Díaz used the character SAMO as an alter ego to comment on their environment. Graffiti signed by SAMO started to appear along train lines and in various enclaves. Phrases like "9 to 5 Clone" caught people's attention. The graffiti works were known as poetic defacements. By the 1980s the art world took note, and Basquiat began selling his paintings from his apartment.

His work—vivid, loud, with broad strokes and often chaotic undertones—was influenced by graffiti and the street culture surrounding him. Because his pieces were saturated with color, critics sometimes described his work as primitive. But Basquiat's style was intentional, capturing a spontaneity that struck discerning viewers as visceral, timely, and urgent. In a 1984 self-portrait, his head is rendered as lurking on the edge of death or despair. The energy in the eyes, painted a deep red, appears trapped. There is pain present in the image, even as the blue-and-white background suggests that transcendence might soon come.

Basquiat was a student of the moment—in interviews he claimed to be inspired by "real life"—but he also referenced important figures from other rich artistic periods and genres, such as Dizzy Gillespie and Charlie Parker. He died at only twenty-seven years old of a tragic drug overdose. But Basquiat's work continues to offer a rich reserve. Chaédria LaBouvier, the first Black woman to direct a solo exhibition at the Guggenheim, opened "Basquiat's 'Defacement': The Untold Story" in 2019. The show used Basquiat's 1983 painting *The Death of Michael Stewart*, inspired by the death of a young Black man after a mysterious encounter with New York police, as a launchpad to engage with racism in the 1980s and still endured by Black people today.

ROMARE BEARDEN

(1911–1988)

"The artist has to be something like a whale swimming with his mouth wide open, absorbing everything until he has what he really needs."

Using the medium of collage, Romare Bearden was known for blending recycled fabrics, bits of paintings, and magazine clippings to render scenes of Black American life in Harlem, influenced by the southern origins of much of his community. His work suggests nothing so much as jazz on paper, with the swirling of texture, mood, and intensity.

Bearden grew up in New York City, where his family had moved from North Carolina. For some time, he had a studio above the Apollo Theater in Harlem. The jazz and blues that wafted up from below provided more than just atmosphere; they were transformed into his art. In pieces like *Empress of the Blues*, which depicts the blues icon Bessie Smith in front of an orchestra, and *Showtime*, the energy of the bandstand is alive with the rocking and swaying of the musicians. Rich, bold tones convey the urgent mood of a nightclub. Through Bearden's eye, movement is captured by angle and pattern, the repetition of shapes to convey a kind of backbeat, and the guttural feeling that pushes blues singing into its own realm of beautiful agony.

Bearden was educated at the historically Black Lincoln University, Boston University, and New York University. He later attended the Sorbonne in Paris, and he worked as a cartoonist for the *Baltimore Afro-American*. The influence of artists such as Picasso, Cézanne, and Matisse is apparent in his work, as are the African mask and textile inspirations that shaped the work of those European creatives. Like many Black artists of the era, Bearden supported his work by making a living doing something else: he was a social worker in New York City.

I am an artist too, and as such, I approach this pioneer with a unique set of questions. Why collage? Why the bits of this, the scraps of that? Bearden was a student of canonical literature and traditional artistry, but he was also a Black man. I think he fundamentally understood that our way has always been to comprehend traditions and imagine them anew. We can see ourselves in places that make no space for us. This ability is a gift. In America, Black people serve and circle prosperity. This outsiderness both allows Black folks to riff on the conventional and also provides inspirations that are culturally brand new. It is important to remember that Bearden was building collages out of magazine clippings when the medium of collage was new to the scene. His first solo shows were in New York and Washington, DC, and he counted the master composer Duke Ellington as an early patron. His collages are featured in the collections of the Whitney Museum, the Metropolitan Museum of Art, and the Studio Museum of Harlem, among many others. He received the National Medal of Arts in 1987.

1936 BERLIN OLYMPICS ATHLETES

"We all have dreams. But in order to make dreams come into reality, it takes an awful lot of determination, dedication, self-discipline, and effort."
—Jesse Owens

Sometimes the game isn't a plaything. The US Olympic team, consisting of 359 competitors, arrived at the 1936 Berlin Olympic Games in Nazi Germany with eighteen Black athletes. At the time—as well as now—the United States was not living up to its promise of equal opportunity. We are a country that professes that all are created equal, that each and every one of us is allowed to pursue happiness and freedom. But Black people were (and still are) being ruined by the fine print in America's principles. In the early twentieth century, the tyranny of share-cropping forced millions of Black families to toil on farms, forever trapped in debt. Jim Crow laws dictated the segregation of everyday Black life. Despite that context, in 1936 the United States decided we had something to prove. We wanted to show the world that America's democracy was better than the dictatorship of Nazi Germany. And when we decided to engage in this political contest, the United States proved something to itself too: the truth is, when our country needed participants who were the fastest, brightest, and best among us, Black folks were on that Olympic roster.

Most famous among them was Jesse Owens, the dynamic track star who handily won four gold medals. But the other athletes who made the trip joined Owens in a deep commitment to dutifully pursue their sport and represent Black America in defiance of the segregation they suffered at home and the racist beliefs perpetuated by the Nazi regime.

In addition to Owens, the Black athletes comprised fifteen men and two women: Dave Albritton, John Brooks, James Clark, Cornelius Johnson, Willis Johnson, Howell King, James LuValle, Ralph Metcalfe, Art Oliver, Tidye Pickett, Fritz Pollard Jr., Louise Stokes, John Terry, Archie Williams, Jack Wilson, John Woodruff, and Mack Robinson (the older brother of historic baseball player Jackie). Altogether, their stories were the makings of legend. Adolf Hitler reportedly refused to shake the hand of gold medalist Jesse Owens, and when Archie Williams heard of the slight, he replied, "Hitler wouldn't shake my hand either." Woodruff won a gold medal for the 800-meter race despite being handicapped by the slowness of his fellow runners. Because of the rules, he wasn't allowed to break free from the pack, lest he accidently foul one of his fellow runners. So what did he do? "I didn't panic," he said. "I just figured if I had only one opportunity to win, this was it. I've heard people say that I slowed down or almost stopped. I didn't almost stop. I stopped, and everyone else ran around me." Then Woodruff ran around everyone else. And while Ralph Metcalfe won his medals, he couldn't freely enjoy them, because his teammates who were Jewish hadn't been allowed to participate with him in the sprint relay race. Hitler made it clear that Jewish competitors shouldn't participate in celebratory victories. On and on, every win, every gold, silver, and bronze medal had an asterisk of a story, an unexpected tragedy, a triumph that occurred despite the anti-Semitism and racism that surrounded it.

Hitler, in trying to prove white national exceptionalism, revealed the opposite: Johnson won gold for the high jump, and Albritton took silver in the same event. In the 100-meter race, Metcalfe finished one-tenth of a second behind Owens, winning the silver medal. In the 200-meter race, Robinson was four-tenths of a second behind Owens—he took the silver medal. Metcalfe also earned a second medal, taking gold in the 4 × 100-meter relay. (Decades later, he became a US House representative for the state of Illinois.) Despite the historic and patriotic nature of these achievements on the global stage, President Franklin Roosevelt never invited the athletes to the White House or extended a congratulatory communication.

These historic eighteen had more than just their particular events to occupy their minds. Their safety in Nazi Germany was a serious consideration. They endured racism from the team's coaches, their white American teammates, and the global media, which cast doubt on their ability to perform well. The whole ordeal seemed like an insurmountable quest for these young athletes. If they lost, it would lend weight to absurd notions of white superiority. And if they were successful, it could support the idea, perpetuated from the era of enslavement, that Black people were somehow equipped with superhuman athletic prowess.

The athletes' achievements did little against persistent racist beliefs, and their return home wasn't attended with the glory and fanfare they deserved. But they felt they had a responsibility, and they honored it. In 2016, then president Barack Obama heralded the group's achievements at the White House in a ceremony to which surviving family members were invited. He drew a direct link between the contributions of the 1936 Black teammates and the political advocacy of figures like John Carlos and Tommie Smith, who raised Black Power fists during the national anthem on the winner's dais at the 1968 Olympics, and Muhammad Ali, who refused to be drafted during the Vietnam War and was stripped of his heavyweight title as a result. Their grit and achievements show us that mother country and fatherland are not places of respite and home; they are proving grounds. The excellence of the 1936 Berlin Olympics athletes gave Black people a road map.

Fighting for equality in lands both foreign and domestic. Aching for the gold—and thus recognition—that is what we are so often denied. And yet, we excel.

MARY MCLEOD BETHUNE

(1875–1955)

"If we accept and acquiesce in the face of discrimination, we accept the responsibility ourselves. We should, therefore, protest openly everything ... that smacks of discrimination or slander."

Mary McLeod Bethune was a testament to the astonishing leap that can happen for Black people in America. This Black woman was a vital force in the accomplishments of Black educators and women's rights leaders in the twentieth century. She ultimately founded a college dedicated to serving African Americans. She led the National Association of Colored Women's Clubs in 1924 and founded the National Council of Negro Women in 1935. She befriended Eleanor Roosevelt and held the highest role by a Black woman in the federal government when President Franklin Roosevelt appointed her director of Negro Affairs in the National Youth Administration. She was not the daughter of doctors or politicians. Her parents were former slaves. Only in America.

One of seventeen children, Bethune was born ten years after the end of the Civil War near Maysville, South Carolina. She grew up working alongside her family, picking cotton for the same landowner who had once owned her parents. With the aid of a benefactor who helped pay for her education, Bethune graduated from a boarding school in North Carolina in 1894. There's so much of Bethune's life that reminds me of how Black people make a way where there is none. She studied in Chicago to become a missionary but wasn't able to find a church to sponsor her travels, so she returned to South Carolina and began teaching. She married Albertus Bethune,

a fellow educator, but they split in 1904. By then the mother to one son, Bethune founded a boarding school in Florida, the Daytona Beach Literary and Industrial Training School for Negro Girls. As the curriculum expanded, the school became a college and then merged with the Cookman Institute. The resulting institution, Bethune-Cookman College, was opened in 1929.

One of the things that jumps out at me, beyond the number and scope of her accomplishments, is that she managed so much as a single mother. Divorced and raising a child alone was an unenviable position during her time. But nothing deterred her. That she refused to let her ambitions shrink in the face of her circumstances speaks volumes. And she was ambitious for her fellow Blacks too: her mission in life was to pass it on—share the word, share the opportunities, share the power. Bethune opened doors and windows for Black people who had known nothing but struggle before they met her. She pushed for federal antilynching legislation and for a formal end to segregation laws. As a representative of the National Council of Negro Women, she was the only woman of color at the 1945 United Nations founding conference. It is supremely fitting that a memorial statue in her honor sits in Washington, DC, and that she was commemorated with a US postage stamp in 1985.

BLACK LIVES MATTER COFOUNDERS

(PATRISSE CULLORS, 1983–PRESENT)
(ALICIA GARZA, 1981–PRESENT)
(AYỌ TOMETI, 1984–PRESENT)

"Black Lives Matter is our call to action. It is a tool to reimagine a world where black people are free to exist, free to live. It is a tool for our allies to show up differently for us."
—Patrisse Cullors

I am a Black man. And when I was a Black boy, "stranger danger" and "in by streetlights" (meaning "get home before dark") were instructions that could have meant the difference between life and death. How to comport oneself in public, how to deal with the police, how to react to microaggressions that could spring up anywhere—in a grocery store or café, at the library—are constants that shape my life. In 2013, a trio of Black women decided to tell the world what I already knew: if, as a Black person, you smoke, drive, cross a street, wear a hoodie, drink iced tea, bird-watch, play in the park, barbecue, experience a manic episode, hold a cell phone, or get drunk in public, you can be stopped by the police. Black people have experienced state-sanctioned violence throughout their time in this country. And there have been protests against such violence for that same duration. Perhaps never before, though, has the reach of a global political movement to protect and liberate people of African descent been more inclusive, vigorous, and bold than Black Lives Matter.

Black Lives Matter was cofounded by Patrisse Cullors, Alicia Garza, and Ayọ Tometi in 2013 as a hashtag and online community. In 2012 seventeen-year-old Trayvon Martin was stalked in the dark, physically attacked, and fatally shot by a white man named George Zimmerman while the teenager was walking home from a convenience store during a visit to his father's home in Sanford, Florida. Martin was unarmed. Zimmerman was acquitted of Martin's murder in 2013. When the verdict was announced, Alicia Garza, a Black and queer political organizer, went to Facebook and wrote what she called "A Love Letter to Black People." "I continue to be surprised at how little Black lives matter. . . . [S]top giving up on black life." At the end of her series of posts she wrote, "Black people. I love you. I love us. Our lives matter."

Patrisse Cullors, who had met Garza at a Black Organizing for Leadership and Dignity conference, wrote in the Facebook comments the now-iconic: #BlackLivesMatter. The next day, the two women reached out to fellow activist Ayọ Tometi. She knew all the ins and outs of social media and began to post #BlackLivesMatter on all platforms. #BlackLivesMatter was born.

Not long after, when eighteen-year-old Michael

Brown was fatally shot in Ferguson, Missouri, by white police officer Darren Wilson, Black Lives Matter emerged as a supportive network for the communities in Ferguson and nearby St. Louis to organize and protest the brutal policing conditions that had shaped the lives of so many Black citizens in the region. Over fifteen days, hundreds of courageous Black protesters endured abuse by law enforcement, including pepper spray and tear gas, and were dismissed by major media organizations and their reporters for speaking out against the terrorism Black people endure not just in Ferguson, but all over the United States. The organizing and community development that took place over those two weeks in 2014 helped define the international decentralized network for Black lives (and other marginalized sectors of society) that today has the support of millions.

To affirm that Black lives matter is to acknowledge that they have *not* mattered to so many, for so long. After the virally witnessed cell-phone recording of George Floyd's 2020 murder by a white police officer named Derek Chauvin, who suffocated Floyd to death with his knee pressed against Floyd's neck, #BlackLivesMatter became not only a galvanizing rallying cry for Americans, but also one for people living in Brazil, France, Syria, New Zealand, Kenya, and beyond who recognized the brutality of racism in their own communities.

In the days following the 2020 murders of Floyd, Ahmaud Arbery, and Breonna Taylor, people marched and protested against the taking of these lives, stolen so violently yet so casually, but behind the action loomed the fear of who could be next. The righteous anger of Blacks and many whites felt even more pervasive in the economically unstable period of the coronavirus pandemic, which left millions vulnerable to conditions that had already wreaked disproportionate havoc on Black communities nationwide: an unjust criminal justice and prison system, inequitable health care and education, and limited access to healthy food. The notion that Black lives matter wasn't simply a reaction to police brutality; rather, it was a holistic claim on the full rights of citizenship so long overdue for Black people in the United States.

The movement has eclipsed its founders. It's telling that no one really knows who these women are. Black and Brown folks—and, after Floyd's murder, young and old white people—marched the streets all over America, all over the *world*, and chanted the rallying cry "Black lives matter!" But that the originators of that cry aren't as known as their movement is exactly what these founders wanted. In 2016 Cullors wrote, "Soon after [Ferguson], Opal, Alicia, [writer and fellow activist] Darnell [Moore] and I helped create the BLM network infrastructure. It is adaptive and decentralized with a set of guiding principles. Our goal is to support the development of new Black leaders as well as create a network where Black people feel empowered to determine our destinies in our communities." As a result, each chapter adapts to the racial crisis in any given town or city. Some groups are involved in local politics; others are concerned with national campaigns and reaching out to senators, congressional representatives, and the like.

"Each and every one of us was made for such a time as this," Ayọ Tometi has said.

They have revived a chant by Assata Shakur, a former incarcerated Black Liberation Army (a Panther splinter group) member:

> It is our duty to fight for our freedom.
> It is our duty to win.
> We must love each other and support each other.
> We have nothing to lose but our chains.

BLACK LIVES MATTER

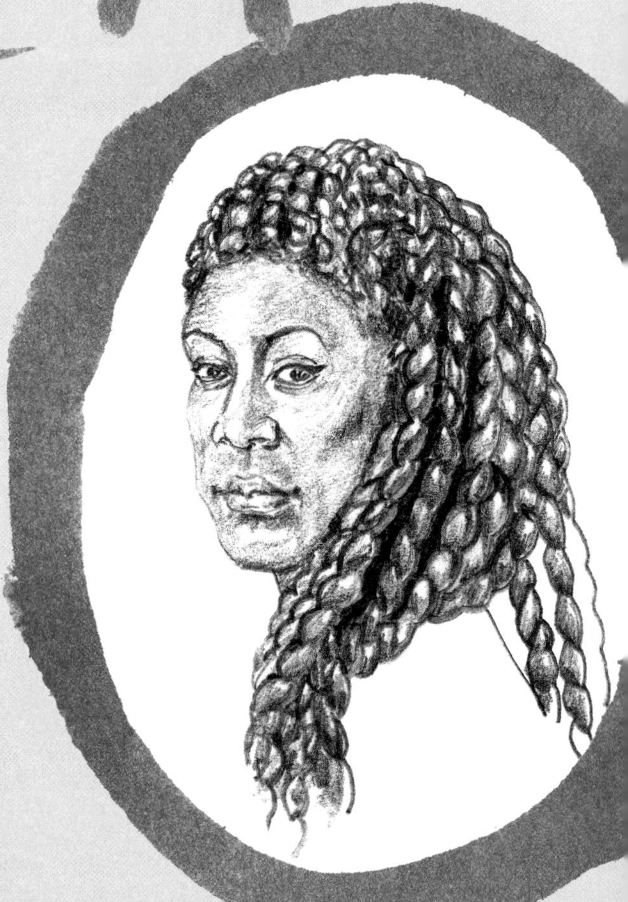

TERENCE BLANCHARD

(1962-PRESENT)

"The music itself is created to help people heal, and help people deal with their frustrations."

Terence Blanchard has, to date, seventy-seven film and television credits to his name, making him one of the most prolific musicians to take on the role of composing and arranging film scores. Around twenty of those works are films by director Spike Lee, with whom Blanchard has been a creative partner for over three decades. His oeuvre includes original scores to Lee classics like *Jungle Fever* and *Malcolm X* and movies such as *Love & Basketball*, *Barbershop*, and *Eve's Bayou*. A multiple Grammy-award winner, he received the 2019 Grammy for his composition "Blut und Boden" for *Da 5 Bloods*.

Originally from New Orleans, Blanchard started playing the trumpet as a child, then studied at the New Orleans Center for Creative Arts. But he made a fateful friendship early. Blanchard grew up with jazz superstar Wynton Marsalis. They went to summer music camp together as children. I imagine the get-togethers and sleepovers where Wynton and his brother Branford, along with Terence, played their instruments and honed their craft under the constant watch of legendary jazz pianist, educator, and father Ellis Marsalis.

Blanchard carved out a niche for himself while studying music at Rutgers University. His influences included greats like trumpeter Clark Terry. Blanchard toured with the Lionel Hampton Orchestra before Wynton Marsalis referred him as a replacement in Art Blakey's Jazz Messengers in 1982. His solo career took off: he would release more than twenty albums. He hadn't considered a career in film scoring until he was exposed to the process as a session player for *Do the Right Thing* and *Mo' Better Blues*, on which Lee's father, Bill, served as music director.

Blanchard went on to write music for Broadway and opera, dispelling the often misplaced assumption that musicians who choose to play jazz lack the skills or sensibility for Eurocentric classical music. His second opera, *Fire Shut Up in My Bones*, was based on *New York Times* columnist Charles Blow's memoir. The 2021 showing made Blanchard the first Black composer in the history of the Metropolitan Opera in New York to lead a production—a bittersweet honor, considering the legacy of Black composers across genres.

Following a slew of leadership roles as artistic director for multiple music institutions, Blanchard was named, in 2019, the inaugural Kenny Burrell chair in Jazz Studies at UCLA's Herb Alpert School of Music.

I'm struck when I listen to Blanchard's film scores and albums from throughout his broad career how his music soundtracks Black living. His lyricism seems meant to act as constant inspiration. This pioneer bears witness to our troubles, our loves, our woes, and our triumphs; he hears the melody of our lives.

GUION STEWART BLUFORD

(1942–PRESENT)

"I'm an engineer, and I'm Black and I'm lonely out there."

Guion Stewart Bluford has the kind of life that, if looked at from a certain vantage point, cleverly hides the magnitude of his bravery and sacrifice. In fact, he's a rare man. He smuggled two lives inside one and is rather humble about this astonishing achievement.

His first career was that of a military man. During pilot training at Williams Air Force Base in Arizona, he learned how to fly on the F-4C Phantom, then a brand-new fighter airplane. He was also trained in survival skills—how to eat in the jungle, how to escape and evade the enemy, and how to survive as a POW. Then, piloting a fighter-bomber, he was sent to Vietnam, where he served for nine months. He remembers his final missions, his plane being shot in the wing, being scrambled (which is fighter-pilot speak for hiding from the enemy) while dropping bombs on an active, triple-A site in the demilitarized zone between North and South Vietnam. (When he talks now about these exploits, he doesn't sound scared. But I was, just listening to him.)

Here's the crazy thing—his sterling military record isn't why Guion Stewart Bluford is in the history books. His family's communal sacrifice as they followed him hither and yon to new assignments isn't why folks know his name. Bluford is a man revered for his *second* career. From a pool of more than ten thousand applicants, Bluford was selected as one of thirty-five people to compete to become a NASA space shuttle astronaut. It was 1979, and by then Bluford had already earned multiple degrees in aerospace engineering, flown the above-mentioned combat missions in the Vietnam War, and become a commissioned US Air Force officer. In 1983, he flew in a space mission to reach a communications satellite, becoming the first Black person to launch into outer space.

That 1983 mission to space was with the STS-8. The crew launched in the space shuttle *Challenger* from the Kennedy Space Center in Florida, marking NASA's first night launch and subsequent night landing. Over the next decade, Bluford often served as mission specialist on his space flights, and he carried out a series of classified and unclassified assignments for the Department of Defense. Upon his final flight in 1992, he had logged more than 688 hours of flight time in space.

J. MAX BOND JR.

(1935–2009)

"Architecture inevitably involves all the larger issues of society."

Buildings tell stories about who and what matters. How buildings are conceived, where they're located, and what spaces and amenities they feature—all these things reveal the interests and priorities of the people who design, build, and use those spaces. J. Max Bond Jr. was inspired to consider the possibilities of making buildings while growing up in Tuskegee, Alabama. Both his parents were educators; his father held a deanship at Tuskegee Institute, an appointment that would eventually take the Bond family to countries such as Liberia, Afghanistan, and Tunisia. But it was the large-scale buildings at the Tuskegee Institute that first captured his imagination.

Bond graduated from Booker T. Washington High School in Atlanta at the age of thirteen and continued on to Harvard University at the age of sixteen. He graduated in 1955 but stayed on at Harvard, earning a master's degree in architecture from the Graduate School of Design in 1958—but not before a professor at the school cautioned Bond to pursue another, more suitable career, lest he struggle to find work as a Black architect. Fortunately, Bond ignored this advice and went on to become one of the most celebrated figures in his profession. His intention was to make buildings—their mission, their spaces, and their representations—more inclusive of the communities in which they existed.

In 1970, Bond and Donald Ryder cofounded Bond Ryder & Associates, a Black-led architectural firm. Their work centered on incorporating the Black experience at every level of their project. For the Martin Luther King Jr. Center for Nonviolent Social Change in Atlanta, Bond chose brick as the façade material in an effort to hire brickmasons. To keep King's memorial aligned with the family's wishes that it be fashioned of the materials of everyday life, Bond employed locally sourced wood and limited marble to the crypt. Similarly, at the Schomburg Center for Research in Black Culture in Harlem, the interior paneling features sapele, an African wood.

In 1990 Bond Ryder merged with Davis Brody & Associates to become Davis Brody Bond. During Bond's tenure and with his leadership, the firm was selected to develop the National September 11 Memorial and Museum in Lower Manhattan and codesigned (as part of the team Freelon Adjaye Bond/SmithGroup) the Smithsonian's National Museum of African American History and Culture (NMAAHC). For that latter project, Bond collaborated with David Adjaye and Phil Freelon on the early concepts that would allow the team to win the assignment in 2008. Bond died in 2009, before the NMAAHC was fully realized, but his imprint on the space—the only museum in the United States fully dedicated to depicting the comprehensive journey of Black people in the US—is unmistakable.

NATHANIEL AND ARTHUR BRONNER

(NATHANIEL BRONNER, 1914–1993)
(ARTHUR BRONNER, 1917–2006)

"Getting together is progress; working together is success."
—Favorite saying of Nathaniel Bronner

Today the Bronner Bros. International Beauty Show, a multiday, biannual event attracting thousands of hair enthusiasts and licensed professionals, is the country's biggest beauty event geared toward Black women. In its seventh decade, it offers attendees classes led by the industry's trailblazers, the chance to experiment with new products, and, most famously, the opportunity to watch or compete in the iconic hair show. If the Battle of the Bands is where Black college marching bands throw down on the football field, then the Bronner Bros. hair show is where stylists compete to take locs, weaves, fros, and fades to new heights or achieve astounding colors, all as excited audience members watch. Over the decades, this show has attracted many major speakers, including Martin Luther King Jr. and Jackie Robinson.

Nathaniel and Arthur Bronner founded the Bronner Bros. hair-care brand in 1947 after noticing how profitable the hair products from their sister Emma's shop were, compared to the newspapers Nathaniel was selling. The brothers began teaching classes in cosmetology at an Atlanta YMCA. So successful were the classes that they grew into a yearly trade show for the ethnic beauty-product industry.

As the show grew, so did the Bronner Bros. line of products specifically designed for Black hair.

I'm fascinated by these two brothers. One worked the front and the other worked the back of the shop. But whether front-facing or behind the scenes, they had a swagger. Two straight Black men created an empire for Black women. Their lives were concerned with what made a Black woman feel beautiful. *Girl, what am I going to do with my hair?* was not only a constant question; its answer was forever complicated. Styles changed from year to year, from decade to decade, but the question of Black female beauty remained. And because the question of Black beauty was monetized, the Bronner brothers went to where the women were. And they listened.

For years, extensions and chemically treated hair were the mainstays of the demos and product lines. More recently, a shift to natural hairstyles, a trend buoyed by the self-care educational videos of YouTubers, resulted in new products and training for stylists, who needed to adjust if they wanted to stay in business.

Today Bronner Bros. is under the leadership of the second generation of Bronners, led by president and CEO Bernard Bronner, who continues to be a leading voice in the world of Black hair care.

LERONN P. BROOKS

(CA. 1975-PRESENT)

"I have found it beneficial to use my scholarship, understanding of historical contexts and curatorial practice, to examine the intersections between representations of African-American visual cultures and society."

Black art isn't rare, but its historic absence from galleries, museums, and the canon of art history taught in schools and universities shows serious Black underrepresentation among archivists and curators. This bias can clearly be seen in permanent collections, such as the artwork taken from ancient cultures, and the organization and marketing of exhibitions. In 2018, the Getty Research Institute announced a program to proactively rectify the lack of Black art acquisitions by museums over United States history in its launch of the African American Art History Initiative. For this academic endeavor, the institute partnered with organizations such as Spelman College, the Studio Museum in Harlem, the California African American Museum, and Art + Practice in Los Angeles to collect and curate archival acquisitions. LeRonn Brooks left his position as a professor of African studies at Lehman College, CUNY, to become the Getty Research Institute's associate curator for Modern and Contemporary Collections.

Brooks, with a doctorate in art history and a close study of Black artists such as photographer Roy DeCarava, brings his scholarly and personal insights to the role. During his tenure he is seeking to acquire and place in cultural context the work of important Black figures in the world of American art, such as the groundbreaking Los Angeles–based artist Betye

Saar. Because the narrative of Black art in America is in the process of being written, it is vital to have a person like Brooks—someone with both an invested and an academic understanding of the artists and their works—spearheading the effort. So often the story of Black artists has been told by people who were peering into cultural experiences from the outside. As Brooks has said, "African American archives are as vulnerable as the people themselves."

Moreover, Brooks is aware that his position as curator of African American art means understanding not only the artistry, but also its contexts and artists, most of whom create surrounded by racist circumstances. When speaking about Paul R. Williams, the renowned architect, Brooks wisely opined, "If you don't address the hurdles he had to deal with, you don't understand the history of African Americans in architecture. He had to carry himself in a way that people could trust. He was a genius at architecture—he inspired an entire generation—but he was also a genius at social navigation. One can't be separated from the other." The expansiveness of Black art history demands that the same investment and industry-wide intentional focus be applied to it as is given to the Eurocentric art it so often comes face to face with, and Brooks is one of many shepherds guiding the way.

RALPH BUNCHE

(1904–1971)

"To make our way, we must have firm resolve, persistence, tenacity. We must gear ourselves to work hard all the way. We can never let up."

In 1950, Ralph Bunche became the first African American and the first person of color to receive the Nobel Peace Prize. As a diplomat working for the United Nations, he was honored for mediating the 1949 Arab-Israeli Armistice Agreements and celebrated for his work promoting peace and human rights.

Bunche was born in Detroit, Michigan, and briefly lived in New Mexico, where both his parents died. His maternal grandmother, who had been born into slavery, moved him and his sisters to Los Angeles. He graduated as valedictorian from Jefferson High School and went on to attend UCLA on a basketball scholarship, while also working as a custodian. He graduated in 1927, again valedictorian, with a major in international relations.

Thanks to a scholarship from Harvard University, along with funds from his Black community in Los Angeles, Bunche studied political science in Cambridge and received his master's degree in 1928. He then taught at Howard University in Washington, DC, while completing his PhD. While working on his doctorate at Harvard, Bunche won the Toppan Prize for outstanding research in political science and completed a fellowship; he then performed postdoctoral research in anthropology at Northwestern University, the London School of Economics, and Cape Town University.

Throughout his career, Bunche maintained strong ties with education. He chaired the Department of Political Science at Howard University (1928–1950), taught at Harvard University (1950–1952), and served as a member of various trustee boards (New York City Department of Education, Harvard University, the Institute of International Education, Oberlin College, Lincoln University, and New Lincoln School).

Bunche's deep experience in academia did not limit his investment in civil rights action. In 1936 he wrote *A World View of Race*, a book that examines the concept of race as a social construct. He was a member of President Roosevelt's so-called Black Cabinet but refused President Truman's offer of the post of assistant secretary of state because Washington, DC, maintained segregated public housing. Bunche's professional accomplishments reveal the inherent tension of being an important spokesperson for the United States while being a Black man. I've often wondered what was at stake when he made the decision to march with Martin Luther King Jr. in Montgomery, Alabama, in 1965.

Ultimately, Bunche decided not to live a life that was either/or. He was deeply invested in diplomatic peace between various countries and racial peace here in the US. An adviser to the Department of State, Bunche moved from his first position as an analyst in the Office of Strategic Services to the desk of acting chief of the Division of Dependent Area Affairs.

In 2003, UCLA renamed its Center for Afro-American Studies the Ralph J. Bunche Center for African American Studies.

TARANA BURKE

(1973–PRESENT)

"'Me Too' became the way to succinctly and powerfully connect with other people and give people permission to start their journey to heal."

Tarana Burke is concerned with justice and resti-tution. She created the activist group Me Too in 2006 to help survivors of sexual assault find the resources they need to heal. Burke is a survivor of sexual trauma in her childhood. On her own journey, she saw how, on all socioeconomic levels, Black girls and women were often discouraged from acknowl-edging sexual assault and how women who spoke up were socially shunned, or worse. Survivors were constantly being asked to trot out the details of their pain—a caustic trade-off to get the visibility the issue deserved. But where was the support for these individuals going forward when their vulnerability had been used to abuse them? Why wasn't society interrogating the systems that protected perpetra-tors and rewarded those who knew the truth but remained quiet?

Years later, in 2017, the hashtag #MeToo went viral after accusations against movie producer Harvey Weinstein were published in the *New Yorker*. Most people thought the hashtag had emerged from Twitter, after a call from actress Alyssa Milano to use the hashtag to illustrate that countless women had experienced some kind of inappropriate, unwanted, or illegal sexual aggression in their lives. Millions re-sponded with the words "Me Too." But Black women on Twitter and beyond knew that Me Too had been around for eleven years already, and their voices helped push Burke's name to the forefront of the me-dia's reporting on the very movement she'd started. It's interesting how often this happens to Black people—Black women in particular. They begin a common cause, highlight a long-known injustice, but when the uncomfortable truths they raise become a national conversation, their names are forgotten. That almost happened to Tarana Burke, but she refused to be cast aside. She was able to retake her place, and that's a sign of the Black justice movement in today's culture.

The shift catapulted Burke from her role as a pro-gram director at Girls for Gender Equity in Brooklyn to nationally sought-after commentator and speaker. She and nine other activists were honored at the 2018 Academy Awards, during a performance of the Best Song nominee "Stand for Something." She appeared on multiple magazine covers, including *Time* mag-azine as one of its "100 Most Influential People" of 2018. But Burke had never been out to become a figurehead. Me Too had begun as one way to offer survivors a space to realize they weren't isolated in their pain. As #MeToo expanded, Burke's work began to involve ensuring that Black women weren't excised from the narrative. In the United States, white-dominant institutions have perpetuated biased be-liefs that Black women's pain either doesn't exist or is simply less consequential than that of white women.

The issue of sexual aggression came to the fore again a year after the resurgence of #MeToo during Supreme Court confirmation hearings for nominee Brett Kavanaugh, who faced credible accusations of sexual assault. Professor Christine Blasey Ford testified to her experience of having been assaulted by the nominee when they were both teens. In comparison with Anita Hill's testimony three decades earlier during the confirmation hearings for nominee Clarence Thomas, Ford's emotional statements were seen as more persuasive, powerful, and vulnerable. In spite of that, Kavanaugh was confirmed, joining Thomas on the Supreme Court in 2018. In the cacophony of the politicized debate, the issue of the pervasiveness of abuse against women and how to support victims became sidelined by notions of the "sullying of men's reputations."

Burke noticed this too, and again used her position to speak to the heart of the matter. She maintained that a world where people are safe from sexual abuse is possible only when we don't deny that such abuse happens. She claimed that this was especially true for Black women, indigenous women, and trans women—women in any of the many communities with higher likelihoods of experiencing assault and fewer options for healing. #MeToo was just a step. The movement in action would consist of a network of survivors and advocates not interested in the recitation of case details. The work in action would include full recognition of the spectrum of sexual abuse, from verbal harassment to physical violence, and condemnation of these behaviors, no matter the pedigree of the perpetrator.

Burke has taken the Me Too movement and incorporated it into a larger Black discussion. *You Are Your Best Thing: Vulnerability, Shame Resilience, and the Black Experience*, co-edited with Brené Brown, is an anthology that brings together academics, writers, organizers, and cultural figures who write about shame and vulnerability in Black America. When Burke talks about her inspiration for editing this book, her words resonate: "There had been this intense public unrest happening in the country after George Floyd and Breonna Taylor were murdered. In private, I was having these really heartfelt conversations with Black folks who were just struggling: *I can't watch any more of this. I can't take this anymore. I cannot* . . . And in public, the conversation was, *How can we get white people to be better? How can we get white people to be antiracist?* Antiracism became the order of the day. But there was no focus on Black humanity. I kept thinking, *Where's the space for us to talk about what this does to us, how this affects our lives?* And so I was thinking to myself that I really wanted to have a conversation with you." Burke is fearless with her self-questioning. She asks herself, in regard to reaching out to Brené Brown, "*Why am I hesitating to reach out to her? We have a close enough friendship to talk about anything.* . . . As a Black woman, I often felt like I had to contort myself to fit into the work and see myself in it. White supremacy has added another layer to the kind of shame we have to deal with, and the kind of resilience we have to build, and the kind of vulnerability that we are constantly subjected to whether we choose it or not."

Burke founded Just Be Inc., which offers a website and resources geared toward Black girls' holistic well-being. She continues to speak out about systems of violence, whether they are interfamilial, intercommunal, or externally driven, in her work to raise awareness and create spaces where people can be safe—that is, where they can be truly free.

OCTAVIA BUTLER

(1947–2006)

"Every story I create, creates me. I write to create myself. Every story I write adds to me a little, changes me a little, forces me to reexamine an attitude or belief, causes me to research and learn, helps me to understand people and grow."

The 1979 novel *Kindred* is science fiction author Octavia Butler's best-known book. The story centers on Dana, a modern Black woman writer who finds herself stuck in time in antebellum Maryland. Butler said that the book's premise emerged from hearing younger generations of Black people claim that slavery was something they wouldn't have allowed themselves to be subjected to. In *Kindred*, as in all her work, Butler illustrates what systemic oppression might feel like. She wants people to understand that sometimes survival is its own form of resistance. But *Kindred* is more than its text. The power of this novel is derived from its subtext and context. The story takes place in 1976, America's bicentennial. Though the narrative never draws attention to this banner year, the date forces readers to ask: When we look at race and racism in America, what is there to celebrate?

Octavia Butler's writing also calls attention to the fact that science fiction is a genre that often investigates worlds that are what we might call post-race. Their narrative landscapes are littered with green and purple people; robots control the government; slick flying machines populate the sky. But in Butler's science fiction, we are never more than an arm's reach from our past. Dana's trip into the antebellum South doesn't come about because she built a time machine and felt the pull of curiosity. Her travels back through time are emotionally triggered by a hereditary connection to Rufus, her forefather, who is also a slave owner. As the novel unfolds, Dana watches this young white slave owner grow into a monster. She not only is often helpless to stop his cruelty; she is called upon to save his life over and over again. In doing so, she is saving her own lineage. Clearly, America's family tree is hopelessly intertwined.

In the white-male-dominated field of science fiction, Butler became a singular voice, showing the reading world the scope and depth of her imagination. At the same time, Butler's fiction seems to say that the conversations and the struggles of racism will always be with us. While most science fiction writers are unconcerned with race as their primary subject matter, Butler's work effortlessly details that we Black folks are here too, in these fantastical worlds.

Butler wrote more than a dozen books, and contemporary readers see in her work a clarity and prescience in understanding the direction of American politics. In 1995, she received a MacArthur "Genius" Fellowship, the first science fiction writer to take that honor. She also received two Nebula and two Hugo Awards, the highest honors in science fiction writing.

A HISTORY OF RITUALS

by Marvin K. White

From Africa to Brazil, from Africa to Cuba, from Africa to the Caribbean, from Africa to the Americas, and from Africa back to Africa, we reclaim the Atlantic from the lie that the triangulated slave trade told on her. She was not complicit. History will absolve those waters. We call upon our ancestors from every direction and offer this pouring, this libation for the flow between us and her. History is flow. History is permeable. We remember our drowning because history passes through water.

We call upon our pre-present writers, artists, dancers, teachers, and inspirations to bear witness to what we have done with history. We have continued their stories, and for them, continued to move their stories forward. History is a freewrite and not a form. We are unable to keep history's secrets. History knows that we say more about where we come from than where we are. History is not fixed, unless it has been fixed.

History, this libation we pour, brings into our midst fluidity. You are not a book. You are a brook. We pour this libation for the Creators. We pour for the spilled blood in every direction. *Para los Santos*. For the Saints. We pour for our esteemed ancestors, who are more than history, when they are the truth. Pour out for histories suffering in silence, the atrocities and horrors of slavery and colonialism.

We are libational outpouring. We are the ones who want to remember. We are the ones who have come to history not to speak mere words to change the course, but we show up with a calendar, out of breath and pointing to how long it's all been going on. We know that we cannot run backward and hope to gloss over the DNA-shaping events of history. We are the libation. History is life's long line. We decide now to grow old. We go back with machetes. Recast the iron skillet. Make it right. Know the forced hand that chicken-scratched an X on the curse of a contract. We go back with present flesh and unbroken bones, put the blade tip to the throat of history, pay for our freedom, come to terms, go out and get us out of layaway. We tell history, "We free."

Pour out on all historical contracts entered or tricked into by ancestors and family members who offered our bodies, minds, and souls as collateral; they are null and void. Tell us we are out from under. Tell us we are debt-free. Tell us we owe nothin'. Or tell us nothing at all. No more of our waking or resting. Our minds are not deeded or signed over to anyone. Our minds have never been leased land. We cannot lose our minds. We cannot lose. We will no longer struggle to make payments. We are free. We were sent to breach. We were sent to break. We free.

We are not fighting to hold on to history; we are fighting to break free from history. One day we will be ready to leave this ground that we have built, that has been built on us, this ground that we stomped on, that stomped on us, this ground that we grew into, that grew on top of us. One day we will know that where we come from is only half as far as where we're going.

The course, today we remember the course of history. One day, the people who were crawling on the floor of the ocean got up, and walked out of the water. There is a history, there is a past, and there is a future with us in it. The human plot against us. The holy plan for us. The betrayal of us. The hand on us. The prophecy with us. The debt paid to the course, the way out of no way. The core unbitten. The charge unchanged.

You know how when you're walking along the bottom of the ocean, and you have forgotten all the times that Mami Wata admonished you to not drag your feet on her floor, and you cut into your sole, on a too-late-to-see shard of glass? You know how when your solar plexus flares, and it's not the blood trail that makes you nervous, it's the boy now, who did reflexology on your feet? You know how when the knowing in your foot-gut chakra tells you that it is the same limpswim to shore as to love? You know how when you pull it out, and *National Geographic* takes a picture of it, just as you hold it up to look at it? The sun revealing some codex, some cuneiform, and all of a sudden, you're on the cover, the cut glass, that is the boy, between you and the sun. And it's not an eclipse, and it was an eclipse, but the scientific world goes crazy. Over a fucking shard of glass that you tripped over because you couldn't drown! Not an entire bowl. Not an intact ceremonial chalice. Not a sealed vessel with the holiness inside. Not amphora. Not hydria. A shard that only points to the what it was a part of. And they not hardly disappointed in that shard. Like maybe a Black Nobel Prize in archeology, not disappointed. Like gods hailing it as the most important bleed of 2022, not disappointed. And here, I thought you was supposed to sweep up what is broken and throw it away. But I guess it says something when the pieces are found, undisturbed, where the heart was broken, still embedded, near where it sank.

We bring history forward. It is always relevant. It is never the bad hand dealt. Is never the snake eying you. So, we have not lost anything. Our bodies remember all of the moves. 'Cause mumble and crying and altars and incense and poetry and prayer are history. The ones who chose—and be clear, we as Black folks know this choice—to jump into the arms of ancestors and fly to their next place, rather than be burned or crumpled or enslaved, are history. Those who were beat so much that they turned into drums are history. Each and every one unaccounted and counted for, waking up in somebody's arms who loves them, in this world or the next, is history.

Marvin K. White is a preacher, poet, artist, teacher, and coconspirator articulating a vision of racial, social, prophetic, and creative justice.

CAB CALLOWAY

(1907–1994)

"Music . . . should keep up with the pace and feeling of life."

Cab Calloway had the moves, the voice, the big band music, and the language. The quintessential American bandleader, Calloway brought the spirit of jazz to life. In a white tuxedo, he danced boldly and effusively, smiled generously, and flung his straightened hair around in time with the rhythm. A gifted singer, he led his band not just with a baton, but through his soulful lyrics.

Born as Cabell Calloway III in Rochester, New York, he first started singing in Baltimore, where he spent much of his childhood. He moved to Chicago and met Louis Armstrong, who helped him learn the art of scat, the improvisational style of singing that would become Calloway's calling card. By 1928, Calloway had his own band, the Alabamians. In 1930, he moved to Harlem and started playing the Cotton Club. His band and Duke Ellington's, who played at the Cotton Club during the same period, were the most popular acts to emerge from that scene. In 1931, Calloway's tune "Minnie the Moocher" hit number one, selling a million copies. It featured a distinct call-and-response lyric: "hi-de hi-de-ho."

One of the striking aspects of Cab Calloway's life is that he became so successful at such a young age. He was twenty-four when his band began substitut-ing for Duke Ellington's at the Cotton Club; twenty-five when he recorded "Minnie the Moocher." Yet this sustained success didn't shield him from violent racism. In December 1945, Calloway and a friend were beaten by a police officer and arrested in Kansas City, Missouri, when trying to visit a fellow musician at the whites-only Pla-Mor Ballroom. The officer, William E. Todd, beat Calloway so badly that he was taken to the hospital for his injuries. And then, to add insult to multiple injuries, Calloway and his friend were charged with intoxication and resisting arrest. One wants to be stunned that this happened to one of the famous musicians in America at that time, but such incidents were depressingly familiar. The charges were later dismissed.

That event and other acts of racial prejudice didn't stop Calloway from continuing to lead one of the most popular American entertainment acts through the 1940s. Calloway and his orchestra appeared in several films, including *The Big Broadcast* in 1932, *The Singing Kid* in 1936, and *Stormy Weather* in 1943. Always celebratory of Black people's unique voice in music, he wrote *The New Cab Calloway's Hepster's Dictionary: Language of Jive* in 1944, a Black vernacular dictionary explaining such ideas as "in the groove."

STEVE CANNON

(1935–2019)

"I feel safe around musicians and poets. I'm serious, if an artist is coming down the street, I'll duck behind a car."

In 1990, the writer and publisher Steve Cannon founded a literary magazine, *A Gathering of the Tribes*, a year after glaucoma robbed him of his eyesight. The magazine spawned a come-one, come-all salon and nonprofit gallery of the same name in his East Village apartment, where visitors from the art and literary communities could share inspired conversation. Musicians made impromptu performances. Writers read their works. The reclusive and introverted artist David Hammons made an installation on the property. Something was always getting stirred up.

A New Orleans native, Cannon moved to New York in 1962, where he found a home with fellow creative spirits who shared interests in art, literature, and music. Cannon once answered, when asked why he started his iconic literary magazine, "The people I knew down on the Lower East Side complained about not having any place to publish their work. So I started Tribes magazine. Just to get them to shut up."

A Gathering of the Tribes—the nonprint version—was part salon, part jazz concert hall, and always a space where artists and musicians could get together to have raucous conversation. In 2011, after twenty years of putting on performances and taking in all comers, Cannon learned he was being kicked out of his East Village apartment by his landlord. After four years of legal battling, he was forced to evacuate the building in 2015. Cannon had lived there for forty-four years.

Cannon and his friends decided to give a bit of ceremony to what most people considered an unceremonious ousting: they held a two-night auction and moving party at Cannon's second-floor apartment, packing up and selling off books, artwork, even pots and pans. At the last minute, Cannon found another apartment three blocks away. With just two rooms and a kitchen, the new apartment would require that the gathering of tribes be smaller, but until Cannon's death those gatherings still happened. As his longtime friend Miguel Algarín, a founder of the Nuyorican Poets Cafe, once said, "Yeah, plenty of s— happened here, most of it fights and thunder."

JOHNNIE CARR

(1911–2008)

"Look back, but march forward."

For so many people growing up in a segregated America, upending discriminatory laws was a pressing issue. Freedom was about the life that people were living in the moment. Johnnie Carr certainly understood the impact of immediate change as an Alabama native growing up on a farm near Montgomery. One of her dearest childhood friends was a girl named Rosa Louise McCauley, later known by her married name, Rosa Parks.

After finishing school, Carr became a nurse. During the 1930s and 1940s she was active in early civil rights work with organizations like the NAACP. Four days after Rosa Parks was arrested on December 1, 1955, for refusing to cede her bus seat to a white passenger, Carr heard Martin Luther King Jr. speak at a meeting that resulted in the formation of the Montgomery Improvement Association (MIA), which was responsible for the Montgomery Bus Boycott the following year. The emotional weight of the segregated public transportation system in Montgomery was heavy and burdensome. Jim Crow policies chipped away at people's humanity, creating deep fissures of resentment and dissatisfaction. Citizens like Carr coordinated to support Black residents with private carpools, effectively becoming the Black community's own rideshare service to help keep folks off the buses.

An activist and organizer, Johnnie Carr was a mother first. In 1964, her family challenged school segregation in Montgomery County. Along with attorney Fred Gray, the Carrs sued the Montgomery County Board of Education on behalf of their thirteen-year-old son, Arlam Jr. He wanted to attend Sidney Lanier High School, though it accepted only white students. In the spring of 1966, the courts ruled in favor of the Carrs. The Montgomery County school system was forced to integrate. School buses were ordered to serve each student in the county; children would have access to all services and programs. Arlam Carr Jr. was admitted to Sidney Lanier High School along with twelve other Black students.

The work of Carr and her fellow activists in Montgomery wasn't about making history, though the boycott organizers certainly did. The work was about living a life free from the constraints of discrimination, about being able to get to work and back with your dignity—nothing more, nothing less. The successful boycott resulted in the 1956 Alabama local ruling, in *Browder v. Gayle*, that segregated bus seating was unconstitutional.

The Montgomery Improvement Association was one of several founding organizations that joined forces and ultimately created the Southern Christian Leadership Conference, and it continued to focus on issues of integration and voter registration. Carr was president of the MIA for over four decades. She died at the age of ninety-seven in 2008.

TERRI LYNE CARRINGTON

(1965–PRESENT)

"Our music or artistry should not be disconnected from our lives or ourselves."

I love Terri Lyne Carrington. She's amazing. I had never heard of her before I began this project. And when I listened to her for the first time, I was mad at myself. I want people to look at my portrait of her and then run out, listen to her albums, and get mad at themselves.

Being a Black woman who is taken seriously as a Black musician is no small feat. In the music world, the men are giants and Black women are often treated like eye candy. It's an industry rife with misogyny. But Terri Lyne Carrington isn't having it. Renowned for her groundbreaking musical career as a drummer and a composer—a career spanning four decades—Terri Lyne Carrington carved a path as a jazz musician that has taken her to soaring heights. A repeat Grammy-award winner always exploring new outlets to question, to protest, and to convey the message of love, she has leveraged the language of music rooted in the Black tradition of jazz to create, inspire, and teach.

Her professional drumming began when, as a ten-year-old in Massachusetts, she snagged her first gig with the iconic trumpeter Clark Terry. After a jam session with pianist Oscar Peterson—an opportunity that arose when Ella Fitzgerald nudged her in his direction—she was offered a scholarship to attend the prestigious Berklee College of Music.

The accolades began tumbling in from there. A sought-after session player, she cultivated her own voice, writing music, singing, and playing on her albums, beginning with *Real Life Story* in 1989. She booked a gig as the house drummer for the *Arsenio Hall Show*, toured with Herbie Hancock and Wayne Shorter in the 1990s, and produced a body of work that left no side of jazz unexplored—the R&B side, along with its funk, its hip-hop, its rock.

One of her most heralded albums, *The Mosaic Project*, features an incredible lineup of women musicians and singers, including Dianne Reeves, Dee Dee Bridgewater, Patrice Rushen, and Esperanza Spalding. In her extensive career Carrington has played on more than one hundred tracks. She has received honorary doctorates from the Manhattan School of Music and Berklee. As founder and artistic director of the Berklee Institute of Jazz and Gender Justice, she works toward greater equity in grants, residencies, and honors for jazz, helping to move that genre beyond the patriarchal structure in which it was born. In 2021, she was honored with the National Endowment for the Arts Jazz Masters award.

BEN CARSON

(1951–PRESENT)

"You become valuable because of the knowledge that you have."'

At the age of thirty-three, Ben Carson became head of pediatric neurosurgery at Johns Hopkins Hospital in Baltimore. He made history when, among other surgical accomplishments that created a bright future for otherwise severely compromised patients, in 1987 he successfully separated twins that were born conjoined at the head. Carson's medical work helped support and demonstrate the then groundbreaking understanding of the brain's plasticity—that it has the ability to continuously remake itself—which contradicted previously held beliefs that the brain was a static organ not subject to dynamic change.

He published a memoir in 1990, which Hollywood followed up with a TV movie, *Gifted Hands: The Ben Carson Story*, based on his life. The book was later also adapted for the theater. Carson was heralded as a hero in Baltimore and beyond—especially in his hometown of Detroit, where he and his brother had been raised by their single mother after his father abandoned the family. Carson's account of his early life and subsequent medical feats tells a stunning story of the American dream, a tale of an ordinary person who worked hard, and successfully, to overcome great odds.

Carson pursued politics in the decades after his trailblazing medical career. In 2016 he made a bid for the presidency as a Republican candidate before withdrawing to endorse Donald Trump. After the election, Trump appointed Carson secretary of the Department of Housing and Urban Development. In accepting that role, Carson not only joined an administration that openly supported white-supremacist and -nationalist ideals, but also enacted policies that undermined decades of civil rights protections for residents in subsidized housing. This included proposing rent increases for poor tenants and stalling regulations from the previous Obama administration that were intended to address ongoing racial segregation.

Infamously, in a 2017 SiriusXM radio interview Carson said, "Poverty to a large extent is also a state of mind." Oh boy. His political shift was in direct opposition to the experience of many underserved Americans, especially many Black people, whom he suddenly seemed to be openly hostile toward. This was a departure for the man who seldom missed invitations to speak to groups of Black kids at school assemblies and the like. Watching his latest incarnation as politician and opinionator on conservative news makes my heart hurt. In recent years Carson has used his public position to promote notions that real Black identity can look only one way—his way—and his controversial statements regarding Mannatech, an herbal supplement company that claimed that their products cured autism, have caused him to lose face in the medical field, an arena in which he was once heralded as an icon.

RUTH E. CARTER

(1960–PRESENT)

"Marvel may have created the first Black superhero, but through costume design, we turned him into an African king."

Self-styling is and has been of great import for African Americans. Manners of dress can denote station in life and suggest how individuals or groups think of themselves—this is true for all cultures. But because the impact of fashion for Black people is descended from the history of slavery in the United States, and thus we have a heightened awareness that being "presentable" means being treated in a respectable way, fashion—like all derivatives from this narrative—carries a special weight.

In a society where white Europeans stripped the African men, women, and children brought to the Americas of their native languages, names, religious practices, and social markers such as apparel and adornments, how people presented themselves served as social currency. Personal fashion could suggest poverty or wealth, a lack of education or access to privilege. And for generations of Black people, clothing indicated status as enslaved or free, what kind of work a person did, and which owner laid claim, amid the many ways that clothing could be used for psychological control; certain states even restricted, by station in society, the quality of cloth someone could wear. Clothing was also used to erase individuality and to disempower. Throughout the centuries, though, Black dress was also used to denote both access to self-expression and a rejection of white societal constructs that sought to limit Black physical autonomy.

Black fashion, if one dares to reduce such a wide swath to a single notion, emerges from a mix of passed-down and aspirational ideas from Africa, the constraints and practicalities of life in the United States, and the influence of other cultures. It is this radiant, complex, and heavy history that Ruth Carter so deftly articulates in her work as a costume designer in some of cinema's most important representations of Black people. From historical period films such as *Amistad*, to joyous contemporary reflections of Black culture such as *Love & Basketball*, to the boundless world of Wakanda in *Black Panther*, Carter reveals the Black aesthetic of the past, of the moment, and of the future.

Some actors have commented that they know how to embody character only after they step into wardrobe. Similarly, viewers can often glean who characters are, where they're going, or what they've been through by what they have on.

In *Do the Right Thing*, the 1989 classic film written and directed by Spike Lee, Carter uses protest art to buoy the film's commentary on the bigotry that erupts on a hot summer day in Bedford-Stuyvesant, Brooklyn. Radio Raheem, played by Bill Nunn, wears a T-shirt painted with the message "Bed-Stuy Do or Die," a harbinger of events in the story. His hands are adorned with gold-hued rings that spell "love" on one hand and "hate" on the other, a direct cue from hip-hop street fashion, which was just beginning to influence popular dress.

In *Malcolm X*, Denzel Washington, as a young Malcolm Little, runs the streets of New York in a bright-blue billowing zoot suit, accessorized with cocked fedora and wingtip shoes. That ensemble nods to a life on the hustle before Malcolm experiences the teachings of the Nation of Islam. When he pursues a leading role in educating other Black Americans and challenging the white status quo, his wardrobe reflects a tailored conservative style, with muted, neutral-tone suits and perfectly symmetrical bow ties.

Born in Springfield, Massachusetts, Carter was drawn to theater as a college student at historically Black Hampton University. She hoped her interest in special education might allow her to become a sign-language translator to welcome in deaf audiences. But exposure to costume design and a long-nurtured penchant for sketching sparked in her a desire to see her illustrated creations made real. Though she began her career as the only Black woman in costume design in Hollywood, the culture has since shifted to include more costume designers of color. She is now rightfully viewed as a trailblazer, still hard at work.

Her first film credit was *School Daze* with Spike Lee, who has become a longtime collaborator. This 1988 film wonderfully reveals how style and culture come together at historically Black colleges. Since that debut, working on more than sixty films and TV programs, Carter has dressed Oprah Winfrey,

Eddie Murphy, Forest Whitaker, and Lupita Nyong'o. For her groundbreaking work on *Black Panther*, she received her third Academy Award nomination and won, becoming the first Black woman to receive the Oscar for that category. (Carter also received nominations for best costume design for *Malcolm X* and *Amistad*.) When this trailblazer received her award, her first thought was of others: "Finally the door is wide open and I've been struggling and digging deep and mentoring and doing whatever I could to raise others up," she said. "And I hope through my example, this means that there is hope and other people can come on in and win an Oscar just like I did." Known for her stunning creativity, it is equally important to Ruth E. Carter that Black young people follow in her footsteps.

Her work continues to inspire offscreen too. She partnered with the global apparel brand H&M on a Black liberation–themed line with the iconic trio of red, black, and green colorways. In 2020, the Savannah College of Art and Design fashion museum launched the exhibition "Ruth E. Carter: Afrofuturism in Costume Design," featuring original works from her four-decade career. She is the first Black woman costume designer to receive a star on the Hollywood Walk of Fame.

CHARLESTON CATERERS

(SALLY SEYMOUR, 1779–1824)
(ELIZA SEYMOUR LEE, 1800–CA. 1874)
(NAT FULLER, 1812–1866)
(THOMAS TULLY, 1828–1883)

"Nat Fuller, the renowned presiding genius over many a fine dinner and supper, has a cunning way of fixing up water so as to take all the bad taste out of it."

—The [Augusta, Georgia] *Daily Constitutionalist*, 1866

Apprenticeship is the backbone of the culinary world. No clearer evidence of that is found than in a lineage of Black chefs from Charleston, South Carolina, spanning just over one hundred years. Top chefs of their day, Sally Seymour, Eliza Seymour Lee, Nat Fuller, and Thomas Tully set the standard for fine dining and professional catering before the proliferation of restaurants. Seymour taught her daughter the intricacies of French cuisine; her daughter mentored Nat Fuller, who in turn taught Thomas Tully.

Sally Seymour was born into slavery, and Charleston planter Thomas Martin took her as his mistress. He arranged for her to be trained in French cookery for his own benefit, but she used that knowledge to establish her own pastry shop on Tradd Street in 1795, after Martin freed her and their children. Seymour staffed her catering business with enslaved labor, whom she didn't pay, illustrating the complex power dynamics for Black people of the era. In a time when Black, mostly enslaved people in Charleston outnumbered whites by as much as five to one, it's likely that the only available pool of cooking labor comprised enslaved people. Seymour purchased— yes, this entrepreneur was a slave owner—and then trained dozens of Black cooking professionals who, upon being resold, could claim to have been trained under her tutelage. Seymour certainly profited from these transactions, yet the apprentices received opportunities as well.

Upon Seymour's death in 1824, her daughter Eliza Seymour Lee took over the pastry shop. She married a free Black tailor, John Lee, and established her own culinary reputation in the 1820s, owning and overseeing the Lee House, the Jones Hotel, the Mansion House on Broad Street, and the Moultrie House on Sullivan's Island. Lee used these businesses to host exclusive social clubs and catered gatherings. She rented rooms and sold pies, cakes, and pastries.

As an enslaved cook, Fuller was sent by his owner to study under Lee. Among many skills, which included bartending, Fuller was known for his meat cookery and dishes with a big visual impact. He's believed to have hosted a major feast in 1865, for both Black and white diners, celebrating the end of the Civil War.

Tully, one of Fuller's mentees, came to prominence in the late 1860s and eventually joined forces with Martha Vanderhorst, a Black pastry chef with whom he opened a bakery and dining room.

LEAH CHASE

(1923–2019)

"Food builds big bridges. If you can eat with someone, you can learn from them, and when you learn from someone, you can make big changes. We changed the course of America in this restaurant over bowls of gumbo. We can talk to each other and relate to each other when we eat together."

Even in her nineties, Leah Chase still reported to work at Dooky Chase's restaurant in New Orleans every morning, as she had done for seven decades. One of fourteen children born to Hortensia and Charles Lange, Chase grew up in Madisonville but moved to New Orleans after high school. There she married bandleader Dooky Chase Jr. and went to work at his family's bar and lunch counter before convincing her in-laws to let her take it over. She transformed the sandwich shop into a full-scale restaurant in 1946, and this Tremé gathering spot quickly became one of the city's crown jewels of Creole cuisine.

Inspired by the fine-dining treatments she saw through the windows of whites-only establishments at the peak of the Jim Crow era, Chase wanted to offer Black diners a commensurate level of service and flair. She presented multiple-course meals on beautiful dinnerware and served up gumbo, crab soup, greens, and grilled fish in cream sauce. Dooky Chase's was soon a hit.

This restaurant was integral to the community, not just because of the food and ambience but because of Chase's political involvement. Rejecting segregation laws that made it illegal to serve white and Black people equally, Chase constantly hosted a mix of diners and ensured that those supporting the civil rights activism of the day had a place to eat. Feeding a range of people from NAACP staff and voter-registration volunteers to luminaries such as Martin Luther King Jr., Chase worked to keep the restaurant a safe space for those frontline leaders. They often held secret meetings on the top floor of the restaurant building.

A lover of art who recognized that museums and galleries were discriminating against Black artists, Chase not only patronized folks like the famous Black painter Jacob Lawrence, but displayed their work in the full grandeur that their pieces deserved, making the restaurant not simply a place to dine, but also a place to indulge in the visual storytelling of Black life. She cooked for three US presidents—Bill Clinton, George W. Bush, and Barack Obama—among many celebrities over the decades. *The Dooky Chase Cookbook*, published in 1990, is considered a classic of Black Creole cooking.

SHIRLEY CHISHOLM

(1924–2005)

"I am the people's politician. If the day should ever come when the people can't save me, I will know I am finished."

On January 25, 1972, forty-seven-year-old Shirley Chisholm took the stage at a Baptist church in her Brooklyn district, her petite frame erect behind the podium, her coiffed hair bobbing above a cluster of microphones. She was there to announce her bid to become the Democratic nominee for president of the United States. Supporters applauded when she set forth her campaign intentions and the version of America she hoped to lead. "I am not the candidate of Black America, although I am Black and proud," she said. "I am not the candidate of the women's movement of this country, although I am a woman and I'm equally proud of that. I am the candidate of the people of America."

By this time, Chisholm had amassed a wealth of personal and professional experience that more than qualified her to throw her name in the ring. She was a New York assemblywoman, a US congressional representative, and a cofounder of the National Women's Political Caucus. Born in Brooklyn, New York, to her Guyanese father, a factory worker named Charles St. Hill, and her Barbadian mother, a seamstress named Ruby Seale St. Hill, she graduated cum laude from Brooklyn College and completed a master's degree at Columbia University in elementary education. (Her British-inflected accent was a result of early childhood years spent in Barbados with family, attending British schools.) She worked as a nursery-

school teacher and consulted for New York City's Division of Day Care before being elected to the New York State Assembly in 1964. During her tenure, she worked to pass unemployment insurance for domestic workers, a field that at the time disproportionately included Black women.

While in office at the Assembly, she ran for Congress in 1968 to represent Bedford-Stuyvesant's 12th Congressional District. Her campaign slogan was "Unbought and Unbossed," a refrain that would be associated with her values for the duration of her career. No big-business interests, no backroom deals—Chisholm believed in the true power of the people. She had an approachable sensibility and spoke plainly and directly to her constituents. She was fluent in Spanish and spoke it regularly. When she won that 1968 race, she became the first Black woman to be elected to the US Congress.

During her seven terms in office, she pushed for legislation that protected what she believed was America's most important resource: its citizens. She pushed for Head Start, an early education program that was launched during Lyndon Johnson's administration. She cofounded the Congressional Black Caucus in 1971, established in part to address the systemic underrepresentation of Black people in Congress. When President Nixon refused to meet with that caucus, the thirteen representatives boycotted his State of the Union Address, which made national headlines. Chisholm supported the Equal Rights Amendment and Title IX, which sought to combat discrimination against women in federally funded education and sports programs. She worked on the House Agriculture, Veterans' Affairs, and Education and Labor committees. Her work became highly visible, and she was featured on the covers of *Jet* and *Ebony* magazines. Despite this vast experience, when Chisholm announced her intent to earn the Democratic nomination for president, her candidacy provoked varied reactions.

At the peak of the women's movement, feminists debated whether she was the right pick, despite her track record of advocating for women and children and being the only woman running for the nomination amid challengers that included George Wallace, Hubert Humphrey, and George McGovern. Black people were also not uniformly convinced of her capability. Black men, particularly in the political establishment, debated combining their delegate power during the convention to back a white male candidate they deemed more likely to win. Jesse Jackson and Julian Bond stumped for McGovern. Alcee Hastings threw his support behind Edmund Muskie. When asked what she thought of her Black male counterparts, she said, "While they're rapping and snapping, I'm mapping."

In her announcement speech, Chisholm cited the Nixon administration's broken promises to the American people. She criticized Nixon's "political manipulation, deceit and deception, callousness and indifference to our individual problems" and his divisive approach to politics. Strategically, she understood that her chances of being nominated were slim. Although she had more delegates than Muskie or Humphrey, she lacked sufficient numbers to force

negotiations. After losing the primary, she returned to Congress, where she served until 1981.

But her presence in the 1972 election shifted the discourse. Chisholm spoke about protecting the environment. She encouraged youth to speak out, organize, and vote. She argued for limiting campaign contributions from large organizations—contributions that minimize the impact of individual working-class constituents. She was critical of the administration's handling of the Vietnam War and wanted to bring the troops home and better support their transition from active combat duties to civilian life.

When asked if she recognized a need for more women and Black women in politics, she agreed. She said we'd see more interest in and care for the country's day-care centers, educational institutions, and social and mental health services. She was the target of three assassination attempts during her campaign for the presidency. Conversely, she also inspired multiple generations of women to enter American politics.

Chisholm died in 2005. Yet her leading example is reflected in a legacy of female elected officials: former US senator Carol Moseley Braun, who represented Illinois (1993–1999) as only the second Black senator since the Reconstruction Era; California senator Holly J. Mitchell (2013-2020), who co-wrote and cosponsored the CROWN Act, creating protections for Black people to wear their natural hair in school and the workplace; Stacey Abrams, who campaigned in a difficult race for Georgia governor in 2018, losing only narrowly, and founded a national voting rights organization; and US senator Kamala Harris, the first Black and Indian American woman to become vice president of the United States. In 2015, President Barack Obama posthumously awarded Chisholm the Presidential Medal of Freedom.

KATHLEEN NEAL CLEAVER

(1945–PRESENT)

"There is plenty of work to do to reach what folks used to call the Promised Land."

When a young Kathleen Neal Cleaver first encountered the Student Nonviolent Coordinating Committee (SNCC), she was a college student in New York City. That organization, a major leader in the civil rights movement, had begun to lean toward Black Power liberation, thanks in part to figures such as Stokely Carmichael. It was through Cleaver's involvement with SNCC that, in 1966, she was introduced to the Black Panther Party. She became one of its most prominent women leaders.

Born Kathleen Neal in Dallas, Texas, she was exposed to travel and ample educational opportunities throughout her childhood. Her mother had a master's degree in mathematics, and her father was a sociologist who worked for Tuskegee University and then for the Foreign Service. His work took the family overseas to the Philippines, India, and Liberia.

Cleaver dropped out of Barnard College to help organize a student conference for SNCC at Fisk University in 1967. There she met Eldridge Cleaver, the minister of information for the Black Panther Party. Within the year she had moved to California, the two married, and Kathleen became the communications secretary for the Panthers. She believed in focus on empowering local Black communities and in self-determination in all matters where power had been systemically extracted: housing, education, health, and military service. (The power-sapping of the latter was especially evident during the Vietnam War. The draft, which disproportionately affected poorer youth, was devastating Black communities.)

The Black Panther Party, with its challenge to white authority, was subjected to government infiltration and constant surveillance. After the Cleavers' home was raided, Eldridge was involved in an ambush against the police. Two officers were injured. Charged with attempted murder, he fled the country while on bail and lived in Cuba, Algeria, and France. Kathleen joined him in exile for twelve years, during which time the couple left the Panthers. That organization was disbanded in part due to disagreements among its young leadership over its goals, but also due to FBI counterintelligence efforts, which introduced spies and sowed discord. The two founded the Revolutionary People's Communication Network as an offshoot in Algeria in 1971. Eventually, after a return to the United States, the Cleavers divorced in 1987.

Kathleen returned to school, earning her bachelor's from Yale University in 1984. She got her law degree, with a focus on civil rights and prison reform, from Yale Law School in 1989. She joined the Emory University School of Law faculty in 1992, retiring in 2020.

That same year, Emory University announced the acquisition of Cleaver's personal papers. It features her professional and personal correspondence, speeches, interviews with figures such as Malcolm X and Huey Newton, and photographs of Black Panther Party members. The archive allows scholars to analyze sociopolitical movements, gender roles, and how the media and US government distorted the Panthers' work.

MARY FRANCIS HILL COLEY

(1900–1966)

"She was a step-in Mom. And she did that for people that was not nice to her. That's hard."

—Lamisha Steele, who nominated Mary Francis Hill Coley for the Georgia Women Achievement Award

Mary Francis Hill Coley was a highly sought-after midwife in Albany, Georgia, who, from the mid-1930s to her retirement, delivered hundreds of babies born to Black and white families. Coley had apprenticed under a midwife from Alabama, and she took her calling as a spiritual endeavor. Part of what made Coley so respected was her knowledge of the birth process, as well as the multifaceted care she provided to both the birth mothers and the infants. She returned to her clients' homes in the days after the birth to bathe and dress both the babies and the mothers, prepare food, and essentially keep the household operating while the mothers were in recovery. In the segregated South, she was a rare example of a care worker who would support *any* family through the process, even a white family that didn't treat her well. But her work was especially important for Black families, who were typically unwelcome in white-dominant hospitals, leaving home birth as the only, if not the preferred, option.

Coley's life was dedicated to bringing Black lives into existence. All around her, whether or not Black babies came into being was willy-nilly. But for Mary Francis Hill Coley, Black lives *mattered*. During her lifetime nothing good was happening for Black people. Her work was a singular bright spot. I suspect she knew this in her bones: she was the survivor of a twin birth; she was raised by relatives after both of her parents died; she raised ten children after her husband abandoned her. This is a woman who knew what a difference it could make to be well cared for and well loved from first breath. Her work was so respected that, in 1953, the Georgia Department of Public Health produced a training film for midwives using Coley as an example, *All My Babies*, which followed her activities for several months. In the film, viewers see Coley walking to her clients' homes during all hours of the day or night, depending on the needs of the mother-to-be or new mom. Her manner is kind and warm; she's a reassuring presence that brings smiles to the faces of fatigued, sometimes uncertain women. Coley is shown explaining her hygiene practices, demonstrating how she comforts fussy babies, and sterilizing cloths in a pot in an open fireplace. The film was used as an instructional guide by the health department. The National Museum of African American History and Culture at the Smithsonian features clips of the film in its exhibit recognizing the contributions of Black Americans in medicine.

KATHLEEN COLLINS

(1942–1988)

"The nature of illness and female success and the capacity of the female to acknowledge its own intelligence is a subject that interests me a lot."

Kathleen Collins was a playwright, fiction writer, and filmmaker whose work focuses on the intimate spaces of Black people's lives, but especially those of Black women. Her characters sort through their private doubts and arguments with lovers and try to find their place in a world where home life is always revealing something about identity and self-perception. Though she died of breast cancer at the young age of forty-six, before her work was widely appreciated, Kathleen Collins has become better known through the efforts of her daughter, writer Nina Lorez Collins, who has guided her mother's work to greater visibility in recent years. I find myself pausing, when thinking about this young artist. What would life have been for her had she not died so young?

Collins's writing wasn't published while she was alive, but she did get to see her work as a screenwriter and filmmaker emerge before she passed away. Her 1982 *Losing Ground*, which she both wrote and directed, was one of the first feature films directed by a Black woman. And yet *Losing Ground* didn't receive distribution in theaters when it was made. Collins's story of a female philosophy professor feeling overshadowed by marriage and her painter husband aired publicly for the first time when it played to a sold-out crowd at Lincoln Center in 2015. Its reemergence was thanks to her daughter's efforts.

When Nina Lorez Collins began excavating her mother's creative archive in 2006, the question she faced was, What could be published or restored? A great deal, as it turns out. In 2015, A Public Space posthumously published Collins's short story "Interiors." The Film Society of Lincoln Center's showing of *Losing Ground* was described by the *New Yorker* as "the great rediscovery of 2015." In December 2016, a collection of Collins's short stories was published by Ecco, an imprint of HarperCollins, titled *Whatever Happened to Interracial Love?* The title story was also published in *Granta* magazine in July 2016. Huffington Post, *New York* magazine, the *Boston Globe*, Literary Hub, and *The Millions* couldn't wait to read it. The collection received starred reviews in *Kirkus Reviews* and *Publishers Weekly*. Every literary organization was waiting to put this publication on its list of most anticipated books of the year.

In the collections *Whatever Happened to Interracial Love?* (short stories) and *Notes from a Black Woman's Diary* (fiction, plays, screenplays, and diary entries) published in 2019 by Ecco, Collins allows her characters to live imperfectly. These stories, by capturing the nuance of being a Black woman, draw in readers. The collective modern embrace of Collins's work is indicative of both her timelessness and the promise she had that is still being fulfilled.

JOHN WILLIAM COLTRANE

(1926–1967)

"My music is the spiritual expression of what I am—my faith, my knowledge, my being.... When you begin to see the possibilities of music, you desire to do something really good for people, to help humanity free itself from its hang-ups.... I want to speak to their souls."

When *A Love Supreme* was released in 1965, it was clear that it was a defining album for jazz saxophonist John Coltrane. The musician had written a letter to listeners as part of the record and used the work, at once both cohesive and wildly lacking form, to articulate a spiritual connection that could be expressed only through music. Throughout his prolific career, Coltrane made many albums, of which *Giant Steps* and *My Favorite Things* are among his most iconic. But *A Love Supreme* was his offering of thanks for being able to convey his intended message through his sound. It is inconceivable that there could ever be another artist like him.

He was born and raised in North Carolina, in a religious home. His father was John R. Coltrane and his mother was Alice Blair. He expressed musical interest early on, especially in the saxophone. In high school, he also started playing the clarinet in a community band. Soon he was playing professionally at a cocktail lounge.

In 1945, Coltrane enlisted in the Navy and shipped off to Pearl Harbor. When he left the Navy in 1946, he went to Philadelphia, falling into the bebop scene. There he was both student and accom-plished musician. He once said of this time, "A wider area of listening opened up for me. There were many things that people . . . were doing in the '40s that I didn't understand, but that I felt emotionally." He practiced all the time, but nothing prepared him for meeting the musical giant Charlie Parker. "The first time I heard Bird play, it hit me right between the eyes."

Coltrane came of age in the big band era, and the sounds he heard as he grew older included the urgent bebop of artists such as Parker and Dizzy Gillespie. But Coltrane was always after something original in his own expression, and that commitment appeared on the bandstand as an obsession with revisiting musical phrases that some read as too raw for performance. Others saw in the rawness of his music perhaps what a practitioner of sport sees in the repeated drill—that every time it's different because nothing can be as it was, even if it *just* was.

Coltrane described *A Love Supreme* as his effort to say, "Thank you, God," after he'd recovered from a bout with drugs. In four parts, listeners get the world of his gratitude and humility, every nuance of the experiment that is a human life laid bare.

CLAUDETTE COLVIN

(1939–PRESENT)

"I'd like my grandchildren to be able to see that their grandmother stood up for something, a long time ago."

On March 2, 1955, in Montgomery, Alabama, nine months before the venerated civil rights legend Rosa Parks refused to surrender her seat on a segregated city bus, fifteen-year-old Claudette Colvin refused to give up her place to a standing white woman when confronted by the bus driver and then a pair of police officers. Remembering the incident decades later, she recalled, "It felt like history had me glued to the seat." In response to repeated demands that she give up her seat, she said, "I paid my fare and it's my constitutional right to sit here." White passengers weren't silent witnesses: Colvin said they chimed in, yelling, "She's gotta move. It's the law!"

The police officers arrested Colvin. She was locked in a cell with no opportunity to phone her parents, but her classmates alerted her mother, Mary Ann Colvin, who was working as a domestic, caring for a white family's children. The classmates stayed with the children so that Mrs. Colvin could fetch her daughter, which she did with her pastor, who drove her to the police station.

For years, Black activists had been reflecting on the issue of segregated buses in Montgomery and strategizing about what to do. An organized event would need to take place. But there seemed to be concerns about using the young Colvin as the face of this new action. After all, she was a kid, and in the days after her singular protest, she wasn't the most beloved individual in Montgomery.

Rosa Parks, who was an esteemed figure in the NAACP, seemed to better fit civil rights leaders' ideas of who could best personify the issue of the Montgomery Bus Boycott. She was a longtime member and, at the time of her arrest for her bus protest, the Montgomery chapter's secretary. Critics say that as a fairer-skinned, married adult woman, she was more palatable to the organization's decision makers.

So Claudette Colvin was not the name that accompanied the historic boycott, nor was much credit extended her way. It was a kind of erasure, Colvin thought, and she felt stigmatized. Other important women too failed to get credit: think of Georgia Gilmore's coordinated cooking efforts that raised funds so that Black people could pay for transportation alternatives and didn't have to break the bus strike to get to work.

Colvin's courageous contributions are on the record, and history is starting to catch up. Individual choices shape the course of Black liberation just as much as, if not more than, large-scale structural ones. Just over a year after the start of the Montgomery Bus Boycott, Colvin served as a witness, alongside coplaintiffs Aurelia Browder, Susie McDonald, and Mary Louise Smith, in the landmark *Browder v. Gayle* case, which outlawed segregation in public transportation in Alabama—a finding that would later be applied throughout the United States.

THE COMPTON COWBOYS

"At some point in the later 19th Century, one in four cowboys were black. . . . We never got a chance to shine because a lot of it was taken from us, or capitalists took it over, or we just got overshadowed."

—Randy Savvy

The Compton Cowboys are a Los Angeles–based collective that pays homage to the history of Black American cowboys, with a focus on sharing this legacy with Black youth in South Central LA. The current iteration consists of a group of friends, but their work is inspired by the original Compton Cowboys, who came together almost three decades earlier, in the 1990s. Current members are Ant Dogg, Carlton, CeeJay, Kee, Kika, Lay, Randy Savvy, and Stona Mane, many of whom came to the world of horseback riding as an alternative to gang life and related violence in the area.

Quiet as this aspect of western life is kept elsewhere, this posse gives a nod to the history of the Black cowboy in the American West and Southwest. In the 1870s and 1880s, as many as 25 percent of cowboys in the Old West were Black. The art of bulldogging (a form of rodeo) was created by a Black ranch hand, Bill Pickett. Bob Lemmons, formerly enslaved before settling in Texas, became famous for taming herds of wild mustangs. The Compton Cowboys know these stories and carry on the tradition.

The collective operates from the Richland Farms area, where Black horse riders have been present for more than seventy years. The Cowboys' horses are often donated and sometimes come from situations where they were abused or neglected. For the kids learning to care for the horses under the guidance of the Cowboys, the healing practice of caring for an animal can help create a meaningful and safe space to project and receive empathy, which can be particularly life-changing for kids in environments that expose them to increased trauma and loss. The group also aims to consistently compete in rodeos, but both the high cost of horses and their limited resources—they operate on a donation-based model—make it difficult.

The Compton Cowboys ride around the city when they're not at the farm working with the horses and the kids, and they're known for their decisively Black aesthetic. Often in lieu of boots and denim button-downs, they wear designer accessories and baseball caps. In a community where Black people are over-policed and underserved, the highly visible Compton Cowboys offer a reminder to youth that sometimes other options are available, that young people don't have to abandon everything about themselves to try those other avenues, and that, in fact, becoming a cowboy can mean *embracing* Black culture.

FANNY JACKSON COPPIN

(1837–1913)

"Good manners will often take people where neither money nor education will take them."

Nothing about the circumstances in which Fanny Jackson Coppin entered the world would suggest she'd become a national leader in education. But despite being born enslaved in 1837, when it was both illegal and dangerous for Black people to attempt to become literate, she not only educated herself, but taught others, so that generations of Black educators could pursue their own opportunities.

Born in Washington, DC, Coppin was fortunate enough to have an aunt who was able to purchase the younger woman's freedom. She went north to Newport, Rhode Island, and worked as a domestic laborer before moving to Ohio, where she enrolled at Oberlin College. Coppin understood that, because Black people had been denied formal learning opportunities for centuries, it was critical to take advantage of them when they presented themselves. At Oberlin, she also taught a night class in reading and writing for freed slaves while pursuing her own studies.

Fanny Jackson Coppin spent her formative years relentlessly pursing an education. It was clear that she wanted more than what was normally offered to a young woman. In her autobiography, *Reminiscences of School Life, and Hints on Teaching*, she writes, "The faculty did not forbid a woman to take the gentleman's course, but they did not advise it. I took a long breath and prepared for a delightful contest. All went smoothly until I was in the junior year in College. The Faculty informed me that it was their purpose to give me a class, but I was to distinctly understand that if the pupils rebelled against my teaching, they did not intend to force it. Fortunately for my training at the normal school, and my own dear love of teaching, tho there was a little surprise on the faces of some when they came into the class, and saw the teacher, there were no signs of rebellion."

Despite her love of learning and teaching, Coppin felt the weight of being a pioneer and a Black woman: "I never rose to recite in my classes at Oberlin but I felt that I had the honor of the whole African race upon my shoulders. I felt that, should I fail, it would be ascribed to the fact that I was colored."

Upon graduating in 1865, Coppin was appointed to the Institute for Colored Youth, a Quaker school for young women in Philadelphia (which is today Cheyney University). Within four years, she was promoted to head principal. The school focused on training future educators, and she created curricula that allowed women to hone technical and artistic skills alongside their academic studies. In 1881 she married Reverend Levi Coppin, a minister of the African Methodist Episcopal Church, and after her retirement in 1902 they traveled to South Africa to work as missionaries. It was during this period that Coppin wrote her autobiography.

A teacher-training school in Baltimore, Fanny Jackson Coppin Normal School, was named for Coppin in 1926. After decades of curriculum expansion, it was renamed Coppin State University in 2004.

HANNAH CRAFTS

(CA. 1830S–UNKNOWN)

"Words cannot express how meaningful this is to African-American literary studies. It revolutionizes our understanding of the canon of black women's literature."

The Bondwoman's Narrative, written perhaps in the late 1850s, is one of the earliest autobiographical fiction narratives, and may be the first novel written by a Black American woman. As far as historians can ascertain, it's the only known novel authored by a fugitive enslaved woman.

The story follows a lighter-skinned girl who flees a North Carolina plantation and passes as a young white man to achieve freedom and safety in the North. Hannah is a house slave in North Carolina, and the novel tells us how she grew up. We learn that she was taught to read and write by Aunt Hetty, an old white woman.

Hannah is a lady's maid at the Lindendale plantation. While serving there, she discovers a secret. Mr. Trappe, a lawyer, has found out that the lady of the house is a fair-skinned mulatto, passing for white. Hannah and her mistress escape from the plantation, get lost, and take refuge in a shack. When they discover that their hiding place had been the scene of a murder, Hannah's mistress goes to the brink of insanity from fear.

Much later the women are found by slave hunters, who take them to prison. The two women, after a long while in captivity, suddenly understand that their warden is Mr. Trappe. This discovery so distresses the mistress that she suffers a brain aneurysm and dies. But wait! That's not the end of the novel. Hannah is sold to a slave trader, who subsequently dies during a horse accident. It takes other turns from there until Hannah escapes, runs away to the North, and finds her biological mother. She then marries a Methodist minister and they live in New Jersey.

In the preface, Crafts writes that she hopes "to show how slavery blights the lives of whites as well as the black race." The book is signed "Hannah Crafts"; but in 2013, an English professor, Gregg Hecimovich, found that the identity of the author was likely Hannah Bond. Among the experts who peer-reviewed Hecimovich's research, which was reported in the *New York Times*, was Henry Louis Gates Jr., a leading scholar of African American history, who was responsible for the novel's publication in 2002. The book's story reflects many of the experiences Bond herself had as an enslaved young woman in Murfreesboro, North Carolina. She escaped in 1857, eventually relocating to New Jersey.

The existence of *The Bondwoman's Narrative* illustrates that, across modalities, Black figures found ways to ensure that their stories could be preserved and retold.

CELIA CRUZ

(1925–2003)

"When people hear me sing, I want them to be happy, happy, happy. I don't want them thinking about when there's not any money, or when there's fighting at home. My message is always felicidad—happiness."

Celia Cruz, "the Queen of Salsa," was born Úrsula Hilaria Celia de la Caridad Cruz Alfonso de la Santísima Trinidad in Havana, Cuba. Through her roughly seventy-five albums, always in her native Spanish, she established herself as the godmother of Afro-Latin music. Known for a booming voice, colorful stage costumes, a grand smile, and a creative willingness to develop her sound, she grew to become a beloved and cherished symbol of Latin pride throughout the diaspora.

When Celia was a child, her father wanted her to become a teacher, so she attended the Normal School for Teachers in Havana. She soon dropped out, however. Although she was only a teenager, her live and radio performances were already gaining widespread attention. In an effort to combine both her father's dreams for her and her own passion, she enrolled at Havana's National Conservatory of Music, studying voice, theory, and piano. Her time there wasn't long either. One of Cruz's professors told her that she should devote herself to a full-time singing career. She took that advice.

Early in her career, she was known for *guaracha*, the Cuban genre of music defined by fast-paced tempos and funny, illustrative lyrics. It was during this period, in the late 1940s and into the 1950s, that she began exclaiming "¡Azúcar!" ("Sugar!") as a rallying cry during her performances, a stylistic signature if you will. That word, with its connotation of sugar plantations, was a kind of salute to the an-cestral enslaved Africans whose culture had shaped the music she grew up hearing in her working-class neighborhood—a history that continues to influence Cuban culture today.

Cruz was singing with the ensemble La Sonora Matancera when, in 1960, they publicly renounced Fidel Castro and his socialist agenda while on tour in Mexico. The cost of that transparency was severe—the band was exiled from Cuba. As a result, Cruz and her partner and fellow band member Pedro Knight relocated to the United States.

In New York, Cruz became an influential part of the salsa scene, recording solo and in collaborations with musicians that included Tito Puente and Willie Colón. When she died in 2003 from brain cancer, her funeral was attended by thousands. Her mausoleum in the Woodlawn Cemetery in the Bronx is often visited by fans. They consider her a voice for the people. That's no small feat when one considers the male-dominated industry in which Cruz rose to acclaim. She was awarded the National Medal of Arts in 1994 and a posthumous Lifetime Achievement Grammy.

Despite the awards and acclaim, she felt responsible to her father's desire that she become a teacher. In a 1997 interview, she said, "I have fulfilled my father's wish to be a teacher as, through my music, I teach generations of people about my culture and the happiness that is found in just living life. As a performer, I want people to feel their hearts sing and their spirits soar."

DOROTHY DANDRIDGE

(1922–1965)

"Prejudice is such a waste. . . . It gives you nothing. It takes away. And it is superficial like so many of our responses today."

Looking at pretty much any photograph of Dorothy Dandridge, one might understandably assume that she was destined for show business: her perfect, short dark curls; a shocker of a smile; and a svelte figure that seemed effortless. Her mother, radio and television entertainer Ruby Dandridge, had ushered her along the way. Ruby had raised her daughters, Dorothy and older sister Vivian, to sing and dance.

Dorothy and her sister performed a song-and-dance act throughout the country, first as the Wonder Children and then as part of the young trio the Dandridge Sisters (with Etta Jones, a family friend). Their success was clear: they opened for famous acts such as Cab Calloway. In 1935, the trio began appearing in films.

In 1942, Dandridge married Harold Nicholas, of the dancing Nicholas Brothers. Their daughter, Harolyn, was born with severe brain trauma. Harolyn's compromised development and the prevalent mental-health guidance at the time led Dandridge to eventually send her daughter away to a private residential hospital. (She and Nicholas had split by then.) Dandridge remained haunted by that decision throughout the rest of her life.

A showstopping 1951 performance with bandleader and actor Desi Arnaz helped spotlight Dandridge's talent. She'd been working in the movies for years but landed a starring role only in 1953, in the film *Bright Road*. The peak of her success came soon after, when she was cast as the lead in the musical *Carmen Jones*, opposite Harry Belafonte. With an all-Black cast, this 1954 film was directed by Otto Preminger.

For her portrayal of Jones—a defiant, saucy vixen type—Dandridge earned a best actress Academy Award nomination, the first Black woman to receive that honor. That same year she was the first Black woman to be featured on the cover of *Life* magazine.

Although Dandridge far exceeded her mother's early aspirations, her career—like that of so many others—was constrained by racist conventions. She should have had the opportunities and reached the heights of any white actors of the period. But opportunities for Black actors to headline films were few and far between, if they existed at all. Dandridge refused to play the role of an enslaved person in the film *The King and I* in 1956. Despite the success of *Carmen Jones*, she wasn't cast as a lead in another film until three years after her Oscar-nominated performance, when in 1957 she starred in *Island in the Sun*. In 1959, she starred in *Porgy and Bess* alongside Sammy Davis Jr. and Sidney Poitier. She died six years later of an accidental drug overdose. She wrote in her autobiography, *Everything and Nothing: The Dorothy Dandridge Tragedy*, "Whites weren't quite ready for full acceptance even of me, purportedly beautiful, passable, acceptable, talented, called by the critics every superlative in the lexicon employed for a talented and beautiful woman."

JULIE DASH

(1952–PRESENT)

"Whenever I do a film, it has to take us one step further to making the world safe for everyone."

When the feature film *Daughters of the Dust* opened in theaters in 1991, it was the first major release by a Black woman director in the United States. A story about the first generation of freeborn Black Americans living on Georgia's Sea Islands, the original screenplay was written and directed by Julie Dash, a descendant of the Gullah Geechee people. She was inspired by summers spent in Charleston with relatives, research she conducted while in film school at UCLA, and Vertamae Smart-Grosvenor's 1970 cookbook-memoir, *Vibration Cooking: Or, The Travel Notes of a Geechee Girl*.

Born in Long Island City, New York, Dash grew up hearing relatives speak the Gullah dialect on summer visits to Charleston, but she didn't understand the depth of her familial history at the time—that her heritage reflected the language, rituals, and culture of West African people whose geographic isolation had allowed them to preserve elements of their history in ways that eluded many other African Americans.

After launching her film studies at the Studio Museum of Harlem's Cinematography Workshop in 1969, Dash attended the Leonard Davis Center for the Performing Arts at City College of New York, where she earned her bachelor's degree in film production in 1974; she went on to earn a master's in film and television at UCLA. It was at UCLA that she began researching her family heritage.

Daughters of the Dust is set in 1902 and focuses on the Peazant family, which is facing a huge transition: the younger generation is ready to pursue life on the mainland, but the family matriarch, Nana, refuses to say goodbye to her ancestral home. The film, sweeping in its blend of natural beauty, Black southern gothic aesthetics, and serene, pastoral imagery, won best cinematography at the Sundance Film Festival and opened to positive critical reviews. The film was selected for preservation in the National Film Registry by the Library of Congress in 2004.

Dash didn't receive the onslaught of work opportunities that such accolades traditionally garner for white male directors. Absent invitations to direct feature films, Dash went on to direct music videos for artists such as Tracy Chapman, Keb' Mo', and Tony! Toni! Toné!; a biopic on Rosa Parks; and works for corporate clients.

When Beyoncé featured referential imagery inspired by *Daughters of the Dust* in her musical album *Lemonade*, it sparked renewed interest in Dash's seminal work that coincided with the twenty-fifth anniversary of her film's release. Dash started developing a documentary about Smart-Grosvenor, whose work had inspired her decades earlier and whose storytelling pays ongoing homage to southern Black life, vernacular, and custom. Dash is guided by a constant principle as she pursues her art: "Every morning I get up and say, please ancestors help me."

CHARLES DAWSON

(1889–1981)

"[I] sought to paint blacks as they are . . . to paint [them] the way Millet painted the French peasants."

A celebrated fine artist and masterful commercial illustrator, Charles Dawson was a prolific voice in Chicago's Black arts scene in the early twentieth century. He shepherded a community of artists who created the New Negro movement, portraying beauty and dignity in African American life.

Born in Brunswick, Georgia, Dawson studied architectural drafting at the Tuskegee Institute before moving to New York in 1907. There he took drawing classes and worked side jobs, including recurring summer stints as a Pullman porter, before heading west to enroll at the School of the Art Institute of Chicago. Dawson cofounded the Arts and Letters Society, a Black artists' collective, with classmates Archibald Motley Jr. and William Farrow. His plan to work as a professional artist was interrupted by World War I. Weeks after he graduated from art school, the United States entered the conflict. Dawson ultimately served in combat in France as a lieutenant.

After the war, he returned to Chicago, where employers had become more inclined to hire women and Black people in the postwar economic climate. Dawson had to take work as a salesperson initially, then sought freelance art assignments. His clients were companies that sought the business of local affluent Black people, such as Annie Turnbo Malone's Poro College, a cosmetology school, and Valmor Products, a beauty company. The bottles, boxes, and tins for which Dawson created imagery reflect the style of the time. The products included Slick Back to cover gray hair; face powders for women that promoted fairer skin; and hair products that restrained the kink of natural hair. Seen from a modern viewpoint, the conflict of colorism seems obvious. But Dawson's approach was considered fresh and subversive—he refused to engage with negative stereotypes, choosing to focus on aspiration and pleasure.

In his fine artwork, he developed a signature style linking iconic figures in African history and mythology with modern-day characters. This is particularly clear in the 1934 concert poster "O Sing a New Song," which features an elegant Black singer dressed in a flowing gown, centered in front of the Sphinx and pyramids of Egypt, while a contemporary audience dances below. The piece is now held by the Metropolitan Museum of Art. Dawson's efforts aligned with the larger national Black arts renaissance of the 1920s, often incorrectly relegated to Harlem, with writers, musicians, and artists reflecting the dignity and pride they witnessed in their own communities.

In 1933, Dawson wrote and illustrated the children's book *ABCs of Great Negroes*, in which each letter of the alphabet cues a contributor to Black history. The work honors figures such as Mary McLeod Bethune and Frederick Douglass alongside the Egyptian queen Nefertiti. Dawson's unpublished autobiography is held in the archives of the DuSable Museum of African American History in Chicago.

DANIEL "DAPPER DAN" DAY

(1944–PRESENT)

"Everything I do has to have the ability to be transformative."

Growing up poor in Harlem, Daniel Day was still young when he understood that, given his circumstances, he needed to look good to have a chance at living good. He was taken by the stylish embellishments of the hustlers and gangsters around the neighborhood. He fell in love with furs, silky shirts, and suits. But new threads were a luxury in his family, even when the old ones didn't fit. When his mother hit the numbers, she'd buy her kids new shoes. The instability of these circumstances affected Day as he got older and developed his own street-running skills. He earned the moniker "Dapper Dan" as a result of his gambling prowess. But hearing a Malcolm X speech changed his behavior.

Day determined that he didn't want the gambling life he'd grown up in, so he traded the dice and drugs for vegetarianism, Black nationalist politics, involvement with the Black Panthers, and a return to education thanks to an Urban League–sponsored program at Columbia University. He visited Africa, spending time in countries like Nigeria and Zaire, as part of the Urban League–Columbia program. Day knew he wanted something different from the life he had been exposed to growing up; he decided to become a clothing designer and retailer.

Rap and hip-hop were emerging in American popular culture, and it was during this period—in 1982—that Day taught himself textile printing and then opened the Dapper Dan Boutique on 125th Street. The shop was often open twenty-four hours a day, seven days a week. He became known for his reversible furs, where the leather inside mimicked the iconography of fashion giants such as Louis Vuitton and Gucci. Soon his wears were sought after by not only the gangsters, but the rappers too: LL Cool J, Slick Rick, Big Daddy Kane. Day's mimicry was evident in a 1989 piece he developed—one that would become iconic—for gold-medal Olympian Diane Dixon. He fabricated a bomber jacket with mahogany-colored fur and balloon sleeves, its fabric etched with a faux Louis Vuitton insignia.

Soon, thanks to his relationships with the hip-hop community, Day was featured on *Yo! MTV Raps*, a popular music program, but the exposure brought Day legal troubles. The fashion brands that Day often remixed into his apparel initiated police raids claiming infringements on their protected work. Day eventually had to shut his business down.

Two decades later, in 2018, that iconic Diane Dixon bomber jacket suddenly appeared on a Gucci runway. In responding to that surprise appearance, Day said Gucci was never one of the brands that had ordered his shop raided. The attention forced a conversation and ultimately a collaboration. Day was offered a deal with Gucci to develop a global capsule collection that worked exclusively with the big firm's fabrics and patterns. Day continues to mentor young designers, his aim being to serve the tastes and desires of the streets from which he came.

WE ARE BLACK HISTORY

by Emil Wilbekin

When I was in the third grade, I remember my parents telling me very matter-of-factly that I wouldn't be going to school on a particular Monday in observance of Dr. Martin Luther King Jr.'s birthday. It was the third Monday in January—the day that the Black community celebrated Dr. King's January 15th birthday. I was obviously grateful to get a day off from school but was confused, because that was not an "official" holiday as noted on the school's calendar, and the rest of my mostly white classmates would be going to school that day. Martin Luther King Jr. Day didn't become a federal holiday until 1983, almost ten years after my parents peacefully protested my school attendance on the birthday of the slain civil rights leader.

You see, my parents, attorney Harvey E. Wilbekin and Dr. Cleota P. Wilbekin, were radical and revolutionary. My mother called the principal of Our Redeemer Lutheran School and let the office know: her son would not be attending that day in observance of the civil rights movement leader's birthday. Period. End of discussion. My parents didn't go to work that day either. They were peacefully protesting in the most nonviolent manner in tribute to Dr. King's work and vision, but also to instill in me a sense of Black pride, racial confidence, and an awareness of Black history, not just for myself, but to remind my school and their own places of employment. They were making a subtle but substantial statement about race, culture, and identity that would inspire and empower me for the rest of my life.

When I was growing up, I didn't think my parents were being radical and pro-Black. I thought they were just being my parents. Taking me out of school for Martin Luther King Day or Three Kings Day, wearing a dashiki, and teaching me about Harriet Tubman, Sojourner Truth, Booker T. Washington, Benjamin Banneker, the Tuskegee Airmen, Shirley Chisholm, Alvin Ailey, Thurgood Marshall, and Constance Baker Motley were what Black families did. I grew up in a mostly Black neighborhood, attended a Lutheran church in a Black neighborhood, was a Cub Scout in a Black troop, played on a Black Little League team, was a member of Jack and Jill, and was clear that I was enough and that the white man's ice wasn't colder than my own. My parents participated in desegregation during the civil rights movement and were active in the NAACP, Alpha Kappa Alpha sorority, Kappa Alpha Psi fraternity, and the National Bar Association—my mother even served a stint as the historian of the NBA.

. . .

My mother was born in Des Moines, Iowa. Her family had migrated from the South post-Emancipation to Illinois and then to Des Moines. Her great-grandfather had been a soldier in the Union Army. Her grandmother was an entrepreneur who had grown wealthy. Her father was the general manager at the post office. My mother would always say two things: "We come from good stock" and "Yes, there are Black people in Iowa." She was a self-described "overachiever" who graduated from high school at sixteen, played on the all-white tennis team (which she integrated), and received her BA and MA from Drake University. She would go on to receive her JD and PhD (psychology), all while raising my brother and me, serving as the minister of music for our church, and actively participating in over twenty civic and social organizations. Eventually, she became a master quilter whose work is housed in the Smithsonian Institution.

My father was born on St. Croix, US Virgin Islands, and was the youngest of thirteen children. His father worked for the telephone company, and our family was prominent in the town of Christiansted on the island—which reportedly had been discovered by Christopher Columbus and was then colonized by the British and later the Dutch. My father attended Hampton Institute—the same historically Black university attended by Booker T. Washington in the Tidewater region of Virginia. The Emancipation Oak tree stands there still, right where it did when newly freed slaves first were allowed to begin their education. My grandparents didn't have enough money to send both my dad and his older sister to college, so my Aunt Beryl deferred, meaning that my father could attend. He studied architecture and would later attend Brooklyn Polytechnic and become an architectural engineer. He would eventually become the commissioner of building and inspections for the city of Cincinnati. Eventually, though, he followed my mother's lead: he attended law school and opened his own private practice.

I tell the stories of my parents because their stories, and millions of other unsung stories, are the threads that make up Black history. They were Black folks who wanted to survive and thrive. They were a part of the burgeoning Black middle class in America, but their Blackness was the root of their existence and identity—the Black community was the cornerstone of our family life, our rock. My parents are my Black history heroes. Their ambition, intellect, creativity, self-actualization, and vision for their lives were light years ahead of their time. They were committed to success, social justice, and a standard of excellence rooted in my mother's midwestern values and my father's West Indian work ethic. They instilled these values in my brother Erik and me. "Don't let anyone tell you that you are less than." My brother and I would attend Hampton University like my dad, my uncles, and an aunt. The university's motto of "The Standard of Excellence" was and is one of the mantras in my life.

• • •

My mother became very ill at the age of eighty-three. She developed congestive heart failure and her decline was steep, quick, and exhausting. It was hard for me to watch this once-vibrant woman literally wither before my eyes. The loss of any parent is difficult, but the death of a mother is especially sharp—especially my mother. It was about my losing not just the woman who had raised me but also the woman who had allowed me to be the quirky, creative, and deeply introspective child (and eventually man) I would become without interference and with great enthusiasm. In many ways, I believe my mother lived vicariously through me. She had a spectacular and very liberated life for a Black woman born in 1927. I love that she was able to see me shift culture and consciousness about being a Black gay man in America. I was able to attend an HBCU, study abroad in London, attend Columbia University's Graduate School of Journalism, become an editor-in-chief of *Vibe* magazine, win a National Magazine Award, and be featured in the *New York Times*; I was able to write for the Associated Press, the *Chicago Tribune*, *Essence*, *Rolling Stone*, and *Town & Country*; I was able to be an HIV+ man and activist, start a movement for Black gay and queer men called Native Son, and live my life as a successful and noteworthy Black creative. Before she died, I remember my mother telling me that I had surpassed my parents' wildest dreams. "You went to New York City and took it by storm," she said.

What made me most sad about my mother's death was that not only did I lose my mom, but America lost a hidden figure, a vibrant piece of the African American quilt, and a visionary, dreamer, and doer who helped change the way the world would see Black people, identity, and culture. My mother very poetically died on the twentieth anniversary of my father's death. I am grateful to have been raised by two incredible Black people who dared to be free, who fought for civil rights, and whose very existence made them my personal heroes. We are *all* Black history, because we survived the generational trauma of our ancestors and continued—*still* continue—to thrive and live lives that are filled with resistance, nonconformity, and Black joy.

Emil Wilbekin is a journalist, media executive, stylist, content creator, culture critic, and human rights activist. He is the founder of Native Son, a platform created to inspire and empower Black gay men. Wilbekin is the former editor-in-chief at *Vibe* and *Giant* and editor-at-large at *Essence*.

ROY DECARAVA

(1919–2009)

"You should be able to look at me and see my work. You should be able to look at my work and see me."

Roy DeCarava didn't set out to become a photographer. Seeing the world through a lens was at first part of his process as a painter and printmaker in 1940s New York: he collected images to reference later. But the immediacy and the visceral quality of photographs eventually literally shifted his focus. DeCarava went on to become a genre-defining artist of the mid-twentieth century. His images captured the spectrum of Black life, from the mundane times of everyday existence to the precious, poignant moments of iconic figures such as John Coltrane. DeCarava's 1961 portrait of that groundbreaking musician—a striking black-and-white image that conveys a vibrational, sonic urgency—is housed at the National Portrait Gallery in Washington, DC. Anyone who's heard Coltrane play will recognize what the image achieves.

DeCarava's 1955 bestselling collaborative work with Langston Hughes, *The Sweet Flypaper of Life*, presents a raw yet tender portrayal of Harlem. Accompanied by Hughes's poetry, which narratively concerns itself with a grandmother character named Sister Mary Bradley, the photographs illustrate a Black neighborhood defiant in its isolation but also whole and celebratory. In "Graduation," one image from the book, a girl wearing a pale dress and pale gloves moves through a street marked with distress: trash and vacancy. An open plot of land seems destined for a looming high-rise, juxtaposed against peeling advertisements and fences. Harlem is in transition, DeCarava seems to say. But for whom, and to what?

Born in Harlem to a Jamaican mother, Elfreda Ferguson, DeCarava worked as a young boy shining shoes and delivering newspapers. Ferguson was an amateur photographer herself. She encouraged DeCarava's interest in visual arts with lessons, and he went on to win a scholarship to study art and architecture at Cooper Union. He later won a 1952 Guggenheim Fellowship, a $3,200 award that enabled him to make photographs full-time. He was the first Black photographer to receive that honor, and he used his access in the art world to push for the acknowledgment of photography as a fine art form by museum institutions and for equity and representation of Black photographers in publications like *Life* magazine. He was active on the Committee to End Discrimination Against Black Photographers.

Just as Frederick Douglass made sitting for photographic portraits an aspect of his work as an abolitionist, to illustrate his own humanity—and by that the humanity of all Black people—one hundred years later DeCarava chose to use the medium of photography to document everyday Black life in his community of Harlem.

In an interview, DeCarava cited the many ways his art had been categorized over the years. He'd been called a documentary photographer, a photographer of people, a street photographer, a jazz photographer, and of course a Black photographer. "But," he said, "I need all of those to define myself."

RUBY DEE AND OSSIE DAVIS

(RUBY DEE, 1922–2014)
(OSSIE DAVIS, 1917–2005)

"You can only appreciate freedom, when you find yourself in a position to fight for someone else's freedom and not worry about your own."

—Ruby Dee

Together, as they always were, Ruby Dee and Ossie Davis created a shared career in entertainment that spanned more than six decades. The couple met in the Black New York theater world in the 1940s and went on to perform, often as a duo, in more than fifty films.

In addition to their omnipresent roles as actors, they were activists offstage and offscreen, staunchly supporting the civil rights movement and befriending its leaders. They supported actor and singer Paul Robeson when he was blacklisted and were close friends of Martin Luther King Jr. and Malcolm X. Davis delivered the eulogy at Malcolm's funeral. He performed a version of that speech in voice-over at the end of Spike Lee's film *Malcolm X*.

Dee was born in New Rochelle, New York, and raised in Harlem. She joined the American Negro Theater in 1940. She graduated from Hunter College with a degree in romance languages in 1945.

Davis was from Cogdell, Georgia, and abandoned his studies at Howard University to pursue acting in New York in 1939. (He'd later continue his education at Columbia University.) He landed with the Rose McClendon Players, a performance outfit that was based just a few blocks from Dee's troupe. Their paths crossed when they were both cast in the play *Jeb* on Broadway in 1946, and they married two years later.

Onstage, Dee and Davis acted in eleven plays together. Dee was the original actress in the role of Ruth Younger in the 1959 production of Lorraine Hansberry's *A Raisin in the Sun*, the first play by a Black playwright on Broadway. When Sidney Poitier left his role as Walter Younger, Dee's husband, Davis, stepped in. By the 1970s, they had become part of the Black independent film movement. During that time, Davis wrote and directed several films. They never stopped embracing younger artists.

Spike Lee cast Dee and Davis in his films *Do the Right Thing* and *Jungle Fever*, which introduced them to a new generation of viewers. One of Dee's final roles was as the mother in Lee's *American Gangster*, starring Denzel Washington. For Davis, one of his last roles was as the discerning judge in Lee's *She Hate Me*, starring Anthony Mackie.

Married for fifty-seven years, Dee and Davis demonstrated a mutual tenderness and respect for their work and legacies, and an appreciation for how fortunate they were to have had the ability to perform. Both Dee and Davis were named to the NAACP Image Awards Hall of Fame in 1989; then, in 1995, they received the National Medal of Arts. In 2004, they received Kennedy Center Honors for their lifelong contributions to the performing arts.

THORNTON DIAL

(1928–2016)

"It seem like some people believe that, just because I ain't got no education, say I must be too ignorant for art."

For his art, which he'd been making long before he knew the materials he put together could be called art, Thornton Dial used objects he'd found. Generally, the pieces he liked to pick had once been of use to somebody: old rope, fabric, metal scraps, wood, clothing, toys. He was entirely self-taught. His sculptures and canvases were often several feet wide and long, the texture like the rugged yet beautiful topography of a sky view.

The Beginning of Life in the Yellow Jungle, from 2003, is roughly nine feet wide and six feet tall. A tapestry of bedding, wire, and plastic bottles, it evokes a burnished yellow wasteland with gashes of bright red spray paint. A doll draped in fabric juts out at the top, while artificial flowers imply that something that once flourished will never again be vibrant. The piece evokes the journey of Black people in the American South, fixed to the land but maybe never beyond it. The rural southern life for Black people has been one of struggle, the piece seems to say. There is no nobility in this pain, but it is miraculous.

Dial was born in Emelle, Alabama, on a cotton plantation where his relatives worked as sharecroppers. He didn't attend much school as a kid; he picked cotton and worked on the farm. In 1940, when he was twelve, Dial moved to Bessemer, Alabama, and noted the art along the way in folks' front yards. He lived with relatives and did construction and factory work while making his pieces. He was illiterate.

The artist Lonnie Holley introduced Dial's work to an Atlanta collector, William Arnett, and word began to spread. By the 1990s, Dial's work was beginning to be shown in museum exhibitions. He was in his fifties before he considered what he'd been doing "art." The art establishment often described him as an "outsider" artist—meaning self-taught, with minimal or no influence from art institutions. The term is often used for Black artists; the quilters of Gee's Bend, Alabama, for example, were similarly described. Of course, identifying Black artists as outsiders places white artists squarely on the inside. But outsider status didn't seem to bother Dial: inherent in his work is a subversion, if not a wholehearted rejection, of the qualified acceptance he received.

Dial exhibited at the 2000 biennial celebration of the Whitney Museum of American Art, the Smithsonian American Art Museum in Washington, DC, and many other locations. His son Richard is a sculptor whose art is placed at multiple museums. He lives in Bessemer, making art as his father did.

EMORY DOUGLAS

(1943-PRESENT)

"Recognize that Art is a powerful tool, a language that can be used to Enlighten, Inform, a guide to Actions."

The Black Panther Party, founded in Oakland, California, in 1966, is often summarily depicted as an armed organization. But in the group's effort to achieve full liberation of Black people through gainful and fair employment, proper housing, access to education, the end of police brutality and state-sanctioned murder, and the abolition of prisons, it used artwork to convey its message. Emory Douglas was its revolutionary artist and minister of culture.

From 1967 to about 1980, Douglas was art director for the party's newspaper, which achieved a circulation into the hundreds of thousands nationwide. His choices didn't shy away from righteous and indignant criticism of US law enforcement—the institutions and the individuals that brought daily violence and harassment into Black communities throughout the country. "It may be a provocative interpretation, but it's not a distorted interpretation," he said.

Using silkscreens and collage, he depicted the Black Panthers as revolutionaries and used the visual image of the pig to denote the police. Uprisings were happening all over the country, and word needed to get out. "My art is about enlightening and arming people about issues," Douglas said.

Douglas was born in Grand Rapids, Michigan. When he was a child, he moved with his family to the Bay Area on the advice of a doctor who said the warmer climate would make his asthma easier to manage. The change of climate worked, but improved health also created opportunities for Douglas to get

into trouble. He was arrested as a thirteen-year-old, which landed him in a correctional facility of the California Youth Authority. During his fifteen-month sentence, he worked in the juvenile center's print shop, where he coincidentally received an introduction to design and illustration. He later took commercial art classes at the City College of San Francisco and was greatly influenced by the work of artists such as Elizabeth Catlett and Charles White in telling Black people's stories from and for a Black perspective.

He developed a bold visual look that mimicked woodcuts. His use of only one color was a result of budget constraints, but it became a signature style. A 1969 cover of the Black Panther newspaper shows a Black GI wearing a helmet with superimposed images of white police beating Black people. A protest sign in the background bears the words, "Our fight is not in Vietnam." Notably, the cover image depicts the Black soldier with tears streaming down his face, acknowledging the deep wounds incurred by so many who returned from the war.

Douglas's posters were often wheat-pasted throughout Oakland, conveying a countermessage to the one the white media propagated about who the Panthers were and what they aimed to achieve. Not all his images were born of struggle and pain. In one poster, captioned "We shall survive, without a doubt," bright rays emerge from behind a photograph of a smiling Black boy. The message is one of inherent joy and enduring hope.

FREDERICK DOUGLASS

(1818–1895)

"Freedom now appeared, to disappear no more forever. It was heard in every sound, and seen in everything. It was present to torment me with a sense of my wretched condition."

The child of an enslaved Black woman and likely her white owner, Frederick Augustus Washington Bailey was one of the most complex and celebrated figures of the nineteenth century. He became famous under the name Frederick Douglass. He and his wife chose that last name after he successfully escaped slavery; it was distinctive and referenced a Walter Scott poem. Douglass, a prolific writer and orator, esteemed patriot, and champion of equity, rose from the constraints of bondage to become one of the most photographed and likely most well-traveled public figures of the era in his advocacy for Black emancipation and meaningful civil rights for all Americans.

Despite the laws prohibiting Black people from learning to read and write, his owner taught him those skills when Douglass was still young, living in Baltimore. He escaped slavery at the age of twenty and lived another nine years as a fugitive, constantly aware that he could be recaptured. But the outrage Douglass felt toward slavery's brutality and the moral sin he understood the institution to be prompted him to leverage both his ability as a critical thinker and his galvanizing presence to work for abolition at every turn. He achieved international fame as a celebrated writer of three autobiographies, an orator renowned for his command of the podium, and an editor of news and opinion with the *North Star*—all of which helped shift the national conversation toward antislavery and Black liberation.

Over the course of his life, Douglass sat for around 160 portraits—more images exist of him than of Abraham Lincoln. Douglass thought of photography as a democratizing medium. He distributed copies, intending that the dignity and self-respect so palpable in his visage would carry over to other Black people still subjugated within slavery.

Douglass's best-known speech is "What to the Slave Is the Fourth of July?" which he delivered in Rochester, New York, on July 5, 1852. He questioned the rationale of inviting a Black man to celebrate the country that aimed to oppress him. "This Fourth of July is yours, not mine," he said. "Do you mean, citizens, to mock me, by asking me to speak today?" His words continue to resonate, casting unencumbered discernment on what the US *claims* to be versus what it actually *is*. "Could I reach the nation's ear," he said, "I would today pour out a fiery stream of biting ridicule, blasting reproach, withering sarcasm, and stern rebuke. For it is not light that is needed, but fire. . . . We need the storm, the whirlwind, and the earthquake."

At the onset of the Civil War, Douglass helped recruit Black soldiers to fight for the Union, petitioning Lincoln to permit Black men to join the army. Two of his sons eventually enlisted.

In his later years, Douglass served under presidents Rutherford Hayes, James Garfield, Chester Arthur, Grover Cleveland, and Benjamin Harrison.

PAUL LAURENCE DUNBAR

(1872–1906)

A minute to smile and an hour to weep in,
A pint of joy to a peck of trouble,
And never a laugh but the moans come double;
And that is life!

Paul Laurence Dunbar, whose stories and poetry often featured Black vernacular, was one of the first Black poets to receive national recognition.

At sixteen, Dunbar had his poems "Our Martyred Soldiers" and "On the River" published in the local newspaper. After finishing high school in 1891, he took odd jobs to earn money while writing. Given that low-key beginning, how did this young man accomplish so much in so little time? He had help. Dunbar asked a pair of brothers, the famed Wright brothers, to publish his dialect poems in book form. They referred him to the United Brethren Publishing House, which in 1893 printed Dunbar's first collection of poetry.

Charles A. Thatcher, a lawyer, offered to pay for his college, but Dunbar wanted to keep writing. He could have been a lawyer or become a politician, but these professional paths didn't speak to him. Yet pursuing his dreams wasn't easy; despite publishing poems and giving public readings, Dunbar struggled to support himself and his mother.

But success soon came to this poet and storyteller. In 1896, critic William Dean Howells published a rave review of Dunbar's second book, *Majors and Minors*, in *Harper's Weekly*. This brought national attention and encouraged the young writer. By the late 1890s, Dunbar was writing both short stories and novels.

Though the Wright brothers chose not to publish Dunbar's first book, the three men maintained a life-long friendship. Dunbar also became acquainted with some well-known Black people. Through his poetry, he met Black leaders such as Frederick Douglass and Booker T. Washington.

Inspired by his parents and pushed to succeed by personal ambition, Dunbar eventually garnered enough success to tour England reading his poetry. He then took a position as a clerk at the Library of Congress. But his triumph was short-lived; his health deteriorated, forcing him to vacate his position in Washington and return to his writing and performative readings. A prolific writer even when unwell, he wrote three more novels and three short-story collections before dying from pneumonia at the age of thirty-three.

His 1896 poem "We Wear the Mask" in some ways sums up his life:

We wear the mask that grins and lies,
It hides our cheeks and shades our eyes,—
This debt we pay to human guile;
With torn and bleeding hearts we smile,
And mouth with myriad subtleties.

KATHERINE DUNHAM

(1909–2006)

"[My aim was to] make the individual aware of himself and his environment, to create a desire to be alive."

Dancers training today are exposed to the Dunham technique, if they're fortunate. A singular form of movement born of Afro-Caribbean dance, classic European ballet, rhythmic movement, and pulsing isolations, the style was created by Katherine Dunham in the late 1920s. The Joliet, Illinois, native studied anthropology at the University of Chicago, where she concurrently studied dances of the African diaspora. While in Chicago, she was introduced to dance traditions from Indonesia and India that supplemented ballet classes she was taking. Her dance teacher, Ludmilla Speranzeva, was one of the earliest teachers to accept Black dancers.

Katherine Mary Dunham was born June 22, 1909, in Joliet. In high school she joined the Terpsichorean Club and began to learn modern dance based on the ideas of Europeans. At fifteen she organized "the Blue Moon Cafe," a fundraising cabaret to raise money for her Methodist Church in Joliet.

Dunham earned a grant after college that allowed her to go to the Caribbean to study African dance in countries such as Trinidad, Martinique, and Haiti. In 1930 she founded one of the first Black dance companies, Ballet Nègre, and went on to create other touring companies and schools during her career. She performed in ballets, including being featured as the lead in *La Guiablesse* in 1934, and she choreographed

and produced her own ballet, *L'Ag'Ya*. Later she appeared in films with her dance troupe—including in American films like *Stormy Weather* and *Casbah* and Italian films like *Mambo*.

As Zora Neale Hurston brought enthusiasm and respect to folkloric approaches to documenting Black vernacular in writing, Dunham was unique in the dance world for her intense and rigorous care in the treatment of the vast subject of Black dance. She appreciated the differing dance styles and histories that emerged in countries such as Brazil and Jamaica, while simultaneously possessing the physical skill to both absorb these movements herself and create a wholly new discipline. Beyond that, she had the academic grounding to place these dances in their historical context, seeing them as the product of generations of African people who, although forced to migrate, themselves retained ancestral movement while incorporating the traditions of their new communities and countries.

Her method is still taught today, no surprise, in dance schools like the Debbie Allen Dance Academy, where Allen, a prolific educator and choreographer, champions a learning environment in which young dancers are exposed to global forms of dance.

Dunham was a recipient of a Kennedy Center Honor and a National Medal of Arts.

YLA EASON

(CA. 1950–PRESENT)

"I made up my mind then that I would create Black superheroes for my son, and for all the other youngsters, so when they fantasize about good and evil, and strengths and weaknesses, they will understand that Blacks are equal to anyone else, on or off this planet."

When Yla Eason's nine-year-old son told her that he couldn't be strong and powerful like He-Man, a popular action hero of the late twentieth century, because He-Man was white and the son was Black, she decided something had to be done. It was 1985, and Eason couldn't find an action figure anything like the strapping and capable He-Man that looked like her son. There were no major Black action toys. Undaunted, she created Sun-Man, a superhero whose melanin-rich skin got its strength from the sun's rays, empowering him to be just as exciting as the white action heroes on the market. The company she founded to produce Black toys became Olmec Corporation.

Eason entered an industry in the early 1990s that was reluctantly just beginning to discuss so-called ethnic dolls. Big-box manufacturers such as Mattel and Tyco Toys were rolling out diverse dolls, but many parents felt that the range of new options, which included Black-, Hispanic-, and Asian-appearing dolls, wasn't sufficient. There were differences in skin tone, yes, but not in features; and that lack perpetuated issues of self-regard and beauty.

"My belief is that the manufacturers continue to give us a Black version of a white product," Eason told the *New York Times* in 1993. "Just as we're not Black versions of white people, Black dolls should not be versions of white ones." Attention to detail was required to ensure that darker-skinned dolls accurately reflected the cultures they aimed to represent.

Eason had science behind her. Groundbreaking studies in the late 1980s had conveyed how crucial it is for children to see and play with dolls who look like them. In one study, Black children were asked to select a doll from a group of Black and white dolls. The majority of the children chose white dolls, snubbing not only the Black dolls but their own Black identity. Eason's company worked to change the options available for young Black children and their families.

In addition to Sun-Man, Eason and Olmec also created a doll called Imani (a fashion model) and a host of other dolls and action figures. In fact, Eason eventually developed the toy industry's biggest selection of Black and Hispanic figures. The Olmec brand coined the term "ethnically correct," meaning that a doll's skin tone and facial features accurately resembled those of the ethnic group being represented. Although the company's products were featured in major retail stores nationwide, Olmec unfortunately went bankrupt within a few years. Still, the mark Eason and her brand made on the industry was indelible. Early on, Eason encountered toy buyers who told her that Black people wouldn't buy Black-inspired toys for their children. Eventually, though, Eason gained the attention of Mattel, one of the largest toy companies in the world. Now that Sun-Man has joined the He-Man universe, it's clear how misguided those early naysayers were.

LEE ELDER

(1934–2021)

"I certainly hope that the things that I have done have inspired a lot of young Black players and they will continue on with it."

In 1975, Lee Elder became the first Black golfer to play in the Masters at the Augusta National Golf Club in Georgia. That moment had been a long time coming. Elder's previous hopes of playing in the tournament had repeatedly been thwarted by changing qualification rules that blocked his participation, a thinly veiled attempt at discrimination.

Born in Dallas and raised in Los Angeles, Elder worked as a caddie and became increasingly interested in the sport. He met Teddy Rhodes, an early Black professional golfer who helped guide his technique. Elder was drafted into the army but was able to play during his enlistment. When he was discharged in 1961, he set out to play golf professionally, winning eighteen of twenty-two tournaments as part of the United Golf Association. The tour was created because Black golfers were being shamefully denied the ability to play in the Professional Golfers Association (PGA), which had "Caucasian Only" written in its bylaws.

Throughout the 1960s, Elder endured overt racism while playing. Threats, insults, and name-calling were everyday occurrences on the golf course. People sent him hate mail. At times he wasn't permitted to access golf properties without significant back-and-forth. During tournaments, spectators sometimes interfered with the placement of his ball.

In his pioneering appearance at the Masters, he performed reasonably but didn't qualify for the tournament. But he repeated his attempt for the next five years, ultimately reaching a ranking of nineteenth in 1977 and a tie for seventeenth in 1979. Although Elder's appearance at the Masters marked a significant moment for American golf, such an opening wasn't available to players like Charlie Sifford, who was the first Black golfer to play on the PGA Tour, as well as Rhodes and presumably multiple unsung Black golfers who never got an opportunity to test their true mettle against the best in the field.

Elder once commented about his pioneer status, "I didn't realize how important it was at the time, because all I really wanted so badly to do was play in the tournament. It didn't dawn on me what had happened until after I played."

In 2020, on the heels of George Floyd's murder and subsequent protests, the Augusta National announced the funding of two endowed scholarships in Elder's name at Paine College, a historically Black school in Augusta.

FRANCINE EVERETT

(1915–1999)

"There are ever so many beautiful colored girls who would have a good chance of winning any of the current beauty contests if they were invited."

Like so many entertainers of her day, Francine Everett could sing, dance, and act. But unlike many of her time, she was a star of the so-called race movies of the 1930s and 1940s, films with an all-Black cast destined primarily for Black audiences.

Everett was so beautiful that the owner of the world-famous Savoy Ballroom in Harlem, Charlie Buchanan, allowed Everett and her friends to hang out in his dance hall even though they were teenagers. Having such a good time, Everett found it hard to study at school. She dropped out of high school and joined the chorus of another Harlem establishment, Small's Paradise.

She was a chorus girl for only a month, leaving Small's to join a touring nightclub variety act called Four Black Cats. While on the road, she married a man from Harlem, Booker Everett. They had been married for only a year when he was killed in an accident.

Regaled for her beauty, Everett performed in films like *Keep Punching* in 1939, which featured the boxer Henry Armstrong, and *Big Timers*, in 1945, starring Moms Mabley and Stepin Fetchit. She famously shunned playing a maid or a domestic.

Because race movies were often low-budget, independently financed productions, with the passing of time they slowly faded away. But Everett continued to model and sing. As a vocalist, she recorded more than fifty short musicals, including *Ebony Parade* in 1947 with Dorothy Dandridge, Cab Calloway, and the Count Basie band.

Stephen Bourne of London's *Independent* called her "a woman most black audiences—especially women—could identify with." And William Greaves, filmmaker, producer, and former actor in race movies, remarked to the *New York Times* that Everett "was a true legend of black film and theater, one of the top stars of the 40s race movies. . . . She would have been a superstar in Hollywood were it not for the apartheid climate in America and the movie industry at the time."

Everett eventually left show business when her mother became ill and needed someone to care for her. During that period, Everett spent so much time at the hospital that she became friends with the staff. When her mother passed away, the hospital management offered her a job. Everett accepted it, working in an administrative role at the Harlem Hospital until she retired in 1985. She died in the Bronx at the age of eighty-four.

ABBY FISHER

(1831–UNKNOWN)

"This book will be found a complete instructor, so that a child can understand it and learn the art of cooking."

The San Francisco Mechanics' Institute Fair bestowed two competitive medals upon Abby Fisher in 1880: silver for best jellies and preserves and bronze for best pickles and sauces. The high praise was, at that point, no surprise. Fisher had established her pickles and preserves business in California after moving from Mobile, Alabama, with her husband, Alexander, and their eleven children. After their arrival on the West Coast, she founded that business under her own name, Mrs. Abby Fisher & Co.

Fisher was a well-known and broadly celebrated culinary expert with decades of cooking experience. Prior to winning the medals named above, she netted the highest honor at the Sacramento State Fair in 1879, among other regional accolades. Formerly enslaved and unable to read or write, she expertly dictated her cooking knowledge, which yielded her 1881 cookbook, *What Mrs. Fisher Knows About Old Southern Cooking*. Her collection, published by the Women's Cooperative Printing Office, featured straightforward guidance on ingredients and technique, with more than 150 recipes that ranged from beaten biscuits, pies, and sauces to gumbo, jambalaya, calf's-head soup, and roast venison.

Little is known about Abby Fisher's life, but the events that we do know boggle the mind. How on earth did this culinary pioneer achieve so much while raising eleven children? Part of her success can be attributed to her phenomenal memory. She was able to recall and recite precisely the exact details of all her culinary creations. Her publication was long believed to be the first African American cookbook. But the 2000 discovery of a work from 1866, *A Domestic Cook Book: Containing a Careful Selection of Useful Receipts for the Kitchen*, by Malinda Russell, a free woman of color in Memphis, shifted that narrative. Both publications reflect a muted history in which Black women became expert in (and were in demand for) culinary knowledge nationwide. Fisher and Russell wouldn't have been able to publish their cookbooks without the support of white patrons. That these pioneers were able to formalize such an effort at a time when Black people had only recently secured legal freedom suggests the high regard in which they were held.

The publication of Black-authored recipes at that period in history shows the deep interest in southern, and specifically Black, cooking that existed throughout the country. Apparently Fisher dictated her knowledge to satisfy requests from friends and customers (read: white women). She went so far as to list the names and addresses of several in the book, conveying the social standing she maintained for herself and the confidence she carried in her extensive repertoire.

JOHN STANLEY FORD

(1919–2000)

"Only when more people of color and other minorities ascend to the boardrooms and C-suites of high-tech firms . . . will the systemic changes required to end racism and bias [there] begin to take place."

—Clyde W. Ford

When John Stanley Ford was hired at IBM in 1946, he became the company's first Black software engineer—in fact, the first in the United States. His work initially focused on accounting machines, but he later contributed to what would become IBM's first business computer. Ford's career was marked by overt discrimination. In the memoir *Think Black*, written by his son and fellow engineer Clyde, accounts of Ford being underpaid, treated poorly by white colleagues, and overlooked for promotions abound. But for Ford, excitement about the actual work and the opportunity to secure economic stability for his family outweighed the abuses he suffered.

Ford served as a first lieutenant during World War II in the army's 369th Infantry Regiment—the segregated regiment in WWII—after graduating from Officer Candidate School in 1944. He received his bachelor's degree in 1946 from the City College of New York, then (after he'd been at IBM for several years) earned a master's in business administration from New York University. During his tenure at IBM, Ford helped other Black people secure employment there. Black women who had learned technical skills during World War II were especially smart hires.

But Ford's accomplishments were diminished by what his son described as "a unique form of post-traumatic stress disorder as a result of being the first Black systems engineer"—the stress of always being made to account for his race, of always needing to be on display. It's admirable to celebrate iconic firsts, yet the accomplishments of Black people who are placed on pedestals of exceptionalism certainly come at a high personal cost. Working in technology—or any field, really—shouldn't require trailblazers to constantly defend their racial identity, but that's the scenario in which Ford found himself for the nearly forty years he worked at IBM.

In 2020 the Flatiron School, a coding boot camp in New York City, announced that it was launching the John Stanley Ford Fellowship. This fellowship is meant to support the advancement of Black tech professionals. Flatiron partnered with a range of companies, including Citi, IBM, Datadog, fuboTV, TrialSpark, MediaMath, Justworks, and Codecademy, to create apprenticeships and ongoing mentorship. Ford knew better than most that to achieve success, one first needs access and opportunity. This is perhaps especially true in the tech community.

ARETHA FRANKLIN

(1942–2018)

"Being the Queen is not all about singing and being a diva is not all about singing. It has much to do with your service to people."

Watching the film *Amazing Grace* is a way of reintroducing oneself to the iconic, seemingly ever-present voice that belonged to Aretha Franklin. In 1972 the "Queen of Soul" recorded a live album in South Central Los Angeles at the New Temple Missionary Baptist Church. The gospel record and the subsequent movie, which due to technical issues wasn't released before her death (but thanks to advances in cinematic technology *was* released soon after), are gorgeous testaments to a specific moment in the wide-ranging career of one of America's most treasured musicians.

On the record and in the film, audiences witness not just the deep spiritual reverence that Franklin brought to the music of her youth—she was raised in the church by her father, the popular and highly respected Reverend C. L. Franklin, who emceed the recording. Audiences also witness the high standards to which she adhered and which she expected of her band and accompanying choir. Whether through a glance or a sung ad-lib directive, her command is on full display. And her performance is truly a religious experience.

By the time of *Amazing Grace*, Franklin had already sold millions of records and garnered countless accolades for songs like "(You Make Me Feel Like) A Natural Woman," "Ain't No Way," "I Never Loved a Man (The Way I Love You)," and, of course, her eclipsing interpretation of the Otis Redding song "Respect." So *Amazing Grace*'s definitive return to Franklin's gospel roots—which some argue she never left—felt magical and special. She didn't *need* to do a gospel album—except that she did. That sound, that ministry, was always at the core of her offerings, the source from which all her glory came.

Her songs soundtracked every decade she sang. Her voice was capable of crooning a lullaby, only to then leap and become holy. Despite her outsized presence on the stage, Aretha always made her music feel as if it were yours alone. Only *you* could hear her grace, her loneliness, her ache, her triumph, her ferocity. At her funeral in Detroit, one couldn't help but observe how the world took notice. The funeral was carried live on many television stations; the Band of the Welsh Guards, a British army band, performed "Respect" at Buckingham Palace. The band wrote on their social media accounts, "This morning [we] paid tribute to a musical icon and one that has been of huge influence and inspiration to our musicians— Aretha Franklin, whose funeral was being held in Detroit 3,748 miles away, at the same time of the Queen's Guard Change. In the Army Respect for others underpins all that we do, so there was only one tune that would do for today's ceremony: . . . a declaration from a strong confident woman who knows that she has everything." Yeah, we all miss her.

LENORA BRANCH FULANI

(1950–PRESENT)

"I have a lot of faith in ordinary people."

Lenora Fulani had already forged a career as a psychologist when she ran for US president in 1988 as part of the New Alliance Party. She was the first Black woman to appear on every ballot nationally, and in her bid she secured 225,000 votes. That's more votes than any other female candidate received until Jill Stein in 2012. Lenora's mother was a nurse and her father was a railway baggage handler. A graduate of Hofstra University, she earned a master's degree at Columbia University's Teachers College and a PhD in developmental psychology at the City University of New York. She then worked as a researcher at Rockefeller University before becoming involved in politics.

Fulani saw great value for disenfranchised American voters, specifically Black people, in shifting to an independent party in lieu of supporting either Democrats or Republicans, whose rhetoric and policies had consistently failed those voters. Believing strongly in her cause, she made a second attempt at the presidency in 1992.

In an interview on *PBS NewsHour* she described her platform, which included same-day and automated voter registration, extended election times (shifting from a single day to a week), and functional policies such as guaranteed jobs and wages, higher minimum wages, accessible and affordable health care, and free education. The interviewer agreed that such notions sounded good but questioned how things like paid medical care and education could be implemented, given the potential cost. Fulani responded:

It's kind of shocking to me that every time we talk about improving the quality of life for the American people, the issue that gets raised is how do we pay for it. George Bush found a billion dollars a day that . . . most people didn't agree with at a time when there was an AIDS crisis in this country and we could have spent a good portion of that money to find a cure. So I think that we're brainwashed whenever it comes to issues that would improve the lives of ordinary people into saying, "Oh, we can't do that." The Congress has free day care for its children, they have free health care, and they make more money than the average citizen. Maybe one of the places that we take the money from is these elite, polished politicians who get into office and then screw up our economy.

In 1994, Fulani cofounded the Committee for a Unified Independent Party, a network for independent voters. She was very active in the Independence Party of New York.

ALTHEA GIBSON

(1927–2003)

"To be a champion, you have to have intensity."

Like many before and after her who earned the designation, Althea Gibson wasn't interested in being labeled "the first." She just wanted to play tennis. She wasn't drawn into notions of being a pioneer or a spokesperson for other Black people. But when Gibson became the first Black tennis player to compete at the US National Championship in 1950 and the first Black player to compete at Wimbledon in 1951, she was placed in that elevated spot. In 1957, after Gibson won the women's singles and doubles at Wimbledon and received her trophy from Queen Elizabeth II, she was greeted by a parade upon her return home to New York.

Gibson started out as a table-tennis player when she was a little girl in Harlem, before taking her skill to the courts. She was known for her athletic, dominating serves. Gibson won her first tournament in 1942 in a series sponsored by the Black-founded American Tennis Association and held the championship title in that association from 1947 to 1957. She played while studying at Florida Agricultural and Mechanical University, where she earned a bachelor's degree in 1953. Her accomplishments were major— she was the first Black player to be ranked number one worldwide. She was the first Black player to win a Grand Slam title, in the 1956 French Open. She also won the US National Championships in 1957 and 1958.

In 1958 she retired from tennis. A talented vocalist and saxophonist, she began exploring opportunities in the entertainment industry. Her rich alto can be heard on the album *Althea Gibson Sings*, from 1959; she also appeared on the iconic *Ed Sullivan Show* twice. She then turned her sights to golf, becoming the first Black woman to join the LPGA Tour, a series of tournaments run by the Ladies Professional Golf Association, in 1964.

Unlike tennis players today, who net high figures and lucrative brand partnerships for winning global tennis tournaments, Gibson played during a time when prizes were few and far between. She had little income to show from her time, dedication, and reluctant fame— she never pursued the spotlight, and she resisted overtures suggesting that she use her position as a galvanizing political force. But her athletic presence, rendered noticeable by her gender and race at a time when so few Black people had access to the sport, helped shift ideas of tennis that still permeate an era that now features such luminaries as Serena and Venus Williams. Gibson didn't seek out groundbreaking, but she broke ground anyway. She was elected to the International Tennis Hall of Fame in 1971.

ELOYCE AND JAMES GIST

(ELOYCE GIST, 1892–1974)
(JAMES GIST, 1907–1937)

"Their goal as filmmakers was more than entertainment; their mission was one of moral and spiritual education for men and women."

—Gloria J. Gibson, president at Northeastern Illinois University

Mayme Eloyce King was born in Texas. We know very little about her personal life other than that she studied music at Howard University before turning to beauty care as a means to support herself. In 1911, she married Roscoe C. Patrick but then divorced him in 1930. But in 1932, Eloyce married James Gist. Eloyce practiced the Bahá'í faith and her husband James was an evangelical Christian. Combining the two religious beliefs, they created a unique ministry. And then they came upon a rather ingenious way to spread the Word. They would make films that carried a moral message for an audience of Black churches and other religious gatherings.

Hell-Bound Train was the first collaboration between married couple Eloyce and James Gist—a cautionary tale of intemperance, jazz, and bad decisions, set on a train filled with unrepentant sinners hurtling toward damnation. Elements of this 1930 film can only be described as surrealistic.

Each car of this train is depicted with its own sin. Sexy dancing is named "indecent" in the first car, where a group of revelers smoke cigarettes and get too up-close and personal. In another car, bootleggers imbibe to the point of many a bad decision. Men are shown to corrupt innocent women with liquor and careless whispers. A woman driven to follow the

whims of her body is later shown to have an infant nestled beside her; the mother is presumably unwed. Violence and rage emerge in other scenes, giving the devil (adorned with a mask with horns and a cape, no less) something to rejoice over. Joy for the drunkard is short-lived—money spent on booze isn't available to pay the overdue rent, and scenes of sickened people convey the risk of alcohol poisoning in the middle of the Prohibition era.

As was the case for silent films of the late 1920s and early 1930s, music plays an important role in the film. Pulsing organ notes accentuate the action onscreen, creating a sense of urgency in this sixty-minute feature made with a handheld camera that has a clear message for viewers: live a teetotaling life or pay dearly for your moral failings.

As the story proceeds, title cards convey bits of dialogue, as was customary for the form, but the story of the hell-bound train is told through the performances of Black amateur actors. A modern-day subtitle of the film could be "When Living It Up Goes Wrong." Implied humor is always close at hand, but the underlying takeaway is intended to be serious.

Historians note that, although the quality of the movie pales when compared to those of independent filmmakers such as Oscar Micheaux, the Gists enjoyed significant reach and impact. They planned screenings of their films with the NAACP and took their work on the road in presentations that combined live music, a film presentation, and then a sermon by James.

The Gists are commonly referred to as amateur filmmakers, because they lacked studio backing, professional equipment, and industry training. But at a time when Hollywood was a defiantly segregated industry and the preferences of Black audiences were ignored (or presumed nonexistent) by a white-dominant industry, it's difficult to know just how widespread Black films actually were and to what aesthetic standard Black filmmakers might have been holding themselves. And because even dedicated scholarship in the area of Black filmmaking is a relatively recent subject, the preservation of old "race films" has been rare. The Gists seem to have had their own style and criteria. Relying on sixteen-millimeter film, they wrote, produced, directed, marketed, and distributed their own work. It's believed that Eloyce led the creative work in developing the stories and directing the films, while James managed more of the production.

Around 1933, they released the short film *Verdict: Not Guilty*, in which a woman who has died giving birth out of wedlock is on trial to get into heaven. As the devil tries to convict the woman for her sins, scenes of her life flash back. In the Gists' third (uncompleted) film about 1935, *Heaven-Bound Travelers*, Eloyce cast herself in the role of a wife and mother wrongfully facing charges of adultery.

The Gists' films were one of a kind, in that they weren't reproduced for wide distribution in theaters. Their screenings took place using a projector that traveled with them on the road. In 1974, the remaining physical film was donated to the Library of Congress, but the decades-long wear had seriously compromised viewing quality. Even with advances in restoration technology, only fragments remain, representing a time in American cinema history when Black artists ignored social constraints to use media and technology as a means to reflect their own lives and portray values that mattered most to them.

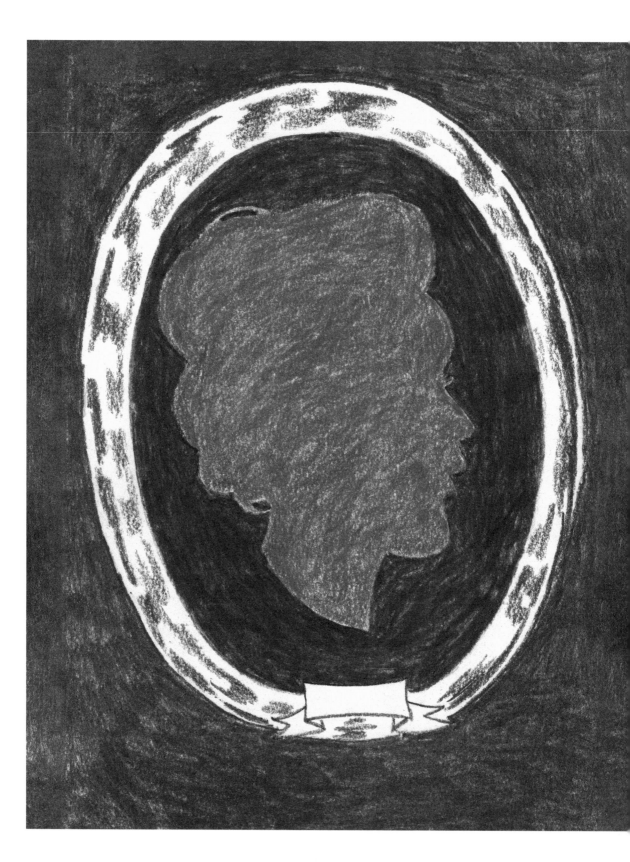

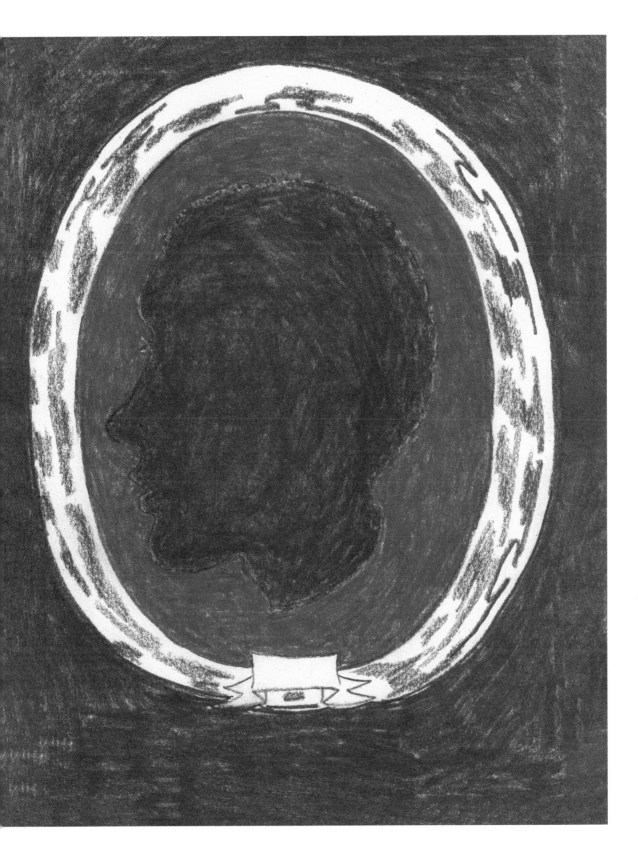

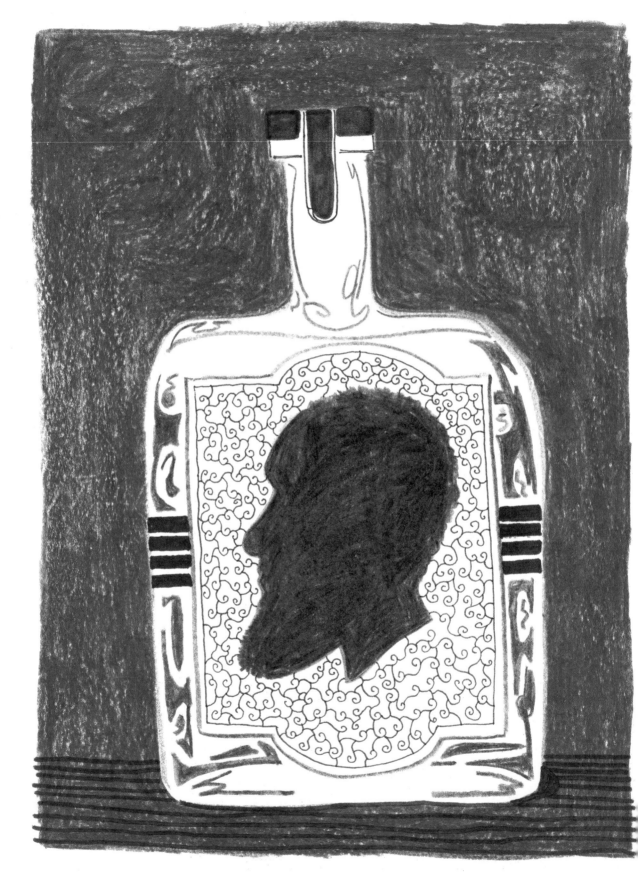

NATHAN "NEAREST" GREEN

(CA. 1820–1890)

"Nearest Green . . . put in everything he had. Most of all, he put in his heart."

—Jeffrey Wright, actor

Nathan "Nearest" Green, a founding father of the recipe and practices that would launch the iconic Jack Daniel's company, was locally well known long before he became national news in 2016. Uncle Nearest, as he was known to friends and family in Lynchburg, Tennessee, was a master distiller of the sugar-maple charcoal-filtering method believed by historians to be a derivative of African charcoal water-filtering practices.

It's unclear just how Green, who was born in Maryland around 1820, came to be enslaved on a farm in Tennessee in the mid-1800s making whiskey. But on this farm, Green encountered a young white chore boy named Jack Daniel. Green was asked to teach Daniel his distilling methods, and the youngster went on to become skilled at selling the whiskey in the region. Daniel eventually partnered with the farm owner to invest in the distillery, bought the farm outright, and then hired Green to serve as its master distiller. That company was the Jack Daniel Distillery, which opened in 1866, one year after the Thirteenth Amendment was ratified, abolishing slavery.

Today, the company freely shares this complex history, properly recognizing Green as its first master distiller. However, although Green's involvement was never a secret, the company didn't acknowledge Green's contributions until 2016, upon the company's 150th anniversary—a significant announcement that was covered in the *New York Times*.

When businesswoman and author Fawn Weaver visited Lynchburg following this announcement and attended several tours, she heard no mention of Green. This omission led her to pursue the intricacies of the story directly. Weaver, the daughter of a Motown Records songwriter, learned, according to the *Times* article, that Green had never been owned by Daniel; in fact, the record indicates that Daniel spoke openly about being mentored by Green. Some of Green's descendants still work for the distillery, the largest employer in a town of fewer than seven thousand people. So where, she wondered, was his presence? Why hadn't the tour guides made mention of him?

The fact that Nathan Green's historical importance was oddly absent gave Weaver an idea. She launched the Uncle Nearest whiskey brand in 2017. (She opted to use the name Uncle Nearest rather than Nathan in part because that's the name he used on paperwork when identifying himself.) No known image of Green exists, but there's a late-1800s photograph of Daniel seated next to a mustached Black man wearing a wide-brimmed hat. That man could be Green, or perhaps one of his sons who worked for the distillery.

Offerings from the Uncle Nearest brand feature two award-winning varieties, including the 1884 small-batch version distilled by a fifth-generation Green descendant and the brand's master blender, Victoria Eady Butler.

DICK GREGORY

(1932–2017)

"They always ask me why I travel so much and I tell 'em, the fight for freedom is out there—it ain't at my house."

As one of the first Black comedians to achieve widespread fame and success in the late 1950s and early 1960s, Dick Gregory used his platform to confront the inequities of systemic racism in the United States. His revolutionary approach to storytelling was present not only in stand-up sets and television appearances, but also in his protest against the Vietnam War through hunger strikes, his advocacy for healthier food options for Black people, and his authorship of a dozen books, including the seminal *Nigger: An Autobiography*. He was at times ruthless in his manner and delivery, but audiences began to count on him for edgy, uncomfortable truth.

Gregory was born in St. Louis, Missouri. At the local Sumner High School he won the state cross-country championship. He earned a track scholarship to Southern Illinois University, but his life in college was interrupted when, in 1954, he was drafted into the US Army. Gregory got his start in comedy while serving, winning multiple army talent shows. He then returned to college, but dropped out as soon as he understood that the administration cared more about his athletic usefulness than his academic pursuits. "They didn't want me to study, they wanted me to run."

Gregory moved to Chicago and started his career as a comedian. In 1961, while working the Roberts Show Bar, he told what was to become a classic Gregory joke:

Good evening, ladies and gentlemen. I understand there are a good many Southerners in the room tonight. I know the South very well. I spent twenty years there one night.

Last time I was down South I walked into this restaurant and this white waitress came up to me and said, "We don't serve colored people here." I said, "That's all right. I don't eat colored people. Bring me a whole fried chicken." Then these three white boys came up to me and said, "Boy, we're giving you fair warning. Anything you do to that chicken, we're gonna do to you." So I put down my knife and fork, I picked up that chicken and I kissed it. Then I said, "Line up, boys!"

Gregory's satirical delivery is often compared to Lenny Bruce's, and he's recognized for paving the way for figures like Richard Pryor, Bill Cosby, and Dave Chappelle. His career wasn't restricted to the stage, however. He was very active in the civil rights movement. He protested against the Vietnam War. He went on several hunger strikes in the United States and overseas. In 1964, Gregory played a role in the search for three missing civil rights workers, James Chaney, Andrew Goodman, and Michael Schwerner, who had vanished in Mississippi and were rumored to have been murdered. With the help of Hugh Hefner, Gregory announced a $25,000 reward for information. The effort worked: with the help of the public, the men's bodies were found by the FBI.

But his activist work came with consequences.

He was soon on the FBI's hit list. Christian Gregory, Dick Gregory's son, says the family has paperwork signed by J. Edgar Hoover urging his Chicago office to "neutralize" Dick Gregory. Nowhere in the paperwork is "neutralize" qualified to rule out the option of violence, and some of the people getting the message—Hoover had asked the Chicago mob to help with the FBI's efforts—were known for murder.

Gregory also dipped a toe into politics. In 1967 he ran for mayor of Chicago (mostly to make a point about the state of politics), and in 1968 he ran for US president, appearing on the ballot in eight states.

Dick Gregory certainly led a full life. As I try to capture his image, I think about the many versions of him. Comedian, writer, activist, Gregory was the first of his generation of comics to become a "crossover" hit—surpassing the heights achieved by comedic greats such as Redd Foxx and Moms Mabley, who were often relegated to Black clubs on what was called the Chitlin' Circuit. Other Black comic entertainers were expected to sing and dance as well, but Gregory delivered his "entertainment" as biting commentary, without distraction. The civil rights movement was taking place on television during Gregory's heyday. America's inconsistencies in regard to race became more vividly obvious to many white viewers through Gregory's reflection on them, though Gregory maintained that his purpose on the stage was to get laughs.

Gregory was a man who reinvented himself time and time again. But he also had the core principle of being loving and lovable to all living things. Of course, that often came with a heaping dash of comedic truth. *The One and Only Dick Gregory* is a 2021 documentary that tries to capture the enormity of his life. The film is filled with interviews—among them, with Dave Chappelle, Chris Rock, Kevin Hart, Lena Waithe, and Nick Cannon—but most of it is told by Dick Gregory himself. It's powerful. He was a man who firmly believed, "Once I accept injustice, I become injustice." He was also a Black man who represented the successful hustler in the best sense of the word, showing how Black people have always had to be flexible with their skills. Gregory once said of himself and the Black experience, "It's all about metamorphosis." The ability to change, to grow, to show the full spectrum of humanity.

In 2017, Dick Gregory passed away from heart failure. But his achievements, his comedy, his wisdom still resonate. This artist and activist gave his audiences both food for thought and the gift of laughter. "Love is man's natural endowment, but he doesn't know how to use it. He refuses to recognize the power of love because of his love of power." "I am really enjoying the new Martin Luther King Jr. stamp—just think about all those white bigots, licking the backside of a black man." Dick Gregory said both these things. That's his genius.

ELIZA ANN GRIER

(1864–1902)

"When I saw colored women doing all the work in cases of accouchement [childbirth], and all the fee going to some white doctor who merely looked on, I asked myself why should I not get the fee myself. For this purpose I have qualified."

Eliza Ann Grier put forth extraordinary effort to become the first Black woman licensed to practice medicine in Georgia. Born in Mecklenburg County, North Carolina, in 1864, coinciding roughly with the emancipation of the enslaved, Grier initially pursued a career in education and studied at Fisk University. But she shifted her focus to getting a medical education, perhaps understanding how pivotal her impact could be. Grier wrote to the Woman's Medical College of Pennsylvania to explain that she and her family had very little money and wondered if assistance "might be provided for an emancipated slave to receive any help into so lofty a profession."

She completed her education at that college in 1897, after seven years of alternating each year of study with a year of arduous labor picking cotton so that she could afford the tuition. With her degree secured, Grier went on to practice in Atlanta. But she tragically became ill in 1901 and ultimately died at the age of thirty-eight, after practicing for only a few years.

Grier's desire to acquire formal training in order to practice medicine can best be understood in light of the shifting medical landscape in the United States at the turn of the twentieth century. Throughout precolonial Africa and then in the African diaspora, Black women were always at the center of care for their communities. These healers, or medicine women, tended body, mind, and spirit and carried knowledge of remedies and other ancient practices. Even throughout slavery, as African traditions were systematically erased, many African American healers continued community-based care.

But as the medical field advanced and continued to be led by white males (who typically mistreated Black people, seeing them merely as case studies in which personal consent was deemed irrelevant), it pushed Black women healers to the fringes, especially in the field of gynecology and obstetrics. Holistic care grew ever more distant from many Black communities, and women whom we would today describe as nutritionists, doulas, lactation advisers, and so on were barred from practicing without state-approved licenses.

That Black women as midwives were replaced by the medical establishment (which would go on to undervalue Black life in myriad ways more than one hundred years later) was surely not hidden from Grier's view. But one wonders what professionals would have populated the modern-day hospital had Grier lived and thrived in her field. Would her accomplishments and her tireless work ethic have inspired other Black women to enter medicine? Imagine a generation of Black women mentored by this tenacious, intelligent woman. Oh my. History would have had volumes.

FANNIE LOU HAMER

(1917–1977)

"Righteousness exalts a nation, but sin is a reproach to any people."

"If your vote didn't matter," a saying goes, "then people wouldn't try so hard to stop you from voting." Fannie Lou Hamer understood this. A sharecropper for most of her life, Hamer was born in Montgomery County, Mississippi. She was forty-four years old before she knew that Black people could vote, yet she ended up wholeheartedly devoting the latter part of her life to activist causes (against great odds), particularly in support of voter registration.

Hamer was the youngest of twenty children and left grade school to work the plantation on which they lived. As an adult, she recalled how the lynching of a man named Joe Pulliam from Drew, Mississippi, when she was eight years old affected her and her community.

In 1944 she married Perry "Pap" Hamer and the two continued to work on the plantation. When Hamer learned she had a tumor, she went to the Sunflower County hospital to have it removed. Instead of that minor surgery, she instead received a hysterectomy—without her consent. (At that time the forcible sterilization of Black women was so common that it was known as the "Mississippi appendectomy.") Hamer and her husband eventually adopted two daughters.

At a church meeting she attended in 1962, civil rights volunteers explained that "Negro" folks could vote. It almost didn't sound right to her, so distant and inaccessible was the notion that Black people

could determine their representation the same as white people could. With seventeen others, Hamer set out to register to vote in Indianola, Mississippi, in August 1962. They commissioned a bus to make the twenty-six-mile trip from Ruleville, Mississippi, where they lived—twenty-six miles just to register to vote.

Two years later, she recounted her attempt to register to vote in a speech at the local Negro Baptist School. She told of the welcome party that had awaited them at the registrar: "I saw more policemens with guns than I'd ever seen in my life at one time." Hamer was subjected to a literacy test, which she failed because she was unable to reinterpret in conversational language the state code dealing with de facto laws. When the group of nineteen were on their way back to Ruleville, police ordered the bus to turn around. The driver was charged with driving a bus that was the wrong color.

Hamer finally made it back to the plantation where she lived. "When I got there I was already fired," she said. A white man told her she'd have to withdraw her registration or leave. She responded, almost perplexed, "I didn't register for you. I was trying to register for myself." The Hamer family had to leave that very night.

Weeks later, assailants fired gunshots into the homes of other would-be registrants who had joined Hamer in Indianola, Mississippi. The following February, her husband, Pap, was arrested for running up nine thousand gallons of water—although they lived in a home that didn't have running water. The Hamers were being systematically terrorized for attempting to vote.

In June 1963, after returning from a voter workshop in Charleston, South Carolina, Hamer and others were detained in Winona, Mississippi. She described hearing one of her companions suffer beatings in a cell while she was held in another. She was then led to another cell that held three white men and two Black men.

"The state highway patrolman ordered the first Negro to take the blackjack," she said, "and they ordered me to lay down on my face on the bunk bed. And the first Negro beat me. He had to beat me until the state highway patrolman give him orders to quit. Because he had already told him, 'If you don't beat her, you know what I'll do to you.'"

She ultimately endured beatings by all the men in the cell. They held her down. "At no time did I attempt to do anything but scream and call on God. I don't know how long this lasted, but after a while I must have passed out. And when I did raise my head up, the state highway patrolman said, 'Get up from there, fatso.' . . . And after a while I did get up, and I went back to my cell." Ever after, Hamer had a blood clot in her eye and walked with a permanent limp.

Hamer joined the Student Nonviolent Coordinating Committee and became their field secretary that same year, traveling through the Mississippi Delta to register others to vote. In 1964 she coestablished the Mississippi Freedom Democratic Party to increase Black representation within the state party and at the Democratic National Convention.

In the 1960s, in Mississippi, to participate in any kind of community organizing that supported Black liberation was risky. "The only thing they could do to me was to kill me," she said in an oral history archived at the University of Southern Mississippi, "and it seemed like they'd been trying to do that a little bit at a time ever since I could remember."

Like many figures working to create equity for Black people in the 1960s, Hamer saw that food access and land ownership were integral to any chance at economic stability. She used a charitable donation to found the Freedom Farm Cooperative in 1969 and bought 40 acres of land in the Delta. The organization grew, purchased an additional 640 acres the next year, and started a "bank" using money from the National Council of Negro Women. The Freedom Farm couldn't gain institutional backing and so was ultimately unsustainable. But Hamer's approach to addressing the weaponizing of food against Black people to limit their movement and financial stability is one that continues to inspire generations of activists seeking to create food sovereignty for Black communities today. Some would say Hamer was ahead of her time, but in fact she just did what she had to do.

"I don't want to hear you say, 'Honey, I'm behind you,'" she told a group at the Negro Baptist School in Indianola. "Well, move. I don't want you back there. Because you could be two hundred miles behind. I want you to say, 'I'm with you.' And we'll go up this freedom road together."

BETHANN HARDISON

(1942–PRESENT)

"I enjoy being an elder and the wisdom that comes with it, but age is something I just don't give in to."

At a 1973 Versailles fashion show promoted as a fundraiser to restore France's largest palace, American celebrities mixed with European royalty. But in truth the show, later known as "the Battle of Versailles," became a competition between older, established French houses like Dior and Givenchy and designers representing the Americans: Stephen Burrows, Anne Klein, Oscar de la Renta, and Bill Blass.

Eleven models of color were prominently featured by the American designers, adding to the impression of a competition between the old and new guards. Bethann Hardison walked in the Burrows show. Her thin frame, natural, close-cropped hair, and dark-brown skin had made her stand out ever since she began modeling in 1967. A native of Bedford-Stuyvesant in Brooklyn, she'd been discovered while working as a representative for Cabot, a button company. Eventually she became a runway model for Burrows, whose line was joyous—full of color, showing skin—against the rich soundscape of funky R&B.

When it was her turn in Versailles, she walked down the runway with the force of a performer, wearing Burrows's sleeveless yellow gown. At the end of the stage she stared straight at the audience, defiantly throwing down the train of her dress. She held the pose while the music thundered around her. It was a wrap. The audience leaped to their feet, stomping, yelling, and throwing their event programs into the air. It was clear who the winner was, although several designers had yet to present. She had stolen the show.

Hardison was more than a showstopping runway model. In 1984, she launched an agency, Bethann Management. It wasn't a Black modeling agency but a modeling agency owned and led by a Black woman. The company represented diverse models who worked for brands such as Chanel, Issey Miyake, and Yves Saint Laurent.

In 2020, Hardison told *Elle* magazine, "I started getting calls from them: 'Bethann, we need a great Black girl.' . . . I would say things like, 'Okay, how many girls are you using?' And they'd say, 'Thirty-five.' And I'd say, 'Okay, you want one Black girl?' I was very good at turning the tables on them, to let them see how awful that sounds."

With model/entrepreneur Iman, Hardison cofounded the Black Girls Coalition in 1988 as a way to build community among the Black models of that era, including Naomi Campbell and Veronica Webb. But the group evolved to advocate for issues specific to Black people's representation in fashion and in advertising.

In honor of her groundbreaking career, in 2014 Hardison received the Founder's Award from the Council of Fashion Designers of America. Hardison has been recognized by countless organizations for her dedication to diversity and inclusion. "I never thought I was contributing to a movement," Hardison said in a 2020 interview. "I always think when things are happening, we *are* the movement."

FRANCES ELLEN WATKINS HARPER

(1825–1911)

"The true aim of female education should be . . . all the faculties of the human soul, because no perfect womanhood is developed by imperfect culture."

A poet, author, and activist, Frances Ellen Watkins Harper used her prominence as a well-regarded literary figure to advocate for Black women and to voice her opposition to slavery. As cofounder of the National Association of Colored Women's Clubs, she helped formalize a network of Black women dedicated to abolishing slavery, promoting literacy and education, and decrying the punishing impact of lynching on Black communities.

Born in Baltimore, Maryland, Harper was raised by her abolitionist uncle after the death of her freed parents. She was educated at the Watkins Academy for Negro Youth, a Black literary society and school established by her uncle. Harper went on to teach at Union Seminary, a school for Blacks in Wilberforce, Ohio. When the state of Maryland enacted a law that said free Black people entering the state could be imprisoned and sold into slavery, Harper was unable to return home. She found solace in writing.

She began publishing pieces in antislavery journals in 1839, when she was fourteen. At just twenty years old, she published a book of poetry, *Forest Leaves*, also published as *Autumn Leaves*. She left Ohio for Pennsylvania. There she wrote *Poems on Miscellaneous Subjects*, a literary success; it was reprinted several times.

In 1858, Harper refused to give up her seat or ride in the "colored" section of a trolley car in Philadelphia. The incident inspired her poem "Bury Me in a

Free Land." In 1859, Harper's story "The Two Offers" was published in the *Anglo-African Magazine*, making her the first Black woman to publish a short story.

Harper was prolific, continuing to publish throughout her life. She also fought for the right of Black women to vote. Influenced by her abolitionist work and commitment to the unique traumas Black women endured in slavery, Harper's poetry functioned as protest and testimony, much in the way that contemporary music forms such as hip-hop illustrate the circumstances of people who are and feel unseen.

Harper died of heart failure in 1911. Had she lived just nine years longer, she would have witnessed some of the fruits of her labor. In 1920 the Nineteenth Amendment was ratified, giving women the right to vote. There was still a road to travel, but when Frances Ellen Watkins Harper passed away, her wish, told in verse in the poem "Bury Me in a Free Land," came true:

> *Make me a grave where'er you will,*
> *In a lowly plain, or a lofty hill;*
> *Make it among earth's humblest graves,*
> *But not in a land where men are slaves.*
> *I ask no monument, proud and high,*
> *To arrest the gaze of the passers-by;*
> *All that my yearning spirit craves,*
> *Is bury me not in a land of slaves.*

SHRINES TO A KINDRED SPIRIT

by Bryant Terry

You'll find altars to Edna Lewis all over my home. I pour water, tea, and whiskey into my favorite handcrafted ceramic cups and bowls and place them out for her. I offer her fresh fruit and ancestor plates from our family meals. I light candles; arrange bouquets of calla lilies, irises, and assorted fresh herbs cut from our home garden; and burn frankincense and sandalwood incenses to honor and remember her.

Like many chefs of my generation, I hold Ms. Lewis in the highest regard. She protected, celebrated, and elevated Black southern food into the national consciousness. Ms. Lewis also broke barriers for African Americans in the food industry, especially Black women. She deserves all her drinks, flowers, and fresh scents, and I'm here for any project that celebrates her work.

I discovered Ms. Lewis back when I attended the Chef's Training Program at the Natural Gourmet Institute for Health and Culinary Arts. I was the only African American male in our cohort, and my longing for Black role models drove me to research forerunners. When I read *The Taste of Country Cooking*, I was quite taken by Lewis's emphasis on community, her focus on seasonality, and the personal lens through which she wrote. I saw myself in her: we both came from loving, strong Black communities in the South; we both moved to New York City to cultivate our careers; and we both had immense pride in our Blackness.

My adoration of and desire to learn more about Ms. Lewis drove me to reach out to John T. Hill, a dear friend of hers (and now mine), who captured her essence in many of the gorgeous photographs you see of her—gathering tomatoes among sunflowers, wearing West African garb and jewelry while putting the final touches on a Christmas cake, and presiding over a table laden with simple, ingredient-driven southern dishes. He saw her past in my present, noting a similar light in us both, which deepened my connection to her.

With Ms. Lewis as my spiritual guide, I found my stride. I strengthened my focus on fresh food that makes the most of the season's bounty. I strengthened my pride in my African heritage, sharing it even more boldly. I strengthened my writing: her approach to cookbook as memoir inspired me to add the texture of autobiography to my own cookbooks. I strengthened my commitment to doing all I could to shift power into historically marginalized communities so that they could be self-determined in regard to health, food, and farming.

By design, my altars to Ms. Lewis send a strong message to my daughters, Mila and Zenzi. Uplifting Black women is one of my core values. Throughout my two-decades-long career as a chef and author, I have committed to a praxis of confronting the misogynoir—the potent mix of racism and sexism—that Black women have to deal with day in, day out. I make good use of my privilege, power, and platform to champion and celebrate them. It's why I created a primarily Black women leadership team when I founded b-healthy, a food justice organization, in 2001. It's why my first event as chef-in-residence at San Francisco's Museum of the African Diaspora in 2015 was "Black Women, Food & Power," in which we discussed Black women's historical and contemporary role in the production, distribution, and consumption of food and food knowledge. It's why in 2020, the first acquisition of my publishing imprint, 4 Color Books, was a cookbook by Rahanna Bisseret Martinez, a brilliant sixteen-year-old Afro-Latina chef whose spirit reminds me of Ms. Lewis's in so many ways. I understand that the actions I take in the present moment help create the future I want to see, and I will always ride for my sisters.

And I mean *all* my sisters. While the shrines around my home memorialize Ms. Lewis, they also pay reverence to every Black woman who served as an architect of American cooking. I often sit in quiet contemplation, imagining the lives of these ancestral aunties and sending love to them. So as we celebrate Ms. Lewis and other notable Black people in this book, I encourage us all to recognize that behind every ancestor we uplift, there are countless ordinary Black folks who paved the way. We need something like the Tomb of the Unknown Brilliant Black Women Who Held It Down for Their Families and the Community to commemorate the domestic laborers who toiled in the homes of wealthy whites; the home cooks who self-published books as early as the nineteenth century; and the commis chefs in fine dining who didn't receive training and support from their white peers to help them advance in their careers.

I see our entire Black family, from our great-great-greats to our children who are yet to come, alive within the concept of Sankofa, which essentially means to return to the past and retrieve what is useful, or to remember the wisdom of our ancestors as we march toward the future. This is illustrated in the Ghanaian Adinkra symbol of a bird craning her head backward to gather a precious egg safely into her beak, feet planted forward toward the future. Zora Neale Hurston expressed it this way: "The present was an egg laid by the past that had the future inside of its shell."

May Ms. Lewis know that we carry forth her wisdom as we step into the future and work to create a better world, with opportunity and recognition for all.

Bryant Terry is a James Beard & NAACP Image Award–winning chef, educator, and author renowned for his activism to create a healthy, just, and sustainable food system.

DOROTHY HEIGHT

(1912–2010)

"I'm still working today to make the promise of the 14th Amendment of equal justice under law a reality."

Dorothy Height was accepted to Barnard College and scheduled to begin classes in 1929. But there was an issue, she learned that summer. The Richmond, Virginia, native who'd grown up in Rankin, Pennsylvania, was told that the college had met its quota for Negro students that term, and she would not be able to enroll.

While in high school, Height had volunteered in voting rights and antilynching campaigns. Perhaps it was in part that experience that helped her find the resolve to head downtown to New York University, where she was admitted into the education program. She received a bachelor's degree in 1933 and, in 1935, a master's degree in psychology. She trained as a social worker and was employed at the New York City Welfare Department.

By the late 1930s, Height had become assistant executive director of the Harlem YWCA and was interviewed by the *New York Times* for protesting the way Black women were being treated as domestic day laborers in Brooklyn and the Bronx. In 1938, the paper reported that Black women waited at "slave markets" to be hired by white housewives who would drive around in search of help for hire at fifteen cents an hour or one dollar a day. During her time at the Y, Height accompanied First Lady Eleanor Roosevelt to a meeting of the National Council of Negro Women. While attending, she met Mary McLeod Bethune.

In her memoir, *Open Wide the Freedom Gates*, Height wrote about her fateful meeting with Bethune: "On that fall day the redoubtable Mary McLeod Bethune put her hand on me. She drew me into her dazzling orbit of people in power and people in poverty. . . . 'The freedom gates are half ajar,' she said. 'We must pry them fully open.' I have been committed to the calling ever since." Height became a driving force in the Y's desegregation efforts and founded its Center for Racial Justice in 1965.

Height was an integral figure in the broader national civil right movement. She can be spotted in photos near Martin Luther King Jr. at the March on Washington as he delivered the 1963 "I Have a Dream" speech. She herself was an accomplished speaker, but no women were asked to speak that historic day.

Height served as president of the National Council of Negro Women for forty years, from 1957 to 1997. In 1971, she helped found the National Women's Political Caucus with Shirley Chisholm, among other women's movement leaders. An adviser to several presidents on matters of civil rights, she attended the inauguration of President Barack Obama in 2009 and was seated on the dais during the ceremony. She received the Presidential Medal of Freedom in 1994 and the Congressional Gold Medal in 2004. That year, Barnard College made Height an honorary graduate.

JAMES HEMINGS

(1765–1801)

"Wherever the liberated or soon-to-be-liberated people from Monticello went, they became caterers of renown."
—Michael Twitty, culinary historian and author

James Hemings was the first American to be trained as a chef in France. In 1784, when Thomas Jefferson became minister of France, he took the enslaved nineteen-year-old to Paris with him to learn the trade. There Hemings took lessons and learned to speak French. Hemings had been born to Elizabeth Hemings, an enslaved woman, and her white owner, John Wayles, making James a half sibling to Jefferson's recently deceased wife, Martha Jefferson, because they had the same father. Martha inherited James upon the passing of their father. He was also the older brother of Sally Hemings, who would become Jefferson's concubine.

By 1787, still in Paris, Hemings had become chef de cuisine at Jefferson's Champs-Élysées home, where the statesman entertained notables from all over Europe. Hemings experienced some autonomy, and there was the prospect of legal freedom from the French government, but in 1789 Hemings returned to the United States with Jefferson when the latter was appointed the first secretary of state. Hemings cooked for Jefferson in New York and Philadelphia, the seats of government at the time, and at Monticello. His talent and visibility as a chef set the standard for high-society dining.

Hemings introduced the "potage" (or stew) stove, a precursor to the modern stove, to American cooking. He introduced dishes such as crème brûlée, meringues, béchamel-based macaroni and cheese, ice cream, and French fries to the American palate. His cooking style, which blended Virginia country fare with French cooking, would be imitated and popularized throughout the mid-Atlantic region.

Hemings eventually petitioned Jefferson for his freedom, which Jefferson granted on the condition that Hemings would train an enslaved chef to replace himself. Hemings trained his brother Peter extensively, preparing him for three years for that top role. Hemings left Monticello in 1796 and refused Jefferson's attempts to bring him on as chef at the White House once Jefferson was elected president in 1801.

But Hemings did agree to return to Monticello as a paid chef for a brief period. Not long after his return, Hemings was reported dead of an apparent suicide. Some historians believe that the combination of Hemings's talent and the great social limitations on his life as a Black man during slavery—further exacerbated by the contradiction of a more independent life in France and in the northern states in which he worked—may have contributed to a sense of despair and hopelessness. In addition, it was said that he suffered from alcoholism. It's impossible to know the circumstances of his death. But in his creative life as a chef and culinary talent, Hemings inspired generations of cooks who followed him.

JUANO HERNÁNDEZ

(1896–1970)

"If you speak English with an accent people are inclined to laugh at you. So [I] cultivated perfect diction and along the way acquired a knowledge of Shakespeare."

In *Intruder in the Dust*, the 1949 film based on the William Faulkner novel, actor Juano Hernández exhibits the majestic screen presence that propelled his fifty-year career. Hernández plays Lucas Beauchamp, an innocent Black man accused of murdering a white man in the Jim Crow South. The movie follows what happens when a group of white people aim to preempt the judicial system.

In one scene, Beauchamp is marched into the police station, restrained both by handcuffs in front and by a sheriff and a deputy holding his arms on either side. They are surrounded by a crowd of curious white male onlookers whose intent seems to be imminent harm. Beauchamp's fedora blows off and someone hands it back to him. Under the silent gaze of this would-be mob, he accepts his hat, dusts the brim off on the sleeve of his blazer, and returns it to his head. The whole time, his gaze never breaks from those who seek to harm him. It's a powerful wordless performance in a movie insufferably dominated by the voiceover of a young white boy as omnipresent narrator. But in that moment, Hernández seems to say, "Maybe to you all I'm just a nigger. But that's your problem." He earned his sole Golden Globe nomination for the role.

It cannot be understated what it likely took for Hernández not only to portray such a dignified, proud role onscreen but to survive socially in an industry that constantly worked to limit his talent and livelihood even when the cameras were off. (While filming *Intruder in the Dust* in Oxford, Mississippi, white cast members stayed on campus at the University of Mississippi. Black cast members were housed at the homes of Black people in town.)

Born in San Juan, Puerto Rico, Hernández had a range of jobs before becoming a film actor: he was a sailor stationed in Brazil, worked as a circus and vaudeville entertainer, had a stint boxing (using the moniker Kid Curley), and was a radio actor and script writer in New York. Initially starring in all-Black radio shows, he soon found his way to Broadway, where he was cast as a chorus singer in the 1927 production of *Show Boat*. His first "talkie" film, *The Girl from Chicago* (1932), was directed and produced by Oscar Micheaux. He starred in about thirty-six titles throughout his career, though he was cast as a Latino character only twice: in the Micheaux film just mentioned and in *Machete*, in 1958. During his lengthy career, Hernández worked with Bill "Bojangles" Robinson and Sidney Poitier, among many others.

Toward the end of his life Hernández appeared in *The Extraordinary Seaman* (1969) with David Niven, in *The Reivers* (also 1969) with Steve McQueen, and, in his final role, in *They Call Me Mister Tibbs!* (1970) with Sidney Poitier. He died in his native Puerto Rico of a brain hemorrhage, leaving behind a script he wrote about Sixto Escobar, Puerto Rico's first champion boxer.

ANITA HILL

(1956–PRESENT)

"There's someplace in your conscience that says, 'If I don't act, then I will have been a part of something that I don't want to live with.'"

In 1991, Anita Hill was a professor of contract law at the University of Oklahoma College of Law with no expectation of becoming a public figure. After practicing law in Washington, DC, and working for the federal government, she was teaching at the Norman campus after a short period at Oral Roberts University in Tulsa. But when President George H. W. Bush nominated Clarence Thomas to the Supreme Court that year, as a replacement for the retiring Thurgood Marshall, Hill realized that her status as a private citizen would soon change.

Anita Hill was born in Oklahoma, the youngest of thirteen children. After graduating from high school, she enrolled at Oklahoma State University and received a bachelor's degree in psychology with honors in 1977. She then attended Yale Law School, obtaining her JD degree with honors in 1980.

Early in her legal career (from 1981 to 1983), Hill worked with Clarence Thomas as a legal adviser in the US Department of Education's Office for Civil Rights and at the Equal Employment Opportunity Commission. During those two years as his colleague, Hill later claimed at Thomas's confirmation hearings in 1991, Thomas had subjected her to ongoing unwanted sexual advances ranging from repeated graphic depictions of pornography to constantly asking her to go out with him. She had left her position to pursue work in academia, she explained, but now felt a responsibility to speak out against Thomas's nomination, despite the historic nature of his poten-

tial appointment as the second Black Supreme Court justice.

In 1991, the term "sexual harassment" wasn't commonly used. Many people didn't know that it was their right to document offenses and file complaints against those responsible for inappropriate sexual behavior in the workplace. But they would soon know. The October hearings became a media spectacle. They aired in real time, and the nation was riveted. Hill endured questioning from an all-white, all-male Senate Judiciary Committee led by then senator Joe Biden. The striking images from those hearings have become iconic: few can forget Hill's poised countenance in the face of rigorous interrogation that asked her to recount in excruciating detail instances of abuse by Thomas.

Keen observers understood the burden Hill faced as a Black woman reporting the behavior of a prominent Black man nearing a career victory. Criticism came from all sides, and it was loud and endless. It soon became clear that the hearing was more like a trial, and it was Hill, not Thomas, whose future seemed threatened. Thomas received his nomination and was voted onto the Supreme Court, where he still sits today.

But Hill didn't retreat. She lent her voice to a widening chorus of Americans who knew the seemingly boundless range of workplace harassment, no matter the race of the perpetrator. Many found her treatment by the Senate to have been extraordinary in its tonal dissonance and sexism. As a result, more women entered the political arena. In 1992, their representation in Congress doubled (to six seats in the Senate and forty-seven seats in the House).

Hill became a prominent speaker not only on the wide-scale impact of sexual harassment but increasingly on matters of equality—specifically, economic equality. She took a professorship at Brandeis University in 1998, following calls for her resignation from OU, where she'd had a tenured position. Lending her modulated but firm voice to a public discourse that shocked many at the time certainly cost her. But her leadership, consistency, and clarity elevated issues of gender violence and created new language and ways for women to speak and expect to be heard. In fact, Hill's bravery came to have cascading effects that would shape legislation and workplace policy.

After the Thomas confirmation, President Bush dropped his opposition to a bill that gave harassment victims the right to seek federal damage awards, back pay, and reinstatement. This bill became law. A year later, harassment complaints filed with the Equal Employment Opportunity Commission jumped 50 percent, as women gathered the courage to step forward. Companies, large and small, started training programs to deter sexual harassment.

The reverberations from Anita Hill's testimony didn't stop there. Public sentiment turned in Hill's favor. Women and men were spotted all over the country wearing "I Believe Anita Hill" buttons on their lapels. Furthermore, as noted above, many observers attribute the large number of women elected to Congress in 1992 to the Anita Hill–Clarence Thomas controversy. Eleanor Holmes Norton, a DC congressional delegate, said, "Women clearly went to the polls with the notion in mind that you had to have more women in Congress."

Like all national phenomena, folks forget. They go about their lives. They remember the bravery and actions of others in muted tones. But Anita Hill has lived a life that thus far can't be forgotten. In 2019, the presidential campaign team for Joe Biden told reporters that Biden had called Hill to state "his regret for what she endured" in his role as the chairman of the Senate Judiciary Committee, presiding over the Thomas confirmation hearings. She said thank you, but her "no thank you" was felt as well. While she later said she would vote for Biden, she remarked with pointed generosity that she would work with him on gender issues.

Anita Hill, with her bravery, has empowered a generation of women. She didn't leap from tall buildings or save hostages from a bank heist. Instead, she gave women a road map to claiming their self-worth. Her opening statement at the Thomas hearings is instructive: "It would have been more comfortable to remain silent. It took no initiative to inform anyone—I took no initiative to inform anyone. But when I was asked by a representative of this committee to report my experience, I felt that I had to tell the truth. I could not keep silent."

Her leadership continues to be an example to follow.

GREGORY HINES

(1946-2003)

"You know, I think I'm going to tap dance until I can't."

Tap dance, which like jazz and hip-hop is a distinctly American art form, merged the West African percussive rhythms of juba dancing with Irish jig dancing as it evolved from early roots in minstrel shows and vaudeville acts. Throughout the centuries, Black hoofers guided the craft, which developed concurrently with jazz, on its own path. They brought forth swing, that evocative sense of rhythm that allows each musician, dancer, and audience member to intimately experience the "groove" of a performance. In the 1980s and 1990s, one figure represented the face of tap in popular American culture: Gregory Hines.

Hines was born in New York City in 1946. His father, Maurice Robert Hines—himself a dancer, musician, and actor—raised Gregory in Harlem's Sugar Hill section. The gifted younger Hines was tap dancing when he was two years old. He and his older brother Maurice performed together, taking pointers from veteran tap dancers such as Howard Sims and the Nicholas Brothers, when they performed at the same venues.

Like his tap predecessors, Hines could sing, act, and dance, but his skill as a dancer propelled him to new heights in the latter part of the twentieth century. He took advantage of opportunities not available to Black performers of past generations. He appeared on Broadway, won a Tony Award for his portrayal of Jelly Roll Morton in the musical *Jelly's Last Jam*, and starred in major films including *The Cotton Club*, *White Nights*, and of course *Tap*. He later appeared in his own eponymous sitcom. Even with global renown and visibility in other art forms, Hines remained deeply committed to seeing that tap got its proper place in the American story; in 1989 he helped establish National Tap Dance Day.

Like many Black traditions, tap has historically been passed down through visual study and oral tradition rather than formal classes (though that has changed in recent decades, as is also the case with jazz). Although Hines trained as a dancer from the age of three, it was his study of the elder hoofers—Teddy Hale, Jimmy Slyde, James "Buster" Brown, Sammy Davis Jr.—that primarily shaped his own unique style.

When Hines danced, a gold dangly earring often hung from his left ear. He'd smile as he let the rhythm and clarity of his foot sound support or dictate the music as the performance required, his lean frame loose and low to absorb his sways. His genius hides in plain sight. And he made it look so simple. He was effusive in his slides, flaps, shuffles, and devastatingly fast combinations—so much so that audiences often overpowered the sound in their appreciation for his talent. He died from cancer at the age of fifty-seven.

BELL HOOKS

(1952–2021)

"As long as women are using class or race power to dominate other women, feminist sisterhood cannot be fully realized."

Throughout her life, bell hooks used her literary voice and academic grounding as tools to highlight and scrutinize systems of oppression as they related to gender, class, and race, in an effort to dismantle them. In more than thirty books, she offered a mix of personal testimony, spiritual exploration, and scholarly curiosity on the subject of human relationships, how we define love, and ways that perceived roles of gender, especially exacerbated by the construct of white supremacy, limit our capacity to live fully.

Born Gloria Jean Watkins in Hopkinsville, Kentucky, bell hooks was one of six children. Her father was a janitor and her mother, a maid who worked for white families. hooks, a student in racially segregated public schools, was a voracious reader. Later in her life, she wrote that it was during this time she came to understand that education is the practice of freedom. She went on to receive her BA in English from Stanford University in 1973 and her MA in English from the University of Wisconsin–Madison in 1976. In 1983, she completed her doctorate in literature, with a dissertation on author Toni Morrison.

She used her great-grandmother's name as her pen name—bell hooks, in lowercase—as a nod to that woman she greatly admired. In 1981 South End Press published her seminal work *Ain't I a Woman? Black Women and Feminism*, written while she was an undergraduate student. She is frequently quoted by feminists as someone who can truly define feminism. What feminism is and how it's seen bifurcates along racial lines, but hooks said that it's "rooted in neither fear nor fantasy. . . . Feminism is a movement to end sexism, sexist exploitation and oppression."

Beginning in the early 2000s, hooks wrote a series of books focused on love and relationships. *All About Love: New Visions, Communion: The Female Search for Love, The Will to Change: Men, Masculinity, and Love*, and *Salvation: Black People and Love* have become must-read texts that treat love not as a romantic pursuit or a value that inherently exists among family members, but rather as an actionable choice that one must constantly engage in and continually refine. Her message has enormous potential to help people heal, but not through the mere proselytizing of her word; they must engage in courageous and vulnerable acts in their lives.

In her role as distinguished professor in residence in Appalachian studies at Kentucky's Berea College, she brought increased visibility to the rich culture of African American Appalachia, an ancestral heritage that influenced her and from which she countered notions of "nowhere places," places that in fact provided opportunities for people to experience and explore their personal sense of freedom. On December 15, 2021, she passed away. But she will be broadly remembered and quoted as if she were an ancestor, because she had so much wisdom to share.

LENA HORNE

(1917–2010)

"You have to be taught to be second class; you're not born that way. But the slanting process is so subtle that you frequently don't realize how you're being slanted until very late in the game."

One year after joining the Cotton Club's dance chorus in Harlem at the age of seventeen, Lena Horne made her Broadway debut, in 1934. She spent the rest of her life performing, becoming one of the most celebrated actresses and singers of the twentieth century.

By the 1940s she was hotly in demand and crossing color barriers in the process. She sang and toured with the Charlie Barnet Orchestra, an all-white band. She was invited to sing solo at nightclubs in Hollywood. She became a favorite of both Black and white American GIs, and the USO invited her to perform, but she refused to sing until she was reassured that Black servicemen wouldn't be segregated in the audience.

The movie industry soon beckoned. Horne became one of the first Black artists to sign a multiyear contract at MGM Studios. In spite of the landmark occasion, she was still, even as a fair-skinned Black woman, relegated to musical roles that could be cut for screenings in the South. In other markets, her characters were never on par with those played by white actors, reflecting long-held prejudice against Black actors playing roles other than those in which they kowtowed to whites.

But political pressure by organizations such as the NAACP and increasing criticism from Black performers in Hollywood paved the way for all-Black films like *Cabin in the Sky* and *Stormy Weather*; in the latter film, Horne's rendition of the title love song was so expressive that she was associated with the tune the rest of her career.

Like several Black film actresses of this period, Horne did some television, but she returned primarily to live performances and recording as a vocalist. Her 1957 album *Lena Horne at the Waldorf Astoria* was a bestseller. As a singer, she shared the stage with legends like Count Basie, Judy Garland, Tony Bennett, and Frank Sinatra. In Horne's last film role, in 1978, she played Glinda the Good Witch in the all-Black cast of *The Wiz*.

In an interview when she was eighty years old, Horne sounded liberated from her fate as a pioneering Black celebrity: "My identity is very clear to me now. I am a Black woman, I'm not alone, I'm free. I no longer have to be a credit, I don't have to be a symbol to anybody, I don't have to be a first to anybody. I don't have to be an imitation of a white woman that Hollywood sort of hoped I'd become. I'm me, and I'm like nobody else."

LANGSTON HUGHES

(1901–1967)

"One definition of the great artist might be the creator who projects the biggest dream in terms of the least person."

What is there to say about Langston Hughes? He was either a Black poet who shaped your entire childhood or you don't know him at all. He was author of the quotable, memorable poem that every Black child in America knows by the age of seven. His poetry frames and threads every Juneteenth, Fourth of July, Martin Luther King Day, Black History Month celebration, and Kwanzaa. Or . . . maybe you've never heard of this man at all. His legacy lives at these extremes, though that never was his intention. Hughes had bigger fish he wanted to fry. He wanted his poetry to be known by *all*. Black, white, both. What is the point of Black culture if it can't be known to everyone?

Born James Mercer Langston Hughes in Joplin, Missouri, this poet became one of the Harlem Renaissance's most prominent and influential figures. Hughes's ancestry is complicated, like that of most Black people in America. Both of his paternal great-grandmothers were enslaved Africans, and both of his paternal great-grandfathers were white slave owners in Kentucky. His father was an educator and activist for voting rights for African Americans.

Langston Hughes grew up in a series of midwestern small towns. His father left the family soon after he was born. After the separation, Hughes's mother began to travel in search of work. As a result, Langston was raised in Kansas, by his grandmother

Mary Patterson Langston, who taught him to have racial pride. Her message: Black people, despite our circumstances, have something to say. Our hardship ought to be glorified. Most importantly, our stories ought to be heard. It was his duty, she taught, to help his race.

With that weight of racial responsibility on his shoulders, young Hughes turned to reading and writing for solace and to prepare to tell his people's stories. In his 1940 autobiography *The Big Sea*, he wrote, "I was unhappy for a long time, and very lonesome, living with my grandmother. Then it was that books began to happen to me, and I began to believe in nothing but books and the wonderful world in books—where if people suffered, they suffered in beautiful language, not in monosyllables, as we did in Kansas."

After his grandmother died, Hughes moved around, living with various other relatives. He soon found himself in Harlem, his second and permanent home. It was there that his literary career was born and that he made fateful relationships.

Hughes was first published in 1921 in *The Crisis*, the official magazine of the NAACP, with his poem "The Negro Speaks of Rivers." It is a poem I can remember reciting in second grade. It's important to realize that my recitation—and experiences of other Black people who can claim the same sort of childhood memory—was exactly what Hughes hoped to ultimately accomplish. At the height of Hughes's literary prowess, the so-called Negro question was on everyone's mind. And almost every Black person of stature had, if not an answer, a working theory. Booker T. Washington and W. E. B. Du Bois thought of Black people as political creatures. To be political, always, was how we Black folks would make our mark. Langston Hughes had another answer. Along with Alain LeRoy Locke (the godfather of the Harlem Renaissance) and fellow travelers—Zora Neale Hurston, Wallace Thurman, Claude McKay, Countee Cullen, Richard Bruce Nugent, and Aaron Douglas—Hughes thought the way to racial equality was through art.

Hughes wasn't very interested in the Black middle class; rather, he was inspired and animated by poor Black folks. He knew that those folks needed uplifting stories to tell themselves. Hughes understood how detrimental it is to be color-struck in the Black community. We have to love ourselves first, before we venture out into white America for affirmation. In 1926, Hughes wrote "The Negro Artist and the Racial Mountain," a declaration of artistic intent he and kindred spirits would live by.

Hughes's first collection of short stories, *The Ways of White Folks*, was published in 1934. The next year, Hughes received a Guggenheim Fellowship, a financial grant intended to support his creative work, which flourished. For twenty years, he was a columnist for the *Chicago Defender*, mainly writing about segregation, Jim Crow laws, and the treatment of Black soldiers during World War II. He collaborated with friends and fellow artists, writing and staging plays. He wrote novels, short stories, poetry, operas, essays, and works for children.

Inspired by Paul Laurence Dunbar and Walt Whitman, Hughes's work captured the interior lives of Black people. He embraced his connection to the everyday experiences of ordinary, poor Black folks and sought ways to explore Black people's humor, language, pain, and joy, often using the urban Black vernacular to do so. He even found a way to implement the rhythmic energy of jazz into his work. In addition to his many collections of poetry and prose, he wrote eleven plays, including *Mule Bone*, on which he collaborated with Zora Neale Hurston. Hughes died from prostate cancer in New York City in 1967. Today, the Schomburg Center for Research in Black Culture, a research arm of the New York Public Library in Harlem, features the Langston Hughes Lobby and *Rivers*, a memorial in his honor—a section of terrazzo flooring marked by a brass cosmogram with song lyrics and African symbols—under which his ashes are buried.

As I draw Hughes's portrait, pondering this artist's influence and legacy, I can't help but think he was on the right track. We Black folk in America are necessarily political folk; Booker T. Washington was right about that. But when we think about what America has given to the world, we have to acknowledge the importance of Black art.

ZORA NEALE HURSTON

(1891–1960)

"How can any deny themselves the pleasure of my company."

Bearing witness was Zora Neale Hurston's extraordinary calling. "I want to know who you are," she said in 1927 to a man named Oluale Kossola, who was called Cudjo Lewis. Hurston ultimately titled the interviews she conducted *Barracoon: The Story of the Last "Black Cargo"*—an urgent testimony of a man who became enslaved, endured the Middle Passage, lived through the Civil War, and formed a life for himself in Africatown, Alabama. Hurston alone was willing, compelled maybe, to document and illuminate a narrative that challenged long-held oversimplifications of Black people's experiences coming to and surviving life in the United States.

It was not the story most folks wanted to hear, or tell, and it would be ninety years before the book was published. But this needing to know was the driving force in her work, from the acclaimed novel *Their Eyes Were Watching God* to her resilient autobiography, *Dust Tracks on a Road*. Her greatest achievement was her lifelong commitment, as a folklorist, ethnographer, and anthropologist, to telling Black people's stories, including her own.

She was born in Notasulga, Alabama, and raised in Eatonville, Florida, by parents whose parents had all been enslaved. She worked odd jobs to pay for her schooling and earned an associate degree from Howard University, becoming one of only a few Black Americans able to get a college education at that point in history. She later graduated from Barnard College and began a PhD at Columbia University,

studying under anthropologist Franz Boas.

In the mid-1920s Hurston landed in New York City, bringing a resolute interest in ordinary Black folks—their rhythms of speech and their delights— to the Harlem Renaissance. Her intellectual peers sometimes derided Hurston's commitment to capturing Black folks' language on the page. Richard Wright named it a "minstrel technique," because it played to whiteness. But Hurston, known for her wit, sass, and stubbornness, could not be moved.

By the late 1930s, Hurston had established herself as a successful novelist and published many articles and short stories. Funds from a Guggenheim Fellowship allowed her to travel in Haiti; she also spent time in Jamaica, studying the practices of Caribbean voodoo. Southern folklore was her main interest, though, and she traveled to the South regularly to collect recordings of songs, parables, and the life experiences of Black folks, whom she always understood as diverse and distinct people bizarrely linked in the construct of race in America.

When Hurston died in 1960, she was struggling financially, in part due to reduced interest in her writing. But when a young Alice Walker, soon to be esteemed for her own influential work *The Color Purple*, published a 1975 essay called "In Search of Zora Neale Hurston," it sparked renewed understanding of the folklorist's work. For more than thirty years, Eatonville has hosted an annual festival in Hurston's honor, celebrating Black arts and culture.

AMY JACQUES GARVEY

(1896–1973)

"Be not discouraged black women of the world, but push forward, regardless of the lack of appreciation shown you."

Amy Jacques was born in 1896 in Kingston, Jamaica, into a middle-class home. At a young age, she was encouraged by her father to read newspapers and take piano lessons. Her parents insisted that she attend high school, where she excelled, graduating with honors. Soon thereafter, Jacques was approached by a law firm. They wanted to hire her, but her father refused to give his permission; he didn't want his daughter working in a company of men. Fate soon intervened. Her father died, and the lawyer who handled his estate saw promise in this young woman. He convinced her mother to let Jacques work for the firm. She served in their clerical office for four years. In 1917, she moved to New York.

There she was impressed by hearing Marcus Garvey speak and joined the Universal Negro Improvement Association (UNIA), which he founded. She was active in the organization, a central fixture even, eventually becoming his secretary. The two were married in 1922. The next year, Garvey was convicted and incarcerated for mail fraud, following long-standing harassment from government officials who balked at a Black-led organization so openly dedicated to identity-driven nationalism. Amy Jacques Garvey took the reins at the UNIA and undertook arduous work in the areas of feminism and Black nationalism.

In support of her husband and their shared political efforts, she published collections of Garvey's writings and met with public officials in his stead. As associate editor of *Negro World*, she introduced a column focused on women. Presumably, she felt that a dedicated focus would be required to effectively challenge patriarchal structures and male-dominant ideologies. When Garvey was eventually deported to Jamaica because of an untrue, politically motivated charge of mail fraud, Jacques Garvey also left the United States, ultimately joining him in Jamaica after an international tour. She remained there, but her husband moved to England. Upon his death in 1940, Jacques Garvey became a contributing editor with *The African*, a journal that was distributed in Harlem.

JUDITH JAMISON

(1943–PRESENT)

"I believe in spirit and then I believe a manifestation of spirit is dance."

In the solo performance *Cry*, which can be seen as the crystallization of an extraordinary career in dance, Judith Jamison achieved night after night what many professional dancers dream of doing convincingly just once: she embodied spirit. *Cry* was choreographed by Alvin Ailey, the founder of his namesake dance company in New York. Ailey was clear in his dedication: "For all Black women everywhere—especially our mothers." But he developed the routine for Jamison, his muse, whose tall, lean, sculpted body seemed destined for it.

In the three-part piece, set to the music of Alice Coltrane, Laura Nyro, and the Voices of East Harlem, Jamison brought gravitas, grace, despair, and unbridled joy to the portrayal of the distinct path Black American women have walked. Dressed in a white gown and holding a length of white fabric, Jamison alternated between cutting and soft motions, her dark brown body appearing adrift in a tapestry of white. Her debut at the City Center in New York in 1971 commanded ten minutes of applause and cheering from the audience. Decades and dancers later, the iconic piece is still part of the Alvin Ailey American Dance Theater repertoire. But in many ways, *Cry* will always be Jamison's.

Born in Philadelphia, Jamison studied dance from the age of six. By eight, she was dancing "en pointe" and taking classes in tap and acrobatics. Although she began her college education at Fisk University, she quickly transferred to the Philadelphia Dance Academy.

Her professional career began in New York at the American Ballet Theatre but later moved to Ailey's dance company, where she first performed in 1965 (having taken her first modern dance class just three years earlier). In 1980 Jamison left the company to pursue dance and choreography opportunities on Broadway and abroad, including starring in the musical revue *Sophisticated Ladies*. Following Ailey's death, Jamison returned to the company in 1989 as artistic director, eventually establishing schools and outreach programs in multiple US cities.

For the next two decades, Jamison took the Ailey company around the world and enjoyed multiple honors, including a National Medal of Arts, an Emmy, and a Kennedy Center Honor. Under her leadership, the Alvin Ailey American Dance Theater became a household name, a fact that is a testament to Jamison's business acumen. As a dance pioneer, she is proof that one can both be a great artist and build an institution. Judith Jamison was inducted into the Hall of Fame of the National Museum of Dance in 2013.

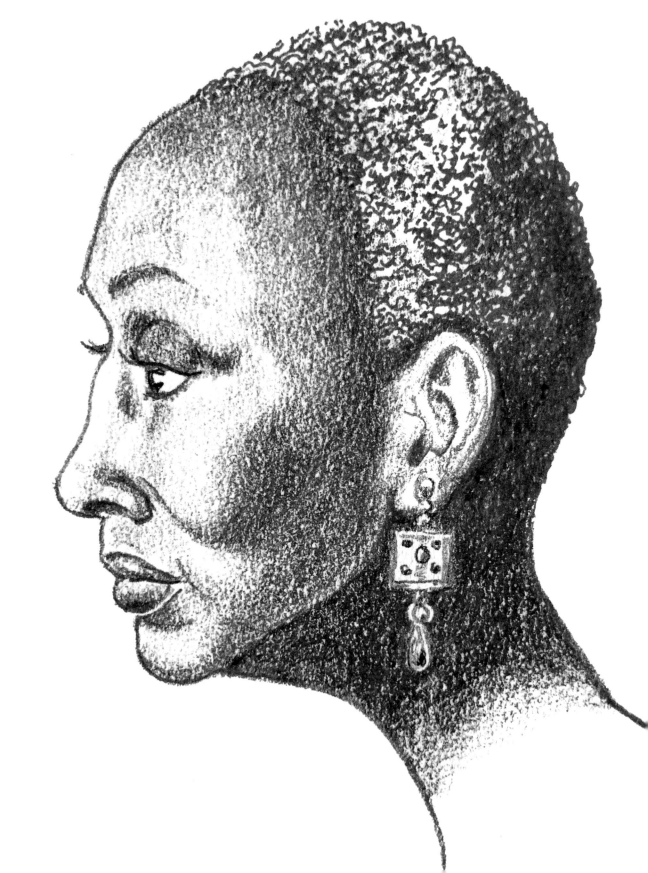

BABY ESTHER JONES

(1918–UNKNOWN)

Baby Esther "has been heralded as the child wonder of Paris and is creating sensation wherever she appears."

—*Chicago Defender*

The popular riff "boop-boop-a-doop," the standard catchphrase of the character Betty Boop, derived from a style of performance that Baby Esther Jones created in her career as a Harlem jazz singer. She was born Esther Lee Jones, in Chicago. Her career began at age six, when she won a dance contest for performing the Charleston. A theater manager spotted the little girl's talent, and soon seven-year-old Jones was on tour. As a youngster, she played venues in Chicago, Detroit, and Toronto. In New York, Jones performed on the nightclub circuit in Harlem, including at the revered Cotton Club. She toured Europe in 1929. The *Chicago Defender* reported that she was the highest-paid child artist in the world. In Europe she performed for royalty. King Alphonso and Queen Victoria Eugenie of Spain and King Gustaf and Queen Victoria of Sweden were all enthralled with her singing and dancing. In Paris people called her a miniature Josephine Baker.

But for me, Baby Esther Jones is an avatar. She's illustrated in this book for a reason. Jones—her life, her art, her signature boop-boop-a-doop (capable of evoking an entire persona)—is a stand-in for every Black person whose artistry has been stolen by white people. She's the embodiment of cultural appropriation and what that does to the sense of self. We Black folks are distressingly familiar with having pieces of ourselves stolen, with no recourse. The inability to attain anything close to justice creates emotional scars. Baby Esther Jones, when she's remembered at all, is seen as a footnote of history; but properly contextualized, her artistry is a pillar of history and American culture. Jones didn't get recognition or remuneration for essentially being the precursor of one of the most enduring cartoon characters in the history of American animation. And although problematic sexual and race-based stereotypes certainly emerge from any oversexualization of a Black child, the stage banter Jones created was part of an influential style of the period; that style was later co-opted by white artists, effectively becoming a complex case study in appropriation.

Baby Esther Jones was more, of course, than the cartoon she inspired. A child star who toured domestically and abroad, she was a true Jazz Age entertainer, employing the arts of dance and song through the 1930s. Her whereabouts after that period remain unknown, but her impact lives on.

BILL T. JONES

(1952–PRESENT)

"Art does for me what religion does—it organizes a seemingly chaotic world."

Bill T. Jones was born in Florida, one of twelve children. His parents were migrant famers who moved to upstate New York when Jones was three years old. After high school, he attended Binghamton University on a special scholarship. During an interview, Jones remarked, "Binghamton was where I first took classes in west African and African-Caribbean dancing. It immediately appealed to me. It was an environment that was not about competition." It was also at Binghamton where Jones met the love of his life, Arnie Zane.

For over four decades, Jones has used dance to explore personal and collective identity. As a performer, choreographer, director, and writer, he is celebrated for creating his own language in the physicality of dance. His stunning moving collages challenge assumptions about the human form. In Jones's work, moving bodies accompany speech and sound effects. Imperfection, rather than crisp unity, is the intent. Dancers perform readings or cry out. Choreography doesn't always adhere to a backbeat or an eight count. To watch a Jones performance is at times to experience serene beauty. At other times, a Jones piece can feel unsettlingly intimate. Jones's ability to portray pain and loss through the passionate motion of dance makes audiences uncomfortable. The pleasure comes in letting go and allowing the inquiry to take you on the journey: What is the body for? Who decides what dance is?

In 1982, Jones and Zane founded the Bill T. Jones / Arnie Zane Company, which became known for creating social commentary arising from their personal relationship and their experience as gay men during the peak of the AIDS crisis. Their collaborations (until Zane's death of AIDS in 1988) brought forth new and urgent depictions of bodies—aging bodies, sexual bodies, gendered and nongendered bodies. Jones's work wasn't always understood or received well by a white-dominant arts establishment fascinated and discomfited by the Black body and unused to gay Black men positioning themselves at the center of their own lives. Jones—or Bill T., as I think of him—has been always very special to me. When I was growing up in the eighties, he was constantly in the *New York Times*. Reading those articles, I began to understand that there was a hierarchy within the arts, and that this Black gay man stood atop the heap. How he approached his work has had a major influence on my own. He taught me this: to bring your entire self—your intellectualism, your culture, your sexuality—to your art is how you fully reveal the complexity of your work. Moreover, he has never failed to keep creating, and his persistence and clarity of mind have made his work unimpeachable. In his lifetime, Jones has been celebrated with a National Medal of Arts, a Tony Award, a MacArthur "Genius" Fellowship, and a Kennedy Center Honor.

GRACE JONES

"I'm always rebelling. I don't think I'll ever stop."

Fully nude, crouched on her hands and knees, a caged Grace Jones stares straight ahead on the cover of Jean-Paul Goude's 1981 photography book *Jungle Fever*. With shreds of raw meat scattered around her dark-brown, iridescent body, she confronts viewers with piercing eyes and a stretched-open mouth, as if to say, "Come any closer, and I will destroy you."

Before Jones took the couture runways by storm in Paris in the early 1970s, she was a young girl growing up in Spanish Town, Jamaica, raised predominantly by her stepgrandfather. Her parents left her in his care while they sought work in the United States. Their household was strict and Pentecostal: Jones knew that being disciplined meant picking a branch off a tree that would be used to whip her. However, her penchant for imaginative play only increased as her environment became more conservative.

At the age of thirteen, Jones moved to Syracuse, New York, to join her parents. With her she brought a deep-seated need to rebel. Over time, she became a go-go dancer; she experimented with drugs; she hung out with nudists. The focused, daring glare she would become known for throughout her iconic career—used alternately as defiant response, punishing rejection, and lighthearted invitation—is one she had internalized from her stepgrandfather's authoritative presence. Even in her full power as a fashion muse, art creator, singer, and consummate performer, she both bared everything and revealed nothing. As a kind of armor, maybe, Jones seemed to always be mocking viewers' opinion of her.

Recruited by a modeling scout in New York after studying theater in college, Jones became part of the fashion elite in Paris. Her presence was always an event. She once appeared nude at a gathering for French politicians, sporting only a bone necklace. She branched out into music in 1977 with the album *Portfolio*. In 1981, after several intervening albums, she followed with *Nightclubbing*, which featured "Pull Up to the Bumper," one of the era's most explicit songs. With *Nightclubbing*, Jones had moved seamlessly from disco to the reggae-influenced "new wave" genre.

During this period, she met artist Jean-Paul Goude, with whom she shared a creative and romantic relationship and had a son. Jones returned to New York, where she took Studio 54 and Andy Warhol's Factory by storm. She appeared in multiple movies, including *Conan the Destroyer* with Arnold Schwarzenegger and, as the villain, the 1985 Bond movie *A View to a Kill*. Even her small roles, like that of Strangé in Eddie Murphy's *Boomerang*, contributed scene-stealing moments that continue to pop up in today's popular culture references.

Often dressed in Egyptian-inspired cyborg ensembles or in androgynous suits subverting her gender, the rocker, runway queen, style setter, and provocateur has always kept audiences guessing, while she challenges the assumptions, and some might say the burden, of race. "I did things for the excitement, the dare, the fact that it was new, not for the money," she told the *New York Times*. "And too many times I was the first, not the beneficiary."

JACKIE JOYNER-KERSEE

(1962–PRESENT)

"Those who know why will always beat those who know how."

Jacqueline Joyner was born in Illinois. The daughter of teenage parents, she endured financial hardship while growing up, but she soon rose above the pack with her athletic prowess.

In high school, she qualified for the finals in the long jump at the 1980 Olympic trials. At the University of California, Los Angeles, Joyner performed both in track and field and in women's basketball from 1980 to 1985.

Joyner-Kersee gradually cemented her place in American sports as one of greatest, most decorated track and field athletes in history. Over thirteen years and four Olympic competitions—Los Angeles in 1984, Seoul in 1988, Barcelona in 1992, and Atlanta in 1996—she won three gold medals, a silver, and two bronze. She was the first American woman to bring home the Olympic gold medal in long jump. She racked up 7,291 points in the 1988 Olympic heptathlon and still holds the world record. But the numbers of points she accumulated, and her gold, silver, and bronze medals in the Olympics, strangely fail to capture the importance of this athlete during this

multi-event Olympic game. Standing at the starting line, Joyner-Kersee wasn't competing with the other athletes on the field. She was literally competing against herself. Winning was a smaller worry; the ultimate prize was to become the stuff of legend.

Joyner-Kersee achieved that legendary status. She has set the standard for athletic prowess. Winning isn't enough. At pivotal moments, it is important to be the best version of yourself. It is little wonder that *Sports Illustrated* named her the greatest woman athlete of the twentieth century. In 2004, she was inducted into the National Track and Field Hall of Fame. In the midst of her groundbreaking career, Joyner-Kersee launched her namesake foundation in her hometown of East St. Louis, Illinois, to help support kids in their academic and student-athlete endeavors. Joyner-Kersee has not forgotten her own humble beginnings. I am certain that she knows what it means when young Black boys and girls across America learn of her achievements and ask themselves: Can I cross the finish line, first? Can I break records?

COLIN KAEPERNICK

(1987–PRESENT)

"I'm going to speak the truth when I'm asked about it. This isn't for look. This isn't for publicity or anything like that. This is for people that don't have the voice."

Colin Kaepernick was born in Milwaukee, Wisconsin, to a nineteen-year-old white girl named Heidi Russo and an African American father who was gone from her life before Colin was born. She put Colin up for adoption when he was five weeks old. He was adopted by a white couple named Rick and Teresa Kaepernick. At age four, he and his family moved to California. At age eight, Kaepernick was already fully involved in the world of sports; that's when he began playing youth football as a defensive end and punter. At nine, he was the starting quarterback on his youth team. In high school, Kaepernick played football, basketball, and baseball. He was named the most valuable player of the Central California Conference in football, leading his school to its first-ever playoff victory.

Colin Kaepernick entered the national stage as a star quarterback for the San Francisco 49ers, where he played for six seasons, leading the team to a Super Bowl appearance in 2013. But attention shifted from his performance during games to his actions on the sidelines when, in 2016, he began opting out of the customary act of rising to stand for the national anthem, a tune that the National Football League and other professional sports organizations play at the start of games. That first time, he simply remained seated on the bench. It was a preseason game, and he wasn't in uniform to play. But preceding the third game of that season, when he remained seated, he responded to a query from the media: "I am not going to stand up to show pride in a flag for a country that oppresses Black people and people of color. To me, this is bigger than football, and it would be selfish on my part to look the other way. There are bodies in the street, and people getting paid leave and getting away with murder."

Kaepernick changed from remaining seated to kneeling after a fellow player—a military veteran—requested that he demonstrate his protest in a fashion similar to the way soldiers honor fallen comrades. But seen through the filter of multiple police shootings and the violent and careless rhetoric of Twitter-obsessed then president Donald Trump, Kaepernick was depicted not as a Black athlete taking part in a long tradition of using his visibility and privilege to bring awareness to issues affecting Black Americans, but as an unpatriotic pariah. He is now loved and hated in equal measure, and yet he hasn't deviated from his cause. He knows his role in the larger cultural conversation; he didn't get lost in this phenomenon. Kaepernick protested throughout the 2016 season and opted out of his 49ers contract at the end of the term. But when quarterbacks with similar records found jobs with various teams in advance of the next season and he remained a free agent, it became clear that no one would sign him to a team. He hasn't played professionally since January 2017.

Kaepernick's decision to protest wasn't without historical grounding. While at the University of California, Berkeley, he had audited an African American studies course about Black representation. He also sought guidance from, among others, civil rights activist Harry Edwards, who was a consultant for the 49ers. Edwards told the *New York Times* that he'd given Kaepernick a reading list, at the player's request, that included *The Fire Next Time* by James Baldwin and *I Know Why the Caged Bird Sings* by Maya Angelou.

It should be noted that Kaepernick's decision to speak out against police brutality follows a tradition of Black athletes speaking out against racism. Our history is dotted with men and women who stood up, spoke out, or acted up against inequities. Their names may be forgotten, but Olympic medalists Tommie Smith and John Carlos and the iconic photo of their Black-gloved fists raised on the winners' podium during "The Star-Spangled Banner" in the 1968 Summer Olympics in Mexico City is seared in our collective memory. Bill Russell and four of his Black teammates on the Boston Celtics were turned away from a restaurant in Lexington, Kentucky. Russell told his coach, Red Auerbach, they wouldn't play in an exhibition game in the city. And what did his coach tell the press? "The Negro boys got real emotional. They said they'd like to go home. We talked for two hours, and I couldn't change their minds." Finally, I can't help thinking about Muhammad Ali's stand against the Vietnam War. Ali was quoted as saying, "Why should they ask me to put on a uniform and go 10,000 miles from home and drop bombs and bullets on brown people in Vietnam while so-called Negro people in Louisville are treated like dogs and denied simple human rights?" This is the path Colin Kaepernick decided to walk when he took the knee.

In 2016, shortly after the initial uproar over his having taken a knee, Kaepernick founded Know Your Rights Camp, an organization focused on supporting young Black and Brown people in communities where they're subject to oppression. The organization's efforts are directed at helping these youth develop political awareness, gain access to educational opportunities, and better understand what appropriate interactions with law enforcement should look like. Camps have been hosted in many cities, including Atlanta, Baltimore, Oakland, and New York, as daylong, action-oriented workshops serving sometimes hundreds of youths at a time and featuring a slate of activists, educators, and entertainers.

Kaepernick's efforts have inspired many in the realm of professional sports and beyond. In 2020, the Milwaukee Bucks NBA team boycotted a game as protest for the police shooting of Jacob Blake in Kenosha, Wisconsin, prompting a wave of further boycotts and protests throughout the league. Increasingly, college athletes, often seen as especially vulnerable in an unpaid system, have been more vocal about advocating for social justice on campus. The NFL itself has become more socially aware as well.

In the wake of Floyd's and Blake's murders in 2020, the widespread critical rhetoric in response to Kaepernick shifted yet again as the world responded to the calls of Black Lives Matter. Kaepernick had sacrificed football, yes—but critics began to see that he'd done what he said he wanted to do: by kneeling, he stood for what was right.

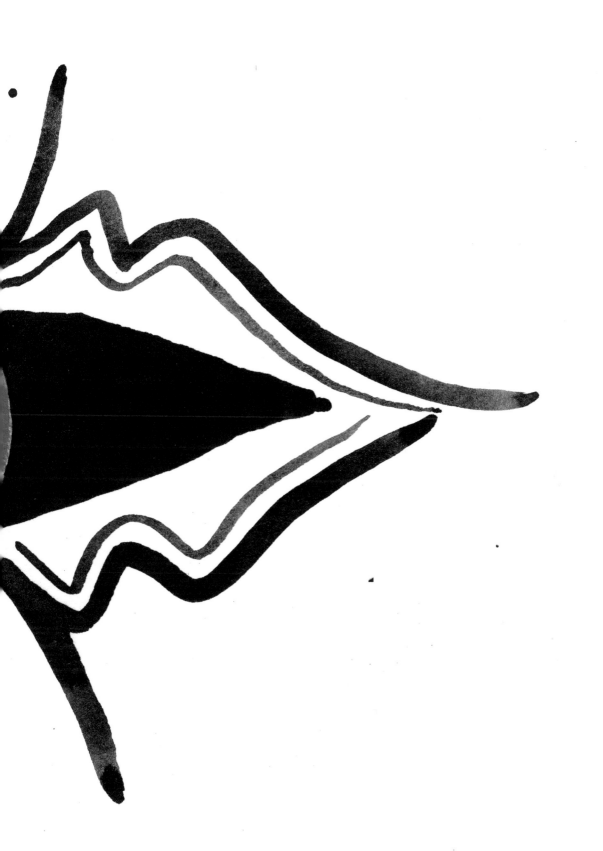

HENRIETTA LACKS

(1920–1951)

"Pounding in the back of their heads was a gnawing feeling that science and the press had taken advantage of them."

—*Jet* magazine

Much has been said about Henrietta Lacks and what her body did for the world of science. Scientifically, she was a miracle. But before her cells became specimens of global interest, Lacks was just a woman, a wife, a mother, making a way for her family on the tobacco farms of southern Virginia—a woman who was diagnosed with cervical cancer at the age of thirty.

This is a moment where the story eclipses the human. In 1951 Lacks sought care at the segregated Johns Hopkins Hospital, where—without her knowledge—a doctor took a sample of tissue from her biopsied tumor for further testing. The lab had routinely been collecting cells from cancer patients to better understand the illness. No one can say why, but Lacks's tissues never died, which was a stunning discovery for scientists who for decades had been trying unsuccessfully to culture human tissues. This cellular peculiarity offered a historic opening in medical research, allowing scientists to test procedures and remedies that would change the face of medical care forever.

But Lacks was unaware of what her body tissues were capable of because medical professionals never told her what they had done with her samples. And without that knowledge, she was unaware that the ongoing requests doctors made of her to return to the hospital for more testing were to extract more of her miraculous cells, not to help in her battle with cancer. Today's standards for consent are quite clear; but even at that time, there were documented stan-

dards of informed consent that should have applied to Lacks. The treatment she received, or the absence of it, is but one shameful example in American medical history of Black people's humanity being denied them in service of industry breakthroughs. Lacks died soon after her cancer treatments began in 1951, at the age of thirty-one.

Lacks's cultured cells became the HeLa cell line, which gave scientists a way to explore the effects of various drugs and treatments on human cells in a lab. For example, HeLa cells were integral in the creation of the vaccine against polio, which in the 1940s had disabled more than thirty-five thousand people each year. The cluster of cells from Lacks's tumor was the first in a line of samples that today anchors a multibillion-dollar industry in biotechnology and medical research.

Lacks and the story of her cells became the focus of a bestselling book, and later a movie starring Oprah Winfrey. But for the initial decades during which the medical community worked with HeLa, the Lacks family had no knowledge of their matriarch's impact. The confusion, grief, and anger at the opportunism involved continues to play out in the Lacks family to this day, even while advancements that came through the use of HeLa cells have saved countless lives around the world. Only recently have some institutions made efforts to make reparations, contributing to a foundation that benefits Lacks's descendants.

JACOB LAWRENCE

(1917–2000)

"The Human subject is the most important thing. . . . I want the idea to strike right away."

In his most iconic work, *The Migration Series* (1940–1941), the painter Jacob Lawrence depicts the mass movement of Black people from the Jim Crow South to industrial cities in the North. Consisting of sixty panels marked by Lawrence's distinct blend of abstract cubism, vivid color, and geometric texture, it takes viewers through the courageous and turbulent experience of more than one million Black Americans over decades.

Lawrence captioned each panel, speaking to the social climate that had sent Black people north. In panel no. 15, captioned "There were lynchings," he depicts a figure crouched in front of a branch on which an empty noose hangs. The figure is wearing burned-orange apparel, in contrast to the airy bluish background. In later interviews, Lawrence was reluctant to add more context to what viewers see. "If you try to talk about them, it diminishes the visual elements," he said. "But in content I can't discuss this work because it's too subjective and we've experienced this. We the American people."

Lawrence was the most widely celebrated Black artist of the twentieth century, with a career that spanned fifty years. His abstract paintings portray the intimate lives of Black people and their historic moments.

Born in Atlantic City, New Jersey, he grew up in Philadelphia and then Harlem, where after classes at Public School 89, he attended an arts program at the Utopia Children's Center, then operated by painter, sculptor, and muralist Charles Alston. During the Depression, Lawrence dropped out of school and joined the New Deal jobs program. He then began to paint scenes of city life. He was encouraged by sculptor Augusta Savage and the lecturer Professor Charles Seifert, who nudged Lawrence to study Black history at the Schomburg Center (part of the New York Public Library) in Harlem, where courses were taught mostly by Black artists. His oeuvre includes a series of paintings from the late 1930s and early 1940s that depict revolutionary Black figures: Toussaint L'Ouverture (forty panels), Frederick Douglass (forty-one panels), and Harriet Tubman (thirty-one panels).

The Migration Series received wide acclaim. Lawrence garnered representation from prestigious galleries, and his work was shown nationally. His career was interrupted in 1943, when Lawrence joined the US Coast Guard during World War II. He was discharged in 1945 and returned to his art. He was reportedly uncomfortable with the juxtaposition of his success with the status of peers who hadn't received anywhere near the same acclaim; options for them seemed unreasonably and permanently limited. Suffering from depression, Lawrence sought treatment in a Queens hospital, where he completed *The Hospital Series*, in which morose and lonely patients roam drab green hallways. After his release from the hospital, he continued to thrive in his career.

Lawrence taught and traveled widely. Over the years he joined the faculty of universities such as the Pratt Institute, California State College at Hayward, Brandeis University, and the University of Washington, where he served as a professor emeritus. His work is now owned jointly by the Museum of Modern Art in New York City and the Phillips Collection in Washington, DC.

EDMONIA LEWIS

(1844–1907)

"My features I take from my father, but my spirit, my industry and perseverance I get from my Indian mother."

The Egyptian queen Cleopatra has inspired countless artworks. *The Death of Cleopatra*, a sculpture by Edmonia Lewis, was first exhibited at the Centennial Exposition in Philadelphia in 1876. The critical reception was positive, but the piece would have an untethered existence for a century. It finally landed in a warehouse of the Forest Park Historical Society, in Illinois. A staffer there contacted the Metropolitan Museum of Art, to see if anyone there had information about the artist, whose name was carved on the piece. The museum employee remembered seeing an earlier query from Marilyn Richardson, an independent curator and expert in African American art who was writing about the artist. The two parties were put in touch. Richardson helped verify the statue, which was donated to the Smithsonian American Art Museum, where it resides now, in a manner befitting Lewis's art.

Lewis was born near Albany, New York, to an Ojibwa mother and a Haitian father. Her half brother earned enough money to send her to Oberlin College in 1859, but her experience ended poorly. She was accused of poisoning white students, for which she was severely beaten in a group attack and left for dead. She was eventually cleared of the charges but was then hounded for stealing art supplies. Lewis left for Boston without finishing her degree. There she encountered abolitionists, including William Lloyd Garrison, and studied with sculptor Edward Augustus Brackett.

But Rome beckoned. There was an expatriate community of American sculptors there, and Lewis believed she would have more artistic freedom overseas than at home. She set sail for Europe in 1865 and stayed there until 1896, though she made regular returns to the United States to exhibit and promote her art.

She was quoted as saying, "I was practically driven to Rome in order to obtain the opportunities for art culture, and to find the social atmosphere where I was not constantly reminded of my color. The land of liberty had no room for a colored sculptor." In a stunning example of stereotyping, the *Times* claimed that Lewis's dying Cleopatra "in some sense typifies the attitude of both races she represents"—as though Lewis's heritage was illuminated by the hopeless despair of a dead woman whose reign had ended.

In addition to Cleopatra, Lewis sculpted Hagar, the enslaved Egyptian woman represented in the Bible's story of Abraham; abolitionists John Brown and Anna Quincy Waterston; Caesar's adopted heir Octavian; and Native Americans, inspired by the epic poem *Song of Hiawatha* by Henry Wadsworth Longfellow—all pieces that still survive today. She enjoyed great popularity—Ulysses S. Grant sat for her, and Frederick Douglass visited her studio. Lewis received many commissions from American and European patrons. She was later known to weave truth and imaginative storytelling into her communications with the media, perhaps because she bristled at their fascination with her for reasons she considered dismissive of her work. According to researcher Richardson, Lewis's death notice indicated that she died in London in 1907 of kidney disease.

EDNA LEWIS

(1916–2006)

"One of the greatest pleasures of my life has been that I have never stopped learning about good cooking and good food."

One of the foremost talents in African American cuisine in the twentieth century, Edna Lewis became known as a New York–based culinary star in the 1990s, decades after she'd already established herself as a southern-trained chef and cookbook author, championing the use of farm-raised, seasonal, local ingredients.

Born in Freetown, Virginia, a town established by a community of formerly enslaved Black people, Lewis grew up on her grandfather's farm. As she later wrote in her now classic 1976 book *The Taste of Country Cooking*, life in Freetown was guided by the ability to grow, forage, harvest, butcher, cook, and preserve one's food. The book illustrated the range of what enslaved and formerly enslaved people ate and how they thought about their food.

Lewis was one of eight children. A few years after her father died in 1928, she left Freetown at age sixteen and joined the Great Migration north. Her first stop was Washington, DC, but the call to go even farther north persisted; she eventually settled in New York City.

After holding various odd jobs (she briefly worked as a seamstress, for example), she was hired as a cook at Manhattan's Café Nicholson in 1949. "Miss Edna," as she became known, cooked food that was inspired by her Virginia upbringing: soufflés and roast meats,

elegant salads, and rice-based stews. Many restaurants didn't serve Black diners and yet hired Black chefs; at Café Nicholson, Lewis served a chic celebrity clientele that included Greta Garbo, Truman Capote, Marlon Brando, and Eleanor Roosevelt. Later in her cooking career, she became chef at Gage & Tollner in Brooklyn.

Her cookbooks are foundational to modern African American cooking, and her writing is refreshing in its lyrical clarity. Lewis is a titan in the culinary world and is revered by Black chefs. Emphasizing her community's traditional country cooking, she focused on the importance of quality ingredients and recipes in which food preparation reveals, rather than conceals, its core elements. Her published works include *The Edna Lewis Cookbook* (1972) and *In Pursuit of Flavor* (1988). She often organized recipes not by dish category, but by season and meal. A harvest-inspired dinner in her *Taste of Country Cooking* features eighteen items, including boiled pork shoulder, "first cabbage of the season," spicy baked tomatoes, corn pudding, biscuits, cucumber pickles, blackberry cobbler, and lemonade.

Among many honorary degrees and awards, Lewis received the inaugural James Beard Living Legend Award in 1999. She died at the age of eighty-nine in 2006.

JOHN LEWIS

(1940–2020)

"When you see something that is not right, not fair . . . you have to do something."

Often heralded as a living legend, John Lewis served Georgia's 5th Congressional District as a Democrat from 1987 until his death, seventeen consecutive terms representing constituents in and near Atlanta. His colleagues called him "the conscience of the Congress." He opposed the 1991 war in the Persian Gulf, and he was among the few to oppose the 2003 invasion of Iraq, asking, "What fruit will our actions bear not just for us, but for our children?"

His life of service was born of the examples set for him. Having grown up in rural Alabama as the son of sharecroppers, he was a young teenager when Rosa Parks refused to give up her seat on the bus, sparking the bus boycotts. He began to think and plan for his own activism. The real spur came a couple years later, when he read, of all things, a comic book about Martin Luther King Jr. Lewis was inspired by both the man and his philosophy of nonviolence as a tactic in confronting segregation and racial discrimination. Following King's example, he committed to a life that sought Black people's true freedom. He cofounded the Student Nonviolent Coordinating Committee (SNCC) at the age of nineteen, organized sit-ins and freedom rides (he was among the original thirteen Freedom Riders), and at the age of twenty-three was the youngest speaker at the 1963 March on Washington. Between the years 1960 and 1966, he was arrested forty times.

In 1965, a series of three marches from Selma to Montgomery, Alabama, took place in response to the police killing of a twenty-six-year-old man named Jimmie Lee Jackson at a February march in Marion, Alabama. Jackson had been trying to protect his mother, who was being attacked by a state trooper wielding a nightstick. The trooper shot Jackson, who died days later. Lewis was then leader of SNCC, and he and his colleague Hosea Williams led a peaceful march across the Edmund Pettus Bridge, aiming for the state capitol in Montgomery. When the six hundred marchers got to the other side, state troopers and local police, many on horseback, tear-gassed the crowd and severely beat protestors, including Lewis, with their nightsticks. Lewis's skull was fractured; he experienced a permanent speech impediment as a result.

The media called the incident "Bloody Sunday," and the national response to images of rampant, unprovoked violence against peaceful Black protestors spurred President Lyndon Johnson's support of the Voting Rights Act, which he signed into law that August. The act was meant to address unconstitutional obstacles, such as literacy tests and poll taxes, that had been placed in the way of Black people's attempts to vote, particularly in the Jim Crow South. The increased representation in the voting rolls that resulted brought into the political conversation millions of Black people who had essentially been denied rights since before the US was formed.

Though increased rights for Black people were the only prize Lewis was striving for, he received a long list of honorary degrees and accolades—among them the John F. Kennedy Profile in Courage Award and the Martin Luther King Jr. Nonviolent Peace Prize. Toward the end of his life, Lewis was still choosing to lead by example, ever mindful of keeping clear the pathway for leaders still to come.

WE'VE MADE PROGRESS, BUT WE ARE NOT THERE YET.

REP. John Lewis

THERE ARE FORCES THAT WANT TO TAKE US BACK. WE DON'T WANT TO GO BACK. WE WANT TO GO FORWARD.

ALAIN LEROY LOCKE

(1885–1954)

"The younger generation is vibrant with a new psychology; the new spirit is awake in the masses."

Alain LeRoy Locke's 1925 publication of *The New Negro*, an anthology featuring the plays, poetry, essays, and music of leading Blacks including Claude McKay, Langston Hughes, Zora Neale Hurston, and Countee Cullen, cemented his position as the father of the Harlem Renaissance. A cultural critic and philosopher invested in the exploration of Black art and literature, he wrote about how to value and assess aesthetically guided work. He countered ideas from peers such as W. E. B. Du Bois who perceived Black art as a tool for promoting the uplift of the community. Instead, Locke believed that Black artists had a responsibility to tell the truth about their own experiences, being as specific as possible about their circumstances and belief systems, regardless of whether that description reflected well on the race. He ultimately understood art as a means to Black liberation.

Locke believed that creative pursuits and Black mobility—the literal freedom to move about this country—would have the greatest impact on Black people's ability to find ways to build their own identities and derive their own sense of progress. He advocated that Black people determine what they want not within the confines of what white systems of power demand, but from their own internal exploration and relationship to the self.

Locke was born in Philadelphia and raised middle-class by his schoolteacher mother and his father who had graduated from law school and was the first Black employee at the US Post Office. From a young age, Locke was a lover of art and literature. In 1907, Locke graduated from Harvard University with degrees in English and philosophy; that same year, he was the first African American to be selected as a Rhodes Scholar. His time abroad wasn't easy. At Oxford, Locke was denied admission to several colleges within the larger university before being admitted to Hertford College, where he studied literature, philosophy, Greek, and Latin. And the American southerners who were also Rhodes Scholars—white men, of course—refused to be in the same room with him. A mama's boy, Locke wrote to his mother every day, detailing his mistreatment. While at Oxford, he traveled all over Europe. Then, in 1910, he attended the University of Berlin, where he studied philosophy.

Locke was known for his immaculate fashion sense. He kept his life as a gay man quiet, but not hidden. In his career, Locke encouraged writers and artists to study African traditions and their pervasiveness in American culture. He believed that Black lives would reveal richer and more meaningful texts if there were more depictions and experiences of Black life. We ourselves are art that is ultimately within our reach.

BLACK PRESS, BLACK HISTORY

by Patrice Peck

I don't remember exactly what age I was when I realized what I wanted to be, but I do remember how it happened. I'd been watching an episode of some random docuseries on VH1 when Nelson George, an award-winning Black writer, journalist, and filmmaker, popped onto the screen. Like the other talking heads on the series, Nelson delivered insightful comments on the topics at hand. But it wasn't what came out of his mouth that inspired me, but instead what lay a few inches below it—a chyron that read "Nelson George, *cultural critic.*"

A light bulb went off in my head. Aha! Until that moment, I had never realized that dissecting pop culture with seriousness could be an actual job. There I was, the young girl whose brain was a sieve when it came to specific historical dates and events but retained the lyrics of a song after one listen or the face of any actor from any UPN series. A young teen immersed in my world of Disney Channel, Tamagotchis, *NSYNC, Destiny's Child, and Harry Potter, all of which served as entry points to the wide world beyond my home, my Jamaican family, my inner-city neighborhood, and my predominantly white school. Pop culture came easy to me, but until the moment I spotted Nelson's professional title, I'd figured it was a wasted passion and useless knowledge.

Discovering the existence of a profession in cultural criticism helped me realize there was a way for me to seriously address the wide range of issues I'd noticed through my obsessive consumption of magazines, music and music videos, television, films, books, and so much more. Because while I was a pop culture stan down to geek out about all my beloved songs, shows, and celebs, it had become increasingly clear throughout my childhood and adolescence that I wasn't represented in the same way that my white peers were, and neither were my experiences. So I figured if Nelson could critique this white pop culture world on cable television or on a popular, mainstream network, so could I. I too could use my voice, particularly my written words, to articulate the dissonance I felt and speak to the larger issues that I knew hid just beneath the surface. And thus, a budding journalist was born.

While Nelson offered me a blueprint, my college professor Marisa Parham provided the tools. In her "Foundations of African American Literature" course at Amherst College, my freshman self had the freedom to let my pop culture geek flag fly in class discussions and in my written assignments. I remember comparing a short story by Zora Neale Hurston to Kelis's hit song "Milkshake" and interrogating the nuances of Eddie Murphy's satirical *Saturday Night Live* sketch "White Like Me." Not only were we required to pen essays on these matters, but in one of her many prescient lessons, Marisa also required us to publish weekly posts on the class blog. The confidence I developed through my professor's belief in the value of our voices motivated me to try out an even more public forum, the campus newspaper, the *Amherst Student*.

The movie *ATL* had just been released. I'd already planned to check out the film in theaters with friends and decided that this would be my first piece of cultural criticism: a film review. I watched closely as Hype Williams's brilliant filmmaking spotlighted unapologetically Black, southern, and hood stories and characters enacted by the same celebrities who informed some of my pop culture references, like hip-hop, BET, video vixens, and code-switching. I carefully and thoughtfully considered and evaluated the film's plot, the performances, and the cinematography. I schooled myself on Williams, a seminal filmmaker responsible for some of the most influential music videos and global culture moments of my lifetime. I researched the history and legacy of roller-skating culture in Atlanta and down south, a major part of the story line, and the city's class structure that led to the wealthy world of Black upper-class folks like New New. And, to my surprise, my review was accepted.

The feeling I had when I saw my words in print, in a half-page spread, in a publication passed around campus and beyond, was indescribable, a concoction of empowerment, shock, satisfaction, validation, and vulnerability. My friends and other students recognized and appreciated my piece because we'd never had anything of ours really discussed in the school newspaper, especially not in our own voices. This lit a fire under me, prompting another Aha! moment. I realized that as a member of the press, I had free access to campus concerts as long as I covered them for the paper. In doing so, I expanded my portfolio, not only reviewing albums, but also interviewing the artists who toured Amherst and four neighboring colleges, including actor and rapper Yasiin Bey (formerly Mos Def), and interviewing artists whose teams sought out coverage, like wunderkind producer Ryan Leslie and comedian Charlie Murphy. Within a year, I was promoted from Arts & Culture staff writer to editor of the section, something I had never even considered but eagerly accepted.

My school didn't have a journalism track, so I married my growing knowledge of my two majors, Black studies and English, with self-taught knowledge cherry-picked from the wealth of magazines telling the kinds of stories and running the kinds of cultural criticism that I aspired to write professionally. I seriously considered and dissected Black popular culture of all kinds for an audience that didn't need a primer on the subject matter or a translation because they simply *lived* it. *VIBE, GIANT, Honey, XXL, Sister 2 Sister*—these publications introduced me to different Black cultures and communities by way of contemporary pop culture rife with references to our rich history and rooted in an unbroken, beautifully evolved legacy of the Black press, the vehicle for telling our stories in fashion, for us and by us. And so, armed with confirmation of the validity and existence of cultural criticism and driven by a passion to join and further enrich this legacy with my own words, I embarked on a postgraduate pursuit of professional FUBU journalism.

I applied for internships and entry-level positions at publications that I'd grown up on, but the year was 2009, and the economic recession meant fewer jobs everywhere—especially in the increasingly volatile journalism industry. I even turned to magazines that didn't often, if ever, feature people who looked like me, but the furthest I got was a second-round interview that resulted in less costly internal hires. But with challenge can also come opportunity. So I took non-journalism jobs and pivoted to writing on the side for free. A simple search using the keywords *pop culture Black girls nonprofit*—all things I hoped to somehow meld into a dream job—led me to the nonprofit organization Black Girls Rock. I became a blogger for their scrappy WordPress blog before being bumped up to editor-in-chief. Never mind that I led a team of two, myself included. The position provided me with the opportunity to recruit and edit contributing writers. With this newfound leadership and the barriers to entry lowered via a blogging platform, I discovered a freedom that allowed me to write important, influential, and impactful Black girls and women into the record of history, people who likely otherwise would have gone overlooked and unknown by major publications, even those that catered to our community.

Over the next decade, I gained more experience and fleshed out my résumé and portfolio from one digital publication to the next: virtual hub Society HAE, the BET channel, *Hello Beautiful*, *Ebony*, Huffington Post's "Black Voices," and TheGrio. I landed my first full-time staff writing position at BuzzFeed as a multicultural beauty writer, a role that had been created to grow and cultivate a female Black audience for the predominantly white-leaning website, and later as a pop culture writer. Although I felt isolated on a mostly white-staffed pop culture team that focused mostly on white celebrities and influencers, the passion that had led me to this calling kept me on course, inspiring me to double down on my cultural criticism and increased knowledge of Black pop culture and history.

Today, I write this as a freelance journalist in a media landscape whose traditional business and editorial models have been disrupted, for both better and worse, by technological advancements, a disruption that impacted the Black press much more than its peer publications that had predominantly white audiences and staff. The coronavirus pandemic revealed this gap left by the crumbling of the once mighty Black press community that I came up in in the 1990s and early 2000s, and so I stepped in with a newsletter, *Coronavirus News for Black Folks*.

Once the COVID-19 data revealed that Black people were disproportionately vulnerable to being infected with and dying from the coronavirus, racial health disparities and inequity became one of the nation's most covered topics, dominating front pages and headlines in newspapers, magazines, radio, and television. Black journalists were in sudden demand in a way they'd never experienced throughout their entire careers. Like many of us who had dedicated our careers to covering our community, I hated that this overwhelming, overnight interest occurred only because of an unprecedented pandemic that continues to devastate the Black community. At the same time, I was encouraged by the widespread acknowledgment of and focus on covering racial health disparities and inequity.

Generations of Black journalists, researchers, academics, scientists, and activists have dedicated their professional and personal lives to not only spotlighting the disproportionate rates of various illnesses and death in the Black community, but also doing the complex, nuanced work of understanding why that disproportion exists, investigating the deeply tangled factors at play: racism, misogynoir, and other biases and discriminations at the intersection of being Black in America and white supremacy. We're also doing this work about a community in which we reside, along with our family and close loved ones, along with strangers who look like us. The stakes of these stories don't stop once we sign off from work.

And yet, because journalism in America is not immune to the systemic racism that has kept the workforces of the most influential, powerful professional industries overwhelmingly white, especially in leadership positions, and aggravated the decline of the Black press during today's media landscape disruption, the Black community has a rich American history of independent health media and nontraditional sources of information distribution born out of a necessity rooted in the resourcefulness and creativity that have been required of the community since the transatlantic slave trade.

I now ache thinking about all the history not being recorded and preserved in all those since-folded publications once dedicated to the archiving of our stories and our voices. At the same time, I see occasional glimpses of that same Black griot tradition reflected throughout social media accounts and YouTube videos celebrating Black history, present, and future and showcasing rarely seen visual archives. The Black pop culture of today does not exist without that of yesterday. Black history is the blueprint of not only Black culture, but American culture, and we are the architects, creating, influencing, impacting and documenting, story-telling, and preserving.

Patrice Peck is a multihyphenate creative with a ten-plus-year background in reporting, cultural criticism, on-camera hosting, and multimedia production. Her cross-platform work centers on amplifying underreported stories at the intersection of race, culture, and identity and can be found at the *New York Times*, the *Los Angeles Times*, *The Atlantic*, MSNBC, *Vogue*, *Elle*, *Wired*, *Businessweek*, and more. She is currently the senior opinion editor at *Cosmopolitan* magazine.

AUDRE LORDE

(1934–1992)

"I am a Black, lesbian, mother, warrior, poet doing my work, coming to ask you if you're doing yours."

Audre Lorde described herself as "Black, lesbian, mother, warrior, and poet." Born in New York City to Caribbean immigrants, Lorde was raised in Harlem. She didn't have a good relationship with her parents, and her tumultuous exchanges with her mother were fodder for her poetry. She began writing as a teenager; her first poem was published in *Seventeen* magazine.

In 1954, Lorde was a student at the National University of Mexico. She then returned to New York to attend Hunter College, graduating in 1959. She received a master's degree in library science at Columbia University two years later. Although already focused on her creative work, she held a job as a librarian in the New York public schools in the 1960s, and then transitioned to teaching. In 1968 Lorde was writer-in-residence at Tougaloo College in Mississippi. She taught young Black undergraduate students, who were very much engaged in the civil rights movement.

Lorde's work espoused a firm belief in exposing the effects of systems of oppression such as racism, sexism, and homophobia. Her own experiences with oppression informed her writing. She understood the way class, race, and gender functioned and wrote about them in influential works that include the essay "The Master's Tools Will Never Dismantle the Mas-

ter's House." Lorde made enduring contributions to feminist and critical race studies. As a Black lesbian feminist who believed that how she identified was central to the work she created, Lorde urged audiences to embrace others' differences as an opportunity to explore their own personal growth.

The first time I read Lorde's poetry, the lyrism made me miss my stop on the subway. Her poem "Smelling the Wind" was tucked in the corner. I remember hanging on to the subway strap for dear life—and not because of the motion of the train. My body was doing what the poem commanded. Lorde's poem was authoritative yet caressing. I read it once, then again and again, and again. When friends or acquaintances struggle to explain how they felt when they encountered this poet's work, I think to myself, I know exactly what they mean. The word "headlong" describes both a mood and a movement. So much of Lorde's poetry captures emotions that penetrate. You forget where you are going; you rethink your destination. You miss your stop on the subway.

Lorde published twelve books of poetry and five of prose. One of the latter, *A Burst of Light* (1988), won a National Book Award. Among other awards, she received a fellowship from the National Endowment for the Arts and served as poet laureate of New York in 1991–1992.

HAKI MADHUBUTI

(1942–PRESENT)

"To maintain the ability to admit and grow from our mistakes rather than let them defeat us represents best the inner strength of a people."

Haki Madhubuti rose to prominence as a leading poet in the Black arts movement of the 1960s. His work centered on Black conscious identity as wholly separate from the invasiveness of white culture. His poetry collections, which include *Think Black*, *Black Pride*, and *We Walk the Way of the New World*, originally published under the name Don L. Lee, articulate a self-led future for and by Black people.

Born Donald Luther Lee in Little Rock, Arkansas, Madhubuti changed his name after a visit to Africa in the 1970s. He grew up in Detroit, Michigan. When he was sixteen years old, his mother died from a drug overdose. His life with his mother served as his inspiration and deepened his initial interest in Black art. In 1963, Madhubuti received a master's degree from the Iowa Writers' Workshop. In 1967, Madhubuti, along with Carolyn Rodgers and Johari Amini, founded Third World Press. This publishing house, dedicated to African American literature, is the largest independent Black-owned press in America. Third World Press has published literary luminaries such as Amiri Baraka, Sonia Sanchez, and Pearl Cleage.

In addition to his publishing company, Madhubuti is the cofounder of the Institute of Positive Education, the New Concept Self Development Center, and the Betty Shabazz International Charter School in Chicago, Illinois. He is also a founder of the National Association of Black Book Publishers and the International Literary Hall of Fame for Writers of African Descent and director of the National Black Writers Conference.

As a poet and writer, Madhubuti has been deeply influenced by Gwendolyn Brooks and Richard Wright. He has published over twenty books and is also an essayist and editor. In addition, he has worked with the Student Nonviolent Coordinating Committee, the Congress of Racial Equality, and other political organizations focused on Black people's civil rights. With an understanding that his responsibility is to document the pervasive challenges of being Black in American society, he copublished the *Black Books Bulletin*, a quarterly published from 1971 to 1980 that celebrated the work of figures in the Black Arts Movement.

ANNIE TURNBO MALONE

(1869–1957)

"[Malone was] recorded as America's first black female millionaire based on reports of $14 million in assets held in 1920 from her beauty and cosmetic enterprises, headquartered in St. Louis and Chicago."

—The Freeman Institute

Annie Turnbo Malone was born to formerly enslaved parents in Metropolis, Illinois, the tenth of eleven children. Her parents died when she was young, and she was raised by an older sister and inspired by an aunt who, as an herbalist, understood the intricacies of plant medicine. Further inspired by her brief exposure to chemistry in her short time in school, Malone launched a hair product that focused on scalp health. She sold shampoo and developed a hair-straightening method for Black women that protected the hair follicles. She named it "Hair Grower."

Malone and her young company moved to St. Louis, Missouri, in 1902. After a successful showing at the World's Fair in 1904, she relied on teams that gave public demos and went door to door to sell her products. By the end of World War I, Malone had become a millionaire, but she was also dedicated to giving back. She launched Poro College, the first cosmetology school dedicated to Black hair care, in 1918, and was known for her philanthropy throughout the 1920s—specifically, at historically Black institutions like Howard University and the Tuskegee Institute.

Without Malone, there would be no Madam C. J. Walker, whose name is most often associated with early-twentieth-century Black hair-care innovations. Malone employed Walker in her first job as a hair-care salesperson, and Walker went on to become a national success story herself. By the 1950s, Poro College had thirty-two locations throughout the country.

Although Black women throughout the African diaspora have always engaged in rituals of well-being, health maintenance, and beautification, Malone developed her forward-thinking business during a time when Black women in America were responding to significant trends in lifestyle and culture created by the industrial and economic growth of the early twentieth century. Espousing the notion of self-care—of doing what made you feel good and look good—was most certainly a revolutionary act. But going beyond sales and service to create a forum for educating others so that they themselves could gain a solid financial footing was another extraordinary step. Malone deserves more credit for that achievement than she's gotten.

54TH MASSACHUSETTS VOLUNTEER INFANTRY REGIMENT

(1863)

"Boys, the old flag never touched the ground!"

—Sergeant William Carney

In mid-1862, the Civil War was entering its second year. Enslaved Black people throughout the Confederate South were fleeing bondage to claim their own freedom behind Union lines. When President Abraham Lincoln signed the Emancipation Proclamation months later, in January 1863, its original intent wasn't to liberate Black people. Applying only to select states, the proclamation was a military strategy to allow Black people to enlist in the Union Army. But the one thousand men who eventually composed the 54th Massachusetts Volunteer Infantry Regiment weren't interested so much in politics; they simply wanted daily life to improve for Black folks. As members of the second "colored" regiment in the US armed forces (the 1st Kansas Colored Volunteer Infantry Regiment was the first), they put their lives in jeopardy to confront the oppression they and their fellow Black countrymen and -women faced every day.

Abolitionist Frederick Douglass advocated for Black enlistment, lobbying the government to allow Black men to take up arms, but a problematic notion was then prevalent. The double-edged perception of Black people at the time was that, if given the opportunity to fight alongside white soldiers, Black men would either cower out of fear or, according to white-held beliefs about Black people's inhumanity, behave savagely during battle and fail to observe standard practices of combat.

Still, by September 1862, Lincoln and his advisers had determined that the best way to leverage the Union's position against the Confederacy was to permit the enlistment of Black fighters. And so word went out. Many soldiers recruited into the 54th were tradesmen—artisans, clerks, and business owners. Many were literate; many were esteemed figures in their communities. Historians note that this regiment didn't consist primarily of runaways, but rather of those who had been living as free men, in spite of the rampant restrictions on residency, work, and travel that they faced. Yet these men understood that they couldn't truly enjoy a life of freedom while any Black people remained subject to slavery. They gathered from Connecticut, Missouri, New York, and Canada. And they went to fight in the South.

Seventeen-year-old Eli George Biddle enlisted from a Quaker community in Boston. James Henry Gooding enlisted at the age of eighteen from New York. Two of Frederick Douglass's sons joined up. None of these men joined as officers. Although Black men could be soldiers, they were thought to be incapable of filling positions of authority; white men simply couldn't conceive of white enlisted soldiers taking orders from Black commanders. This sentiment was rebuked when Lewis Douglass, Frederick Douglass's eldest son, became sergeant major.

Leading the 54th was a white officer named Robert Gould Shaw, who had left Harvard to join the Union Army. He was twenty-five years old. On May 28, 1863, he and the other white officers gathered with the 54th's thousand-plus Black soldiers on the Boston Common. There were celebrations and a parade. "I know not," said Governor Andrew at the parade, "where in all human history to any given thousand men in arms there has been committed a work at once so proud, so precious, so full of hope and glory as the work committed to you."

The men of the 54th became known for their bravery and fighting skills. They are most noted now for the July 18, 1863, Union assault on Fort Wagner, on Morris Island just outside Charleston, South

Carolina. Underestimating the number of Confederate troops that awaited them, the Black troops and accompanying white officers were ravaged in battle. The regiment ultimately retreated. When the Rebels buried the dead, they buried the Black soldiers in an unmarked grave along with the unit's white officers, which was meant as an insult. But reports of the unit's valiant efforts prevailed.

During the battle, Sergeant William Carney was responsible for bearing and ultimately saving the flag, a morale victory for the troops. He took several bullets but never let the flag touch the ground. In 1900, he became the first Black soldier to receive the Medal of Honor for his efforts.

But racist practices continued: When the War Department had originally recruited Black soldiers, it promised a daily pay rate of thirteen dollars. In reality, though, the soldiers were paid only ten dollars and had additional fees deducted for their uniforms. The soldiers of the 54th again banded together, refusing to accept any money until they all got the pay they had been promised. It took eighteen months.

Through their efforts, the members of the 54th Massachusetts Volunteer Infantry Regiment paved the way for thousands of Black men to fight in the Civil War. They represent the pivotal contributions that Black service members have made in the US armed forces since the earliest days of this nation.

OSCAR MICHEAUX

(1884–1951)

"My long experience with all classes of humanity had made me somewhat of a student of human nature."

Just how Oscar Micheaux got his start to become the most prolific independent producer of Black films remains unclear. But during a career from 1919 through 1948, Micheaux wrote, produced, directed, and distributed more than forty films, founded his own production company (the Micheaux Film Corporation), and was one of only a few Black independent creators to survive the transition from silent films. His 1931 film *The Exile* was the first sound film by a Black person. His final film, *The Betrayal*, from 1948, was the first Black-produced film to premiere in white-owned theaters.

Micheaux was born in Metropolis, Illinois, and raised in Great Bend, Kansas. He found work as a Pullman porter, which, despite the low wages and the requirement to wait on white travelers hand and foot, allowed him to travel the country at a time when such movement was inaccessible to most Black people. In 1906, he used his earnings (often better pay than Black service workers earned elsewhere) to buy land in South Dakota, where he became a homesteader, writing as he found time. He lost the land to bankruptcy, but he used the experience to enhance his storytelling skills, writing a novel—his third—about homesteading as a Black man.

Micheaux published *The Homesteader* in 1917, selling it door to door. To counter the effects of D. W. Griffith's racist film *Birth of a Nation*, which applauded the terrorism of a white-supremacist country, Micheaux was inspired to adapt his book himself. It became the first film he directed, in 1919.

Hollywood's cultural influence on Micheaux's movies is noticeable—he created within similar genres and encouraged the promotion of Black performers as versions of white studio stars. For example, Lorenzo Tucker, with handsome features, tall figure, and fair skin, was known as the Black Valentino. Ethel Moses, a Harlem star and former performer with Cab Calloway's band, was regarded as the Black Jean Harlow. And thanks to a sultry delivery and sensual appeal, Bee Freeman was known as the sepia Mae West. Silent movie stars such as Juano Hernández continued their streak as Micheaux's films moved into sound technology, transitioning into "talkies" right along with their filmmaker.

But Micheaux also developed his own style of storytelling, one that spoke directly to a specifically Black audience. Actors such as Paul Robeson and Robert Earl Jones got their start in Micheaux films, tackling themes that addressed the Black experience.

Micheaux's 1931 film *The Exile*, based on his 1913 novel *The Conquest*, explores an interracial romantic affair. In his 1938 film *God's Step Children*, he takes on colorism in Black communities. In his 1939 film *Birthright*, he follows a young man set on founding a rural school but who has to deal with pushback from Black and white communities. What's left of the film is in the Library of Congress archives—some footage, like so many Black independent films from the turn of the century, has been lost to history.

In 1986, Micheaux posthumously won the Directors Guild of America Lifetime Achievement Award.

SCIPIO MOORHEAD

(CA. 1770S)

When first thy pencil did those beauties give,
And breathing figures learn't from thee to live.
—Phillis Wheatley, poet

Not much is known about the Boston portrait artist Scipio Moorhead. We glean insight into his talent and skill from a work commonly attributed to him by scholars: the iconic engraved portrait of Phillis Wheatley, a popular late-eighteenth-century US poet. She had been enslaved in a household headed by a tailor named John Wheatley, who had purchased her soon after she was taken from Senegambia. She worked as a domestic but was taught to read and write. Her poetry was distributed in England first, then in New England.

At the request of a bookseller in London, a portrait was commissioned to accompany her collection *Poems on Various Subjects*. That artist was Moorhead, who was enslaved to Reverend John Moorhead, who lived near the Wheatleys. It's believed that Wheatley and Moorhead knew each other, since the book included a poem titled "To S. M., a Young African Painter, on Seeing His Works." From Wheatley's poem it's easy to see that Moorhead's artistry was valued by many, and that they shared a meaningful connection:

> To show the lab'ring bosom's deep intent,
> And thought in living characters to paint,
> When first thy pencil did those beauties give,
> And breathing figures learn't from thee to live,
> How did those prospects give my soul delight,
> A new creation rushing on my sight?

Still, wond'rous youth! each noble path pursue,
On deathless glories fix thine ardent view:
Still may the painter's and the poet's fire
To aid thy pencil, and thy verse conspire!
And may the charms of each seraphic theme
Conduct thy footsteps to immortal fame!
High to the blissful wonders of the skies
Elate thy soul, and raise thy wishful eyes.
Thrice happy, when exalted to survey
That splendid city, crown'd with endless day,
Whose twice six gates on radiant hinges ring:
Celestial Salem blooms in endless spring.
Calm and serene thy moments glide along,
And may the muse inspire each future song!
Still, with the sweets of contemplation bless'd,
May peace with balmy wings your soul invest!
But when these shades of time are chas'd away,
And darkness ends in everlasting day,
On what seraphic pinions shall we move,
And view the landscapes in the realms above?
There shall thy tongue in heav'nly murmurs flow,
And there my muse with heav'nly transport glow:
No more to tell of Damon's tender sighs,
Or rising radiance of Aurora's eyes,
For nobler themes demand a nobler strain,
And purer language on th' ethereal plain.
Cease, gentle muse! the solemn gloom of night
Now seals the fair creation from my sight.

TONI MORRISON

(1931–2019)

"It was always about African-American culture and people—good, bad, indifferent, whatever—but that was, for me, the universe."

As one of the most gifted writers in American history, Toni Morrison chronicled fictional characters on their journey to personal freedom. Her words, which had an indelible global impact, earned her the Nobel Prize, the Pulitzer Prize, and the Presidential Medal of Freedom.

Her writing could be succinct and pointed, breathtaking and luxurious. She drew from biblical allegories, mythology and folklore, song, and, most noticeably, the patois of Black people, simultaneously singular and varied. In her first novel, *The Bluest Eye* (1970), a dark-skinned girl believes getting herself a pair of bright blues would make her deserving of love. This novel also revels in Black life. We see a Black family falling apart in the Breedloves; we bear witness to a different Black family, the Whoevers, remaining financially sound. In fact, all of Morrison's fiction is invested and interested in Black love and life, death and commerce.

Early in Morrison's career, her passion to tell the story of Black folks was faced with a singular criticism, sometimes stated, sometimes implied: When, just when, was Toni Morrison going to get around to writing about white people? Those critics seemed shocked when she turned the tables on them. Had they ever asked the same kind of question of James Joyce, Tolstoy, Dickens? Sometimes, they seemed rather surprised that she had the audacity to place her writing in their company.

But it was clear from the start: Toni Morrison belongs in the Western canon. *Sula* (1973), the story of two friends, is also a story of how lore is made. National Suicide Day and the origin story of the Bottom, important elements of *Sula*, have essentially become American Black mythology. *Song of Solomon*, published four years later, seamlessly blends together Greek mythology and African folktales. Of course, we can't forget the seminal 1987 novel *Beloved*, in which the ghost of a child rises up in the house of the person who killed her. While it's a ghost story, the novel is also concerned with slavery, American style. The stories of the hunted slaves are varied—Sethe, Paul D, Stamp Paid; but so are those of the slave owners, the hunters, "schoolteacher" and his nephews. Slavery is a tapestry that affects us all, the book says.

In her masterful oeuvre of essay collections, plays, and eleven novels, Morrison demonstrates her unique talent of layering prose with both the deeply personal and the macro effects of time, place, politics, and circumstance. It is a feat that most students of the form can only dream of possessing.

WALTER MOSLEY

(1952–PRESENT)

"A man's bookcase will tell you everything you'll ever need to know about him."

Born in California to his Jewish mother, Ella, and his African American father, Leroy, who came from Louisiana, Walter Mosley has published more than sixty acclaimed books over a span of thirty years. In his first novel, *Devil in a Blue Dress*, Mosley, a Los Angeles native, introduced the character of Easy Rawlins, a private investigator in postwar LA. That book launched him into a creative exploration of Black characters' lives that captures generational and regional nuances while managing to speak broadly to an African American experience of migration and renewing one's identity. He focuses on Black characters because he wants to see the experiences of Black heroes reflected in literature, an important record of who exists and matters in society.

It has always made sense to me that Mosley's Black male heroes find their adventures in California. Easy Rawlins moves in a world that feels expansive and distinctly Californian. The gritty, pulp-noir mystery was normally the stomping grounds of writers like Raymond Chandler, but Walter Mosley made the genre his own. And in doing so, he brought a new tone to Black characters. In his novels, his characters possess the same full lives as their white counterparts. Mosley's prose is steeped in danger, adventure, opportunity. I think I was looking for all those things when I moved to California in 1999 at twenty-eight years old. I had lived in New York since I was eight years old and I was ready to go. Moving to California was one of the most adult things I had ever done. I was sick of living in New York. I was sick of complaining about it. A job moved me out to San Francisco. And California allowed me to become the person that I am. California is its own planet. It gives you spaciousness. It attracts art and creativity. It's a land that inspires. And for Black folk who headed west, California feels like a land that is not haunted. So much of America is steeped in Black folks' toil and tears and blood. But here on the coast, ideas can bloom. You have room to think. In that way, I feel close to Mosley the writer. He is an artist who let his creativity roam.

There are few forms that Mosley has not played with in his career—from novels and plays to nonfiction and artwork, he's done them all. Mosley not only practices mastery of his craft, but teaches it as well; as a leading voice in the art of storytelling, he encourages others to try their hand at writing the novel that's waiting inside them.

Mosley was inducted into the New York State Writers Hall of Fame in 2013 and has received myriad accolades for his work, including a Grammy, multiple NAACP Image Awards, and PEN America's Lifetime Achievement Award.

ARCHIBALD MOTLEY JR.

(1891–1981)

"I'm a person that thinks far into the future. I'm still that way. I don't look to tomorrow or to next week or a couple of weeks from now or a month from now. I'm always looking very far ahead."

The work of Archibald Motley Jr., who is known as a Jazz Age modernist, reflects the lively creativity that helped define Chicago's Black arts scene at the turn of the century. He painted church scenes and portraits, but his most vivid works are scenes of Chicago nightlife, in which revelers dance, drink, and smoke the night away or flood the streets en route to the next soiree. His subjects are captivating, often in vibrant dresses or tailored suits. His work reflects periods he spent in the Midwest, Paris, and Mexico, primarily in the first half of the twentieth century.

The New Orleans–born artist moved to Chicago with his family as a boy and was one of the first Black artists to study at the School of the Art Institute of Chicago. His education in the classroom was deeply rooted in European traditions, but Motley always centered his work around his own cultural identity. Motley is considered one of the major figures of the Harlem Renaissance, a fertile creative period of Black art, literature, and music that also affected the Chicago landscape, where it was called the Bronzeville Renaissance.

In *Gettin' Religion*, he makes a blue-hued night scene feel raucous and lively as people dressed in shades of gray, black, and blue pass under a streetlight. Pops of red appear: in the tight dresses and towering heels of women out on the town, in the lips of folks in the middle of conversation, busking, and heckling. Motley's ability to document the raw energy of street life in near caricature was harnessed for quieter moments too. His personal favorite was *Portrait of My Grandmother*, in which his grandmother is seated in quiet, reserved dignity, her hair pulled back, a white blouse buttoned to the neck. She was born into slavery, and time has worn on her. Her gaze is steady and engaged, but also protective, even fatigued. Motley depicts her with affection and with a sense of honesty and sympathy.

Motley's work, which created space for new archetypes of Black figures in painting, continues to be celebrated in prominent museum exhibitions around the world.

DIANE NASH

(1938–PRESENT)

"There probably was no greater invention during the twentieth century than Gandhi's invention of how to really wage warfare and change society using nonviolence."

For anyone who hasn't experienced the oppressive side of segregation as it was lived and documented in the 1950s American South, deep empathy and a studied gaze down history's path is required to even glimpse the recurring despair. No matter how optimistic you might have been, there it was, your assigned inferiority, just waiting to douse your vibrant flame. It's easy to assume that the distance provided by time is the reason that the era of segregation feels absurd. "I can't imagine living that way," you might say. But distance from that period is not what buffers you from such inhumane treatment. Rather, it is the courage of mainly young people, who in the face of systematic racism and violence decided to begin the work of dismantling America's Jim Crow laws.

Born into a middle-class family in Chicago, Diane Nash began her college education at Howard University in Washington, DC, before transferring to Fisk University in Nashville in 1959. Both were celebrated historically Black universities, but one was firmly based in a region that had long been dominated by Jim Crow laws and practices. It was in Nashville that the effects of segregation began their assault on the twenty-one-year-old student.

Nash learned about, and then learned from, Reverend James Lawson, who was teaching young people various nonviolent protest methods at a church not far from campus. Lawson taught many young people who would become integral to the nonviolent movement in pursuit of equal justice, including John Lewis. In 1960, Nash participated in the sit-ins that sought to desegregate lunch counters in Nashville. Following a march of several thousand people to City Hall, the city became the first in the South to end that segregation. The protest effort helped launch the Student Nonviolent Coordinating Committee (SNCC), which Nash cofounded with Charles Jones, Charles Sherrod, Ruby Doris Smith, and many others. They coordinated more sit-ins in other cities, supporting and training other young student activists.

In 1961, Nash participated in the Freedom Rides, launched by the Congress of Racial Equality (CORE), in which Black and white people together rode buses into the South to protest segregation policies of interstate travel. Freedom Ride buses were often attacked by the Ku Klux Klan, including with firebombs.

During that time, Nash was arrested for teaching nonviolent protest tactics to minors. She was convicted of contributing to their delinquency and faced a two-year jail sentence as a married and pregnant woman. After an open letter in which she restated her convictions and her willingness to serve time "if it may help hasten that day when my child and all children will be free," the judge sentenced her to ten days in jail. She continued her activist work with SNCC from 1961 to 1965. She eventually returned to her native Chicago and worked in education.

To pursue the fight for equality, Nash had dropped out of Fisk. In 2009, the university gave her an honorary degree.

FAYARD AND HAROLD NICHOLAS

(FAYARD NICHOLAS: 1914–2006)
(HAROLD NICHOLAS: 1921–2000)

"My brother and I used our whole bodies, our hands, our personalities. . . . We called our type of dancing classical tap and we just hoped the audience liked it."
—Fayard Nicholas

The 1943 film *Stormy Weather* stars Lena Horne and Bill Robinson, Hollywood icons who broke ground for Black performers. But the scene that steals the show features the breathtaking choreography and tap dancing of the Nicholas Brothers, Fayard and Harold.

Cab Calloway launches into a full-throated call-and-response that beckons every horn player on the bandstand up. Fayard and his younger brother, Harold, emerge from up top to join the fanfare. Airborne, they leap between the music stands, twisting and jumping above the players.

During the nearly six-minute sequence, Fayard and Harold dance in unison, but with fully formed individuality. Their smiles shine. At the climax, the brothers descend a giant stairway, landing on alternate steps in full splits as they leap over each other and rise again hands-free. As if that were not outrageous enough, they gracefully remount the stairs to—again in full splits—cascade down identical slides framing the stairs. It is the most energetic, athletic, stylized poetic dance number in American cinema.

Fayard, born in 1914, grew up watching rehearsals and learned to tap, sing, and act by observing. He practiced his split jumps by clearing fire hydrants. Harold, when he came along, took a keen interest in dancing too, and Fayard taught his sibling everything he knew. They became star attractions, dancing at the Cotton Club, on Broadway, and in multiple films in the 1930s and 1940s. It seemed they did everything. But they should have been able to do more.

Perhaps in a world where early-twentieth-century movies weren't segregated, or in which dance scenes by the duo weren't relegated to easily removable clips for screening down South, audiences might have seen the Nicholas Brothers achieve the mainstream visibility of artists like Gene Kelly and Fred Astaire. But that wasn't *their* world. They were often cast to stereotype their presence and rely on shtick. But YouTube clips reveal the pride and great dignity these young men brought to their work, rivaled only by their humility and love for the art. The pair received Kennedy Center Honors in 1991, recognizing their lifetime achievement. And their legacy is still palpable: watching young Fayard and Harold, one can see their artistic heirs James Brown, Michael Jackson, and Savion Glover. The night the brothers debuted at the Cotton Club in 1932, they were so strong, so good, and the audience so loud and inspired, that none of the classic stage acts dared to follow them. Every single one of the brothers' recorded performances conveys that feat: they opened hearts, brought crowds to their feet, and joyfully, brilliantly shut the whole place down.

SATCHEL PAIGE

(1906–1982)

"Don't look back. Something might be gaining on you."

The star of Negro leagues baseball was unquestionably Satchel Paige. Born in Alabama, he was known for his iconic windup and unstoppable pitch in a career that took him across the United States and to Cuba, Puerto Rico, Mexico, and the Dominican Republic. His sports acumen and self-celebratory manner demonstrated his star power, regardless of whether Black or white fans were watching. Although he wasn't the first Black man to integrate Major League Baseball, his playing created a space for Jackie Robinson and other players to ultimately succeed.

Because there's no official record of early Negro leagues baseball statistics, it's difficult for historians to definitively cite his stats. But it's believed that Paige pitched twenty-five hundred games and racked up two thousand victories, with twenty-two strikeouts in a game. He is believed to have garnered a twenty-one-game winning streak, a sixty-two-inning scoreless streak, and fifty no-hitters, among other incredible achievements.

Age is a factor in comparing the accomplishments of professional athletes, and Paige's age has been famously disputed. He was known to use different birthdates. Records indicate that he may have been born anytime between 1900 and 1908. For many Black people born around the turn of the twentieth century in places like Mobile, such record-keeping wasn't prioritized, and they, as individuals, were sometimes not included in census data. It's possible he may not have known his actual birthdate. But regardless of his age, it's agreed that Paige's four-decade career was incredibly rich. He played with the Birmingham Black Barons, the Baltimore Black Sox, and the Cleveland Cubs. His efforts were most visible at the National Association of Colored Professional Base Ball Clubs's Kansas City Monarchs.

Paige entered a newly desegregated major league in 1948, joining the Cleveland Indians and taking them to the World Series. He became the first of the Negro leagues' stars to be inducted into the National Baseball Hall of Fame in 1971. He was often described by people who watched him as the greatest pitcher to ever play the game.

SUZAN-LORI PARKS

(1963–PRESENT)

"One of my tasks as a playwright is to . . . locate the ancestral burial ground, dig for bones, find bones, hear the bones sing, write it down."

In 2002, Suzan-Lori Parks became the first Black playwright to win a Pulitzer Prize. Her drama *Topdog/Underdog* explores the volatile relationship between two Black brothers: one, Booth, is a shoplifter, and the other, Lincoln, has a job at an arcade playing the namesake president (in whiteface), so that customers can pay to fake-assassinate him. Parks's play landed on Broadway, at varying points featuring actors Jeffrey Wright, Don Cheadle, and Yasiin Bey (then named Mos Def). In 2003, she followed with her debut novel, *Getting Mother's Body*, which tells the story of a young unmarried and pregnant protagonist in 1960s Texas who is trying to change a streak of bad luck to good. Parks's gift for allowing audiences to find bright peaks as well as near despair in her characters' limited worlds is in keeping with the works of writers such as Zora Neale Hurston, whose dedication to dialogue and voice offers characters a real range of humanity.

A Kentucky native, Parks grew up in a military family and attended high school in West Germany. Back in the United States, her family moved often—Texas, California, North Carolina, Maryland, and Vermont. Parks studied writing at Mount Holyoke College, where James Baldwin taught a writing class; he encouraged her to try playwriting. As testaments to her talent, she later received a Guggenheim Fellowship and a MacArthur "Genius" Fellowship.

Parks is noteworthy not just because of her prowess as a playwright/screenwriter, but also because she's an example that Black art and exceptionalism can flourish in any setting. In work that includes screenplay adaptations, many plays, and other stories, Parks explores the absurdity of a society overwhelmingly committed to framing race, but she never loses touch with the tender elements that push it all beyond such constructs.

EVA JEFFERSON PATERSON

(1949–PRESENT)

"People can change deeply held beliefs."

The year 1968 in the United States still manages to defy categorization—it was full of reckoning, replete with tragedies and cultural shifts the country is still working out. That year two sanitation workers in Memphis were killed in an accident involving a malfunctioning garbage truck, exposing ongoing neglectful and prejudicial practices, which then led to a strike. To support the workers, Martin Luther King Jr. traveled multiple times to Memphis, where he was assassinated while standing on the balcony of the Lorraine Motel. More than one hundred cities exploded in uprisings and despondent anger and grief.

Robert F. Kennedy was assassinated after winning the California primary in his bid to become president. At the Mexico City Olympics, US athletes Tommie Smith and John Carlos raised gloved fists to protest violence toward Black people after winning gold and bronze medals; the International Olympic Committee stripped them of their awards. Amid countless university-based protests nationwide, students lost their lives in encounters with the police and the National Guard.

Eva Jefferson Paterson was a sophomore at Northwestern University in this climate of urgent transformation. She served in the student government, becoming vice president in 1968 and then the first Black president in 1970. That latter year, four students were shot dead at Ohio's Kent State University while protesting, followed by two killed at Jackson State College (now Jackson State University) in Mississippi. Paterson became a skilled articulator of the student activists' concerns and was invited on *The David Frost Show*, where she debated Vice President Spiro Agnew.

Paterson more than held her own. Even as a twenty-one-year-old student, she was measured and impassioned. She criticized Agnew for taking out of context past comments on why young people would resort to violence. She deftly summarized the violent history of American politics, saying that people who've seen change arise only out of violence may feel that violence is necessary, even though she didn't believe that herself. She described being "honor-bound" to represent all aspects of her Northwestern constituency, including the so-called radical figures, just as Agnew surely had to think about the cross-section of Americans he was expected to represent. "You're doing us a great disservice because you're making people afraid of their children," she said, to audience applause. The exchange brought many of the nation's divisive issues into focus and literally gave Paterson a national platform.

Paterson went on to become a civil rights attorney, addressing implicit bias on juries, discrimination in the San Francisco Fire Department, and attacks on affirmative action policies. She worked for over two decades (part of that time as executive director) for the Lawyers' Committee for Civil Rights, which provides free legal services to low-income clients. The Equal Justice Society, of which she is the president and cofounder, advocates equity and fairness in correctional and educational institutions.

LEAH PENNIMAN

(CA. 1980–PRESENT)

"We're reclaiming our right to belong to the earth and to have agency in the food system."

Perhaps one of the most damning aspects of slavery and the associated psychic burden its shadow casts is the tragic rift in the relationship between human beings and the land they need to thrive. Working with and caring for land has been crucial to any civilization. But for generations of Black people, that connection has been fraught with the weight of bondage, subjugation, and misinformed notions about mindless, unskilled labor. In fact, Black farming had its roots long before the existence of slavery in the Americas, an understanding that was crucial to Leah Penniman's decision to make organic food, the practice of regenerative farming, and caring for the environment central to her work.

Leah Penniman was born to a Black pastor, Adele Smith-Penniman, and an unnamed white father. Penniman was introduced to farming when she was sixteen years old by her grandmother. Later she worked with the Food Project in Boston. After graduating from Clark University in Massachusetts, Penniman lived under food apartheid in Albany, New York. (The term "food apartheid" decisively rejects the notion that "food deserts" are naturally occurring gaps in food accessibility; rather, they are the result of codified, actively protected policies that privilege the profits of white-dominant corporations over the health and well-being of communities of color—specifically, Black communities.) After giving birth, Penniman was on food stamps. These experiences led Penniman to understand the need for food sovereignty in Black neighborhoods.

A farmer, food-justice activist, author, and educator, Penniman cofounded Soul Fire Farm in Grafton, New York, in 2011. The community farm's mission is to help reclaim an ancestral connection to the land by eliminating systemic racism in the food industry. In her work as co–executive director, she oversees a range of programming and educational workshops that support up-and-coming Black and POC farmers and offers subsidized healthy foods for those suffering under food apartheid.

Educated with a master's degree in science education and a bachelor's degree in environmental science and international development, Penniman received wider recognition after the publication of *Farming While Black* in 2018. The book was the first of its kind, operating as a guide for would-be Black farmers interested not only in recognizing the historic contributions of their ancestors, but also in reclaiming their own relationship to nurturing, restorative agricultural practices. The book references a range of issues, from core practices like soil fertility and seed preservation to the use of plant-based methods for intergenerational healing.

The work of Soul Fire Farm has been recognized by the Fulbright Program and the Soros Racial Justice Fellowship, among many others. In 2019, Penniman received the James Beard Foundation Leadership Award.

RENEE POWELL

(1946–PRESENT)

"I'm not the kind of person who can go out and agitate, it would be so out of character for me, but in my own way I can demonstrate what can be done. I know, in that sense, a lot of people still think of me as a pioneer."

Following the inspired precedent set by tennis champion Althea Gibson, Renee Powell became in 1967 the second Black woman to join the Ladies Professional Golf Association (LPGA). She had been surrounded by golf talent her entire life. Her father, William Powell, had worked as a caddie as a boy, and he went on to build his own course, the Clearview Golf Course, in Canton, Ohio—the first golf facility owned and operated by a Black man. Powell herself played in junior leagues and as an amateur, and then joined her school teams when she was a student at Ohio University and Ohio State University. She qualified for the US Women's Open prior to her arrival on the LPGA circuit.

Powell described feeling welcomed by fellow golfers on the tour but acknowledged racist behavior throughout the country from folks she described as "outsiders" in an essay for the Golf Channel. She recalled being undeterred, however, thanks to the influence and tenacity of her family. Despite her father's service in World War II, during which he was stationed near courses in England and Scotland and able to play at times, he was unable to pursue professional golfing because of the restrictions placed on Black people. When he sought funding for the golf course he wanted to build, he discovered that no GI loans were available for Black veterans, so he brought in investors: he partnered with two Black doctors in the area, and Powell's uncle mortgaged his home to make the land purchase and construction possible. "That was the character of the family that raised me," Powell wrote. "There was never any anger or bitterness, which eats you up inside, only determination. I've always wanted to do likewise, to set an example to others and not let the narrow-minded people define me as a person." Her father's Clearview course is listed on the National Registry of Historic Places and the Ohio Historical Register.

Powell retired from her professional golfing career in 1981 and took over management of her father's Clearview Golf Course; she later began Clearview HOPE (Helping Our Patriots Everywhere), a therapeutic recreational golf program for women veterans. In addition to numerous other accolades, in 2008 she became the first woman golfer and the third American to receive an honorary doctorate from the University of St. Andrews in Scotland, joining golf giants Jack Nicklaus and Charlie Sifford.

HARRIET POWERS

(1837–1910)

"[The quilt] is the work of an aged Negro woman, who put into it the reverence, the fantastic conception of sacred events, and the passion of imagination of her people."
—Lucine Finch, dramatist

Harriet Powers's medium was textile needlework. She was known for quilting and embroidery while a slave in Athens, Georgia, where she was born. Historians believe she was enslaved to John and Nancy Lester in Madison County, and some even go so far as to presume she learned her craft from her white mistress. But others note the similarities between Powers's detail work and that found in techniques by artisans from Dahomey, a precolonial African kingdom that is now in the southern part of Benin. Had she been given other instruction, either through passed-down traditions or a book?

Census records indicate that by the 1880s, Powers had moved with her husband and family into rural Clarke County and owned four acres of land. Eventually, she and her husband split, but Powers continued to work as a seamstress. She exhibited her first story quilt at the Cotton Fair in Athens in 1886. Featuring appliqué, a technique in which smaller pieces of fabric are sewn onto a larger one, her story quilt depicted Bible scenes that she reportedly could recite verbatim. It involved 299 pieces of separate cloth. For four years, Powers was pursued by Oneida Virginia "Jennie" Smith, who was head of the art department at the Lucy Cobb Institute, to sell the piece. Powers refused. After four years of intermittent back-and-forth, Powers accepted five dollars for it, despite having wanted ten.

Smith documented an oral history of Powers explaining the eleven panels on the quilt, which included Adam and Eve in the Garden of Eden, Satan and the seven stars, Cain killing his brother Abel, the crucifixion, and the Last Supper. Smith entered Powers's story quilt in the Cotton States and International Exposition in Atlanta in 1895. Following that public display, Powers was commissioned to create a quilt for the chairman of the board of trustees of Atlanta University. That fifteen-panel quilt illustrated biblical events as well.

Powers's first story quilt is part of the Smithsonian Institution in Washington, DC, while her second is held by the Museum of Fine Arts in Boston.

RICHARD PRYOR

(1940–2005)

"What I'm saying might be profane, but it's also profound."

Richard Pryor is considered by many today to be the greatest stand-up comedian of all time. Unapologetically Black and refusing to be intimidated by the experiences of his life, which he believed to be fueled by a specifically American brand of racism, Pryor brought visibility to the dark humor and deep pain of being Black, being poor, and feeling uncared for by just about everyone.

Growing up in Peoria, Illinois, he was raised by his stern grandmother, who owned several brothels. Being surrounded by pimps, johns, prostitutes, and other characters of the underworld was often painful for young Pryor, especially when he observed his own mother subjected to abuse by his father, who was a boxer and a hustler. His mother, an alcoholic and a prostitute, abandoned him when he was ten years old. He was expelled from school when he was fourteen. When he enlisted in the US Army a few years later, he managed to serve the majority of his time in the army prison. While Pryor was stationed in West Germany, he attended a showing of Douglas Sirk's film *Imitation of Life*. Apparently, a white soldier in the audience found the racially charged scenes quite funny. Pryor, along with several other Black soldiers, beat and stabbed the white soldier, who was injured but didn't die.

In 1963 Pryor moved to New York City and broke into comedy through open-mic sessions. Once he opened for singer Nina Simone at New York's Village Gate. She said of Pryor's performance: "He shook like he had malaria; he was so nervous. I couldn't bear to watch him shiver, so I put my arms around him there in the dark and rocked him like a baby until he calmed down. The next night was the same, and the next, and I rocked him each time."

Pryor modeled his approach to stand-up after the work of Bill Cosby, who had a friendly, mild-mannered shtick that didn't put anyone off. The two were increasingly compared to one another, and eventually Pryor disappeared from public life for a couple of years before reemerging with the assertive, profanity-laced, muscular style of comedic storytelling that would make him an icon. Ultimately, Pryor knew how to tell a good story, and he was willing to reveal to his audiences his darkest secrets, his fears.

Pryor's style was in your face, aiming for the neck. He was bitter and angry, which leavened his comedy but often made him dangerous and abusive to the women in his life. He was addicted to cocaine and often performed high. Though deeply wounded, he was also creative and brilliant.

Pryor, who also starred in more than forty feature films, won multiple Grammys and an Emmy. His groundbreaking *Richard Pryor: Live in Concert*, a film from 1979, set a new standard for comedic performance. When the John F. Kennedy Center for the Performing Arts launched the Mark Twain Prize for American Humor in 1998, Pryor was the first recipient.

DEE REES

(1977–PRESENT)

"Writing is really freeing because it's the only part of the process where it's just you and the characters and you are by yourself in a room and you can just hash it out. There are no limitations."

An award-winning screenwriter and filmmaker who takes on a range of subjects, Dee Rees is particularly known for directing films that feature underseen stories—in particular, stories of women and of Black people that often give weight to emotion and space.

Her first feature film, *Pariah*, is a tender coming-of-age drama that introduces audiences to Alike, a young Black woman learning about her sexuality and how it affects her relationships to the people around her. Rees's work takes cues from the work of groundbreaking directors such as Kathleen Collins and Julie Dash, who place inclusive ideas of Black womanhood at the root of invigorating, realistic, and sometimes funny scripts. Released in 2011, *Pariah* won over a dozen awards.

Originally from Nashville, Rees was born to a scientist mother and police-officer father. She graduated from Florida A&M University with a master's degree in business administration and worked for various beauty companies for a few years before finding her way to film. Once in the medium, she developed her own style, which blends a willingness to ease out of dialogue and frenetic activity, lingering instead on the quiet moments, with an ability to visually stun and mentally provoke.

In 2015, she released *Bessie*, about the legendary blues singer Bessie Smith. The scene that stands apart, despite actor Queen Latifah's penchant for revealing the brassy, bold side of Smith, is when Latifah sits naked at her vanity. At that poignant moment in the story, Smith, despite all that she has achieved, is coming to terms with her limitations. The beauty and the burden of her life—her body's knowledge—is captured in Rees's direction of the scene.

With her 2017 film *Mudbound*, illustrating the complicated interaction between a Black family of sharecroppers and a white family working alongside each other in 1940s Mississippi, she became the first Black woman to be nominated for an Academy Award for writing since 1973. (The earlier nomination went to Suzanne de Passe for *Lady Sings the Blues*.) Demonstrating her talent for storytelling throughout a range of subject matter, in 2020 Rees directed *The Last Thing He Wanted*, an adaptation of a Joan Didion novel in which the protagonist pursues an arms deal in Central America.

BASS REEVES

(1838–1910)

"Maybe the law ain't perfect, but it's the only one we got, and without it, we got nuthin."

Bass Reeves was an American lawman, believed to be the first Black commissioned deputy US marshal deployed west of the Mississippi River. He was born into slavery in 1838 Arkansas, into the household of state legislator William Reeves. Following William Reeves's move to Grayson County, Texas, his son George left to serve as a colonel in the Confederate Army during the Civil War. George took Bass Reeves with him. At some later point—historians aren't sure exactly when, or what occurred—Bass Reeves determined that he was no longer working in the service of George or William. It's said that he lived among Native peoples as a fugitive, learning the languages of tribes including the Creek and the Cherokee, who by then had been forcibly relocated west due to President Andrew Jackson's Indian Removal Act of 1830.

But Reeves went on to experience uncommon freedom of movement in the period between Emancipation and Reconstruction. During that period, Reeves moved back to Arkansas and married Nellie Jennie. The couple had ten children.

By the late 1870s, the western region had become fertile ground for fugitives. Deputies were sought to track and capture purported criminals. James Fagan, newly named US marshal, apparently wanted Reeves to become a deputy marshal. Reeves was reportedly over six feet tall, a clear asset; in addition, he was familiar with the area and spoke multiple languages.

During more than thirty-two years in law enforcement, Reeves worked as a deputy federal marshal in the West, then moved to Texas and finally Oklahoma in 1897. He retired in 1909. He was widely celebrated for his investigative skills, marksmanship, and honor. The biographer Art T. Burton believes Reeves was the true inspiration for the Lone Ranger, as Reeves's exploits and achievements were widely catalogued in newspapers throughout his career. He reportedly arrested more than three thousand people in his time as a lawman.

FAITH RINGGOLD

(1930–PRESENT)

"I didn't want people to be able to look, and look away."

In the "story quilt" medium that Faith Ringgold reinvented, she writes her own version of history. "Art is a visual image of who you are," Ringgold once said. In *Who's Afraid of Aunt Jemima?* Ringgold reimagines the pancake-batter icon as an entrepreneur, baker, and caterer of fine parties for a bourgeois clientele. The stitched acrylic on canvas shows a literal tapestry of the Black people who shaped make-believe Jemima's life; they are beautiful and prosperous, adorned with symbols of success and comfort. "She's just fabulous in my story," Ringgold says of Aunt Jemima. Such representation is just one example of the way Ringgold manifests the world she wants to see in her work, which goes beyond story quilts to include painting, sculpting, and performance arts.

Born during the Great Depression, Ringgold lived in Harlem. Her father bought her her first easel. Her mother, a seamstress and clothing designer, helped her daughter flesh out the story quilt concept, which incorporated the African American tradition of quilt making. Ringgold attended the City College of New York, where she received a degree in fine arts and education in 1955 and an MA in fine arts in 1959. She noted that she learned about seemingly everything except Black and African art. Crossing the white barrier in the country's defining institutions became a hallmark of her career. When she discovered that she couldn't garner the same representation or showing opportunities as male and white artists, she joined in protests against museums such as the Whitney, demanding that they create parity in their acquisitions and open up to more artists of color and Black women.

Ringgold documented the civil rights movement in her career-defining *American People Series*. Her brushstrokes are deliberate and her color choice is often stark, revealing the divide between her subjects. In number 17 of the series, a Black woman and a white woman stand in close proximity, but the vacant stares on their faces reveal a wider fissure between them.

In 1967 Ringgold painted a twelve-foot-long piece in the series, number 20, *Die*. Evoking the violent uprisings of the period, the piece reveals a bloody torrent of Black and white people in the chaos of the streets—in the chaos of America. She showed the piece in her first solo exhibition at New York's Spectrum Gallery. Decades later, the painting was purchased by New York's Museum of Modern Art, one of the museums against which she had protested for the inclusion of Black artists' work toward the beginning of her career.

MINNIE RIPERTON

(1947–1979)

"I've learned it's just as easy to be happy as it is to be unhappy—so we should all try and make that attempt to be happy, right?"

American soul music found an incomparable voice in the five-octave range that Minnie Riperton shared with her audiences. First coming to prominence as lead singer in the 1960s soul-psychedelic band Rotary Connection, she went on to pursue a solo career. Stevie Wonder, for whom she'd sung backup, produced her 1974 album *Perfect Angel*, which found popular success with the melodic "Lovin' You." But it's projects like her first record, *Come to My Garden* (1970), with its dramatic arrangements, and the locked-in fit of *Adventures in Paradise* (1975) that continue to beckon new listeners with lush, funky, soulful grooves and Riperton's playful phrasing, which could convey such urgency and unfettered emotion.

Riperton was born in Chicago, where she grew up studying music, dance, and theater. She was the youngest of eight children. Her parents, Thelma Inez and Daniel Riperton, recognized her singing ability at an early age and encouraged her to pursue music. At Chicago's Lincoln Center, she took operatic vocal lessons. As a young artist, she signed with the Chess label, where she sang background for the Dells and Etta James.

Riperton's vocal range was stunning. But her voice, as an instrument, was also a testament to how much we take Black singing for granted. Though a stereotype, it's true that singing shapes and cradles Black culture. Choral or singular, it comforts us, hones our joy and sorrow. Riperton knew this intimately. There's a reason she was known as "the Nightingale."

She released what would be her last record, *Minnie*, in 1979.

NOTES ON A PRACTICE

by Oriana Koren

James Baldwin once presciently described the antihuman practice of white supremacy as a game that isn't running. To "run game" is to be engaged in cunning as praxis—a skillful trickery used to procure, with limited effort, that which one desires.

In supremacy, the desire is to make *real* a delusion of superiority. Despite the impossibility of transcending that which you are, humans have never stopped trying to get close to what we call the "divine."

When your finite human existence comes to an end and you cease to be, the primary hope of supremacy is finding a way to defeat the finite to become infinite—only "superior" beings can outsmart death—and the only infinite beings we've conjured in our mind are those which are divine.

The divine are not human, but they aren't quite spirit, either.

Divinity is a problem of memory in the same way that photo making and doing language are solutions to that problem. We exist physically and metaphysically, kept alive through "rememory," a concept explored in Toni Morrison's *Beloved*. There's the act of remembering an event or person, and then there's the act of *re*memory, a recontextualizing of an event or, primarily, of a person or people who weren't afforded their humanity and personhood when they were still in their corporal form.

The act of rememory is how Black people ascend to the state of divinity, how we transcend the state of being human.

Those who seek to diminish and destroy us have gotten lost in cunning as praxis, while we have found a home in humanity as praxis. In making humanness our home, we do the necessary work of earning the title of human.

Once that status has been earned, there's room to evolve to the next phase of existence: to become infinite is simply to not be forgotten, but it is to be remembered, throughout time, over time, in a continuous, infinite loop. Rememory is what fascists have been fighting against, and it's why who gets to tell history (and what histories are being told) is constantly fought over.

It's why supremacy hasn't yet uncovered a method to kill Black people in any way that matters.

It is human fate to die, but it is not our fate to be forgotten to time, not when we can be conjured by the language and the art our souls get transmuted into so we may live, eternally.

The legacy of all artists is rememory.

We create and disseminate pieces of our experience that transcend our finite existence in the human world. In these acts of earning one's humanity, what we make becomes the stuff that allows yet other human beings to create themselves and to earn their humanity, too.

In some places in the world, humans call this karma—literally translated as acts, works, and deeds.

Lately, my mind has been preoccupied with what makes a practice. To practice is to engage in something, over time, to both acquire and maintain that something, and the practice I've been especially preoccupied with is that of being human.

Maybe it takes a mass death event—like the ongoing COVID-19 pandemic—alongside the constant and consistent questioning of one's humanity over generations to recognize clearly that to be human isn't a given, but is instead a state of being one must practice in order to achieve. My deepest practice has been that of making art—making photographs and doing language (which, to me, consists of reading, writing, talking, and thinking).

The practice of art making is uniquely human. There are no other animals, that we're aware of, who make art for pleasure or for expression. I'm especially lucky to come from a group of humans who are so consistently engaged in art making that we're widely known as builders of a distinct and global culture: Blackness.

I've been engaged in an artistic practice for over twenty years of my existence, which is to say that most of my existence on Earth has been defined by the act of building the self through art.

I've thought a lot recently about what distinguishes my experience as a Black person from that of a white person or other people of color, as we're all genetically made of the same star stuff.

Our experiences of our humanity, however, are incredibly different.

My lineage consists of world builders, art makers, theorizers of human experience, and survivors of dehumanization. Given that lineage, I'm awed but not surprised when, in the face of yet another attempt at genocide, we make, we create, and thus, we survive.

I am a human being because I do the hard work of being human, not because it's a fact of life that I'm a part of the species. For the last four hundred years of human existence, there has been concerted effort using art and language to delineate me as wholly different from human.

While it's an insult to be called an animal in the pejorative, it's true that I am an animal, because all humans are, in fact, animals. What is far more insulting and dangerous is the idea that I'm so far beneath the title of animal that I'm simply an object.

An unthinking, unfeeling, de-evolved thing with almost no sentience: when I'm seen as such, anything can be done to me. An object is defined as a thing that can be seen and touched but isn't a living being, plant, or person. To be a person, one must first be a human. To be a thing, an object in the human world, is not just to be rendered invisible, but to be in constant danger of total elimination. It's my thingification I'm constantly fighting with and it's the objectification of my humanity I'm in constant struggle against.

Oriana Koren is a photo-ethnographer, writer, and researcher. Oriana has built their own visual archive of Black contributions to American cuisine to correct institutional memory of American culinary art and agricultural technology. They are a founding member of the Authority Collective and Candor Collective, as well as the head curator and founder of the Lit List photo award for emergent BIPOC artists.

PAUL ROBESON

(1898–1976)

"The answer to injustice is not to silence the critic but to end the injustice."

Paul Robeson's résumé reads like a biblical scroll, endless and captivating in its range and authority. Born in Princeton, New Jersey, to a father who had been born into slavery and a mother raised as a vocal abolitionist, Robeson showed impressive athletic ability as an All-American football player at Rutgers University. There he established himself as a track, basketball, and baseball star as well. Upon graduating in 1919, he went on to earn his law degree from Columbia University and lived in Harlem. Encouraged by his wife, Eslanda Goode, to try performing, he started auditioning for theater roles. Soon after, he was performing on Broadway. Robeson became one of the most prolific and dynamic stage performers in his lifetime, defining iconic roles in *The Emperor Jones*, *Porgy and Bess*, and *Show Boat*. And he could sing as well as act: his rich baritone still defines *Show Boat*'s classic tune "Ol' Man River."

In 1943, Robeson became the first Black actor to portray Othello on Broadway, accompanied by a white supporting cast. But Robeson's achievements on both stage and Hollywood screen didn't obscure his view of the plight of most African Americans in the first half of the twentieth century. While he had been living and working in Europe in the 1930s, Robeson observed the rise of Nazism and heard robust debates about socialism, and when he visited Russia, he took particular note of how neutrally people responded to him. He eventually learned Russian, in order to be able to perform in that language, and later described his experience in Russia as the first time he'd felt that he'd been treated like a full human being, relieved of the burden of his skin color—a burden that felt oppressive in the United States.

In his 1949 speech at the World Peace Congress in Paris, Robeson stated: "It is unthinkable that American Negroes will go to war on behalf of those who have oppressed us for generations against a country [the Soviet Union] which in one generation has raised our people to the full dignity of mankind." His remarks there and elsewhere were used to question his patriotic commitment to the United States. He was brought before Congress in 1956 to testify before the House Committee on Un-American Activities, where infamously he was repeatedly asked to acknowledge whether he was a member of the Communist Party. "Oh please. Please, please," he said derisively. "Would you like to come to the ballot box when I vote and take out the ballot and see?" He ultimately invoked the Fifth Amendment. When asked why he didn't remain in Russia, Robeson replied, "My father was a slave, and my people died to build this country, and I am going to stay here . . . just like you."

Robeson had his passport revoked for a period in the fifties and was also blacklisted in Hollywood, echoing treatment that Muhammad Ali received years later as a professional athlete engaged in political activism. Clearly, being good at everything is problematic for a Black person in white America.

Robeson's career as an actor and singer spanned four decades, and he enjoyed global recognition for his iconic roles, his definitive voice, and his steadfast willingness to use his art to promote justice.

DAVID RUGGLES

(1810–1849)

"The pleas of crying soft and sparing never answered the purpose of a reform, and never will."

Born free in Norwich, Connecticut, to David Sr., a blacksmith, and Nancy, a caterer, David Ruggles must have understood from an early age how precarious and unique his circumstances were. Only under such circumstances could he have determined that, as a free Black man, he bore some responsibility to achieve other Black people's freedom.

In 1826, still a young teen, Ruggles moved to New York City and worked as a mariner, then as a grocer, opening his own establishment. His grocery shop, located at 1 Cortlandt Street, became a reading room and library for Black people, to whom the New York Public Library denied access. By the 1830s, he'd turned his attention to the abolitionist movement. He launched his own bookstore, reportedly the nation's first Black-owned, and sold antislavery publications there, but the shop was eventually destroyed by a mob. Interestingly, the mob was composed of white abolitionists who disagreed with his tactics and thought him too extreme.

As a salesman, he sought subscribers for the abolitionist weekly *The Emancipator*, a job requiring that he travel throughout the mid-Atlantic region. He began writing his own articles in 1834. By 1838 he was writer and publisher for the first journal edited by a Black person, *Mirror of Liberty*.

He advocated for "practical abolition," which meant an active and intentional effort to abolish slavery rather than solely speaking out about the institution's injustices. It's reported that in his highly visible work with the Underground Railroad, he aided more than six hundred enslaved in securing their self-emancipation, one of whom was Frederick Douglass. But Ruggles's visible stature as an agitator and constant advocate for the rights of Black people landed him in the crosshairs of other Black people who, like the white mob mentioned earlier, felt that his tactics were too brash. Ruggles pushed back against fugitive slave laws that landed freeborn Black people in bondage and narrowly escaped attempted kidnapping himself. Through the New York Committee of Vigilance, which he cofounded, he worked to support legal remedies for those illegally detained into slavery.

Ruggles didn't live a long life. It's reported that the strain of his efforts coupled with the circumstances of life in mid-nineteenth-century America resulted in poor health. Sick and blind, he died in Massachusetts at the age of thirty-nine.

PATRICE RUSHEN

(1954–PRESENT)

"Music is really a spiritual thing—a connection between your inner self and the projection of that in public."

Over four decades, Patrice Rushen has fashioned a multifaceted career in jazz, pop, and R&B. Oftentimes, musicians don't get their due; their talents are glossed over. Not so for Rushen, who's an incredible and multifaceted musician. A native of South Central Los Angeles known initially for her jazz piano and vocal skills, she has forged a career of firsts, alternating among music director, film composer, producer, bandleader, and bandmate with the likes of Stevie Wonder, Prince, Carlos Santana, Lee Ritenour, Terri Lyne Carrington, Carmen Lundy, and Christian McBride.

It's still news to some that Rushen began her career as a classically trained jazz artist before exploring other facets of popular music. She has sometimes been criticized for what's been perceived as a genre shift, but Rushen has always retained in her work a core musicality and understanding that, for discerning listeners, has its roots in a Black aesthetic and a fundamentally feel-good sound. She is a yeowoman, working steadily through every decade. She's still at the top of her game and will probably be producing hits until the day she dies.

Rushen is representative of the evolution of Black music: Black music lets no moss grow under its feet. Our rhythm and rhyme keep shifting. It's amazing that Rushen's music evolves while it simultaneously refuses to chase trends. Her body of work from the 1970s and 1980s is widely sampled—hits like "Forget Me Nots," "Haven't You Heard," and "Settle for My Love" are the framework for songs by Will Smith ("Men in Black"), Mary J. Blige ("You Remind Me"), George Michael ("Fastlove"), and countless others.

A four-time Grammy nominee, Rushen has been a sought-after musical director for the entertainment industry's top honors, becoming the first woman to serve as music director for the Grammys, the Emmys, the NAACP Image Awards, and the People's Choice Awards. As a composer for film and television, she wrote the music that accompanied Robert Townsend's *Hollywood Shuffle* and Disney's *Ruby Bridges*, among others. In 2001, the Detroit Symphony Orchestra commissioned her work *Mine Eyes Have Seen the Glory*, a sweeping symphonic piece that commemorates Martin Luther King Jr.

Rushen currently serves as chair of the Popular Music program at her alma mater, the University of Southern California's Thornton School of Music. She is also the ambassador for artistry in education at Berklee College of Music in Boston, where she developed a new curriculum focused on teaching burgeoning artists performance, songwriting, production, and music direction, among other disciplines in the field, extending to subsequent generations of artists the same philosophies of multidisciplinary music that have shaped her long and triumphant career.

JASON SAMUELS SMITH

(1980–PRESENT)

"Basically, tap is all about love. It's all about your love for music, your love for dance, and how much you enjoy doing it. It should be about inspiring others to enjoy life. That's really what I've gotten out of tap—the love for and the joy of life."

Both the look and feel of tap continue to evolve even as the art form hovers near its origins. In the work of Jason Samuels Smith, a bridge is visible between a hip-hop- and jazz-based understanding of sound and rhythm and the sharp edges and gentle sway that make up the essence of swing. With accolades that include a Primetime Emmy Award for Outstanding Choreography, an American Choreography Award, and recognition from *Dance* magazine, and countless performances in the theater, on television, and in film, Samuels Smith has earned multiple grants and residencies in support of his dancing vision.

He was born in New York City and began his performing career early, appearing on *Sesame Street* as a child and, when he was fifteen, serving as the understudy to the leading role in the Tony Award–winning Broadway show *Bring in 'da Noise, Bring in 'da Funk.*

In a 2012 project for the Joyce Theater, he paid homage to jazz master Charlie Parker by interpreting Parker's music via tap. "I'm trying to show people what the music looks like," he said in an interview. An evangelist for tap dance, he teaches widely and promotes the idea that tap can embody nearly any narrative. Although its traditions emerge from a Black American story of tragedy and triumph, the tension of tap—the inherent struggle between keeping time, speed, and balance, on the one hand, and pushing for sonic clarity and emotion—is what makes the form so beautiful, most especially when performed by Samuels Smith.

AUGUSTA SAVAGE

(1892–1962)

"We do not ask any special favors as artists because of our race. We only want to present to you our works and ask you to judge them on their merits."

Born in Green Cove Springs, Florida, a town known for brickmaking, Augusta Savage had red clay in ample supply. As a young girl, she formed figurines; this was one way she could amuse herself and pass time in a low-income community with likely little if any access to toys. Her Methodist minister father wholeheartedly disapproved of her clay work, believing it reflective of the idolatry deemed a sin in the Ten Commandments. He often beat Savage for sculpting figures. She would later say, "He nearly whipped all the art out of me."

When she was a teen, her family moved to West Palm Beach, where teachers noticed her skill and put her to work teaching clay modeling to her fellow high school students. She married at the age of sixteen in 1907 and had a daughter with John Moore, who died a few years later. She married a second time in 1915, to James Savage, a union that ended in divorce, but she retained his name. She moved to Jacksonville, Florida, near her parents, intending to sculpt for a living, but couldn't secure consistent patronage. Savage spent a year in Tallahassee at the Florida Agricultural and Mechanical College for Negroes (today known as Florida A&M University) and was recommended for study in New York. Following her passion, Savage left her daughter with her parents and moved to Harlem.

In the North, Savage worked as a housekeeper to afford study at the Cooper Union School of Art, where she honed her craft. Commissions soon came in. Among other assignments, she sculpted a bust of W. E. B. Du Bois for the New York Public Library.

She received a scholarship to attend the Fontainebleau School of Arts in Paris, but her attendance was blocked by the selection committee, whose members worried how white women would feel about traveling, living, and training with a Black woman.

Her friends and admirers shone a light on this injustice, even appealing to President Harding to intervene, but to no avail. Fundraising efforts and a fellowship finally allowed her to study in Paris where she exhibited at the Salon d'Automne and the Grand Palais. She later received a grant to travel in France, Belgium, and Germany.

Back in the United States in 1931, amid the Great Depression, Savage struggled to find consistent financial backing for her work. Like many other Black creatives of the period, Savage chose to work with the Works Progress Administration's Federal Art Project, a program she eventually led, becoming an important community figure for Black artists in New York.

In the 1930s, Savage founded the Savage Studio of Arts and Crafts and became the first Black member of the National Association of Women Painters and Sculptors. She later came on board as the inaugural director of the Harlem Community Art Center.

The New York Historical Society exhibited a retrospective of her work in 2019. Notably, some of her students achieved great feats, including painter and muralist Charles Alston. His bust of Martin Luther King Jr. was the first depiction of an African American to be displayed in the Oval Office of the White House.

GIL SCOTT-HERON

(1949–2011)

"I was trying to get the people who listened to me to realize that they were not alone."

Gil Scott-Heron's music, at the intersection of musical genres, is typically, and even reasonably, described as art that contributed to the US protest culture. From the media criticism he sarcastically stacks in "The Revolution Will Not Be Televised" to the devastating grief that can be heard in "Did You Hear What They Said?" (which chronicles the death of a young Black man in the needless war in Vietnam), Scott-Heron's stylized poetry set to music defined an era and charted a path for the hip-hop generation that followed. But there's a reading of Scott-Heron's oeuvre that doesn't only hover over the anger and despair but instead sees the deep, unbridled love for a community subjected to countless trespasses while still finding a way to innovate, inspire, and simply survive.

Born in Chicago, Scott-Heron grew up in Tennessee and New York. His mother was a librarian and an English teacher; his father was a soccer player. Before he was revered as a musician, Scott-Heron was first a writer. When he was a teenager, Scott-Heron wrote detective stories, and his writings won him a scholarship to the Fieldston School in the Bronx. He then went on to study at the historically Black Lincoln University. He wrote his first novel, a murder mystery entitled *The Vulture*, at age nineteen. It was published in 1970.

Beginning in the 1970s, he recorded thirteen records that firmly solidified his position on the liberal side of politics, but by the 1980s his cult popularity had faded and his apparent struggles with addiction had surfaced publicly. Younger generations refer to Scott-Heron as a precursor to rap, owing to his rhythmic, punctuated speech against a backbeat. But he avoided such comparisons, preferring to think of himself as a contributor to the schools of blues and jazz. That said, "The Revolution Will Not Be Televised" is how most people will remember Scott-Heron. The lyrics are still searing and prophetic.

AMY SHERALD

(1973-PRESENT)

"I want my portraits to create a space where blackness can breathe."

Art is everywhere, but the practice of making art, having that art valued, and earning a living in the business of art is a deeply siloed affair. Amy Sherald was born in Columbus, Georgia, into a religious household where creative pursuits like painting weren't considered viable career options. Art was for playtime, not a reliable, serious pursuit. But Sherald, who'd always found a way to incorporate picture making into her daily life as a child, sought ways to bring art into the foreground. Her distinct style of capturing life-size Black subjects in moments of poise and leisure features people who haven't been given the space to exist in the world of art but have always been present. The concept of painting someone who reflects your background, your heritage, your story should not be radical. But Sherald *is* radical. She's also part of a rich heritage of artists who seek to represent themselves and their Blackness in its myriad forms and imaginative possibilities.

To view any collection of Sherald's works is to witness unfettered love and respect for Black people. Her subjects are caught in candid, unplanned moments, yet they also seem to display a sense of preparedness for their documentation. They are dressed in T-shirts and jeans or dresses and suits with bright, intricate patterns and textures. Skin tones are done in shades of gray and charcoal, but they never appear washed out or reductive. Somehow the absence of brown-toned skin makes the Blackness more evident. What began as an aesthetic decision became a transformative way to both reject and embrace race in the space of portrait making.

In *Miss Everything* (*Unsuppressed Deliverance*), Sherald paints a young, slender woman in a vintage navy dress with white polka dots; wearing wrist-length white gloves, she holds a giant teacup in one hand and a saucer in the other. Cocked to one side on her close-cropped hair sits a bright-red hat, and her skin, rendered in Sherald's unique grayscale approach, shimmers against a turquoise-blue backdrop. The subject looks straight out at viewers, elegant in demeanor but also at ease. The painting won the National Portrait Gallery's 2016 Outwin Boochever Portrait competition. Two years later, First Lady Michelle Obama selected Sherald to paint her official portrait, now on display at the National Portrait Gallery in Washington, DC.

NINA SIMONE

(1933–2003)

"I tell you what freedom is to me: no fear."

Nina Simone was often referred to as "the High Priestess of Soul," a title that many felt acknowledged the regal, authoritative approach she conveyed with her music and live performances. But she didn't care for the moniker. She wished, instead, that audiences regarded her as a folksinger committed to singing the blues. The blues are front and center in her 1960s songs "Take Care of Business" and "I Want a Little Sugar in My Bowl." But the flirtatious, sensual side of her was only one aspect of her artistry.

You can see the scope of Simone's artistry the moment you try to place her music in a particular genre: R&B, jazz, gospel, classical, soul, folk. Simone's music defies category despite its roots. It fits all these categories and none at the same time. As a singer, songwriter, composer, arranger, and activist, she nimbly navigates genres in order to convey the deeper and often political meaning of her work. As a response to the murder of civil rights activist Medgar Evers and the white-supremacist church bombing that killed four Black girls, she wrote "Mississippi Goddam." Her song "Four Women" portrays a multigenerational lineage of characters caught in a powerless trajectory of oppression owing to the legacy of slavery.

Born Eunice Kathleen Waymon in Tryon, North Carolina, Simone learned piano as a young girl and grew up singing in the church choir. She was trained in classical repertoire and, like many Black artists who found their way to jazz, blues, or R&B, expressed a desire to pursue a serious career as a classical concert pianist—an opportunity denied her because of race. A defining event of her childhood happened when she was twelve years old at her first classical performance. During the recital her parents, who had been sitting in the front row, were forced to give up their seats and move to the back of the concert hall to make room for white people. Simone refused to play until her parents were moved back to the front. She considered the moment one of her first acts of civil disobedience.

Simone was known, if not openly criticized, for having exacting standards for her music—how it was performed and how she wanted audiences to respond to her. But her eccentricities, exacerbated by what were later revealed as her struggles with mental illness, helped define her as an artist unwilling to compromise on her work and committed to using that work to support activist efforts in the world. Her voice resonates with a power that's impossible to forget, long after the track stops playing.

NORMA MERRICK SKLAREK

(1926–2012)

"In architecture, I had absolutely no role model. I'm happy today to be a role model for others that follow."

Norma Merrick Sklarek's life as a pioneering architect included a striking list of firsts: she was often the first woman or first Black woman named to a position or assigned a particular role. That meant she had to be the best, even if she was rarely acknowledged for her abilities.

Born in Harlem to parents who'd migrated from Trinidad but had been raised in Uptown and in Brooklyn, Sklarek attended Bard College for one year. That allowed her to earn the prerequisites needed to enroll at Columbia University's School of Architecture. She often did her homework alone or on the subway, while older students, some with advanced degrees, worked together to complete the complex assignments. But she finished the program, a major feat given that she was one of only two women in her class.

After Sklarek graduated, she encountered more obstacles. She racked up nineteen rejections from firms that refused to hire her. Was it because she was a woman? Was it because she was Black? She couldn't know, but of course she did know. And yet she couldn't afford to linger in the doubt either. After settling for a job as a draftsperson in New York's Public Works Department—she knew she was overqualified—she took the architecture licensing exam in 1954. Sklarek passed on her first attempt, becoming the first Black woman architect in New York State. After working at various firms in the city, she moved to Los Angeles in 1960, where she'd been offered a job at Gruen Associates. In that position, she became the first Black woman architect licensed in the state of California.

At Gruen, Sklarek eventually became director of architecture, collaborating on truly groundbreaking projects like the Fox Hills Mall (later rebranded Westfield Culver City), the Pacific Design Center in West Hollywood, San Bernardino City Hall, and the US Embassy in Tokyo. But she was often wrongly credited as project manager rather than designer, a punitive slight that was not uncommon for the few women who managed to make a career in architecture at that time, and a much more glaring slight for a supremely accomplished Black woman like Sklarek.

During her career, Sklarek worked at six firms. As vice president of Welton Becket Associates, she oversaw the development of Terminal 1 at LAX in 1984, which was completed in advance of that summer's Los Angeles Olympic Games. When she left that company, she cofounded the then largest woman-owned practice in the US, Siegel Sklarek Diamond.

MONETA SLEET JR.

(1926–1996)

"My basic feeling ... was ... [that] I was observing ... and trying to record, but I also felt a part of it because I'm black, and it was one way I could pay my dues."

On April 9, 1968, Coretta Scott King was photographed at the funeral of her husband, Martin Luther King Jr. Five days earlier, he had been assassinated while standing on the balcony of the Lorraine Motel in Memphis, Tennessee. Mrs. King is dressed in black, wearing a black veil, and is seated in a pew, surrounded by other attendees. Her poise and grace—her dignity—are all the more striking for the cruel violence her family had so recently endured. The Kings' daughter Bernice, then just five years old, leans into her mother's lap, a sweet face framed by bangs and pigtails. She gazes into what seems like emptiness. Their personal grief, wrapped in a sad, weary beauty, is captured precisely in frame. The photograph became a definitive image from that day. The man who captured it was photojournalist Moneta Sleet, who, during years working as a staff photographer for *Ebony* magazine, had covered countless civil rights protests and marches and had developed a friendship with Dr. King.

Every major news outlet wanted to cover the funeral. But there was very little representation by Black journalists in the white-dominant media institutions that angled for the limited space to document the event, and there were no Black members of the press at Ebenezer Baptist Church that day. Somehow Mrs. King got word of this and made it known that if Sleet wasn't permitted in the church, there would be no coverage of the funeral from inside the building.

Despite his solidly grounded objectivity as a trained journalist, Sleet fought back tears, he later admitted, while he worked that day. His photograph of Mrs. King and little Bernice was published in *Life* magazine and widely circulated in multiple media outlets. In 1969, Sleet became the first African American to be honored with the Pulitzer Prize in Feature Photography. Of his own emotional response to the striking image, Sleet later said, "He was my leader too." After the Pulitzer win, Sleet received job offers from other publishers, but he chose to remain at *Ebony*, where he would work for forty years.

Born in Owensboro, Kentucky, Sleet took an interest in photography when he was given a Brownie camera as a child. He studied the craft while a student at Kentucky State College in Frankfort, took a detour in the army during World War II, and later continued his education in New York at the School of Modern Photography. He earned a master's degree in journalism from New York University. After the Black photography magazine *Our World* closed in 1955, Sleet joined the staff at *Ebony*. He went on to document emerging heads of state during a period when African countries were gaining independence from European colonial rule. He photographed Billie Holiday, Haile Selassie, and Muhammad Ali, among many others. He documented the Montgomery Bus Boycott in 1955 and 1956; Dr. King's Nobel Peace Prize acceptance in Oslo, Norway, in 1964; and the march from Selma to Montgomery in 1965. Sleet documented Black beauty contests, prison inmates, and fashion spreads. He died of cancer at seventy, not long after covering the 1996 Olympics in Atlanta.

VERTAMAE SMART-GROSVENOR

(1937–2016)

"I don't have culinary limitations because I'm 'black.' On the other hand, I choose to write about 'Afro-American' cookery because I'm 'black' and know the wonderful, fascinating culinary history there is. And because the Afro-American cook has been so underappreciated."

Vertamae Smart-Grosvenor used her multiple story-telling and artistic abilities to weave a career that included cultural anthropology, food writing, acting, and broadcasting, the last primarily as an NPR commentator between 1980 and 2013. In the food world, she is perhaps most celebrated for her direct, engaging, and passionate observations about her native Gullah Geechee food culture, which forms the basis for a cultural cross-section of stories in her 1970s *Vibration Cooking: Or, The Travel Notes of a Geechee Girl.*

Self-described as a culinary griot, and known as a dramatic person, Smart-Grosvenor wrote in her now classic autobiographical cookbook, "When I cook, I never measure or weigh anything; I cook by vibration. I can tell by the look and smell of it." She says this not to undermine the technique that must accompany a well-cooked meal, but rather to underscore that cooking knowledge can't necessarily be transcribed on the page. A consistent and attentive use of all the senses is required.

Born in Fairfax, South Carolina, she moved as a child to Philadelphia with her family. At nineteen years old she left for Paris, wanting to become a part of the theater scene in France. Later, she lived in Washington, DC, and New York, where she crossed paths with luminaries that included Maya Angelou and James Baldwin. During one period she sang background vocals for Sun Ra. As an actor, she appeared in the Julie Dash film *Daughters of the Dust*, which tells a multigenerational story of Gullah women, and in *Beloved*, based on the Toni Morrison novel. Smart-Grosvenor was the subject of *Travel Notes of a Geechee Girl*, a documentary that found her once again directed by Dash.

In *Vibration Cooking*, Smart-Grosvenor moves between diary-like entries and brief recitations about preparing dishes, preferring an oral style of instruction in lieu of detailed ingredient lists and measurements. Her tone is frank, sometimes sarcastic, and bold; clearly, she is fully aware that her food culture, Black food culture, has been consistently denied the visibility and elevation that other global traditions have received. Her recollections and recipes illustrate a life filled with friendship, desire, family, and political conviction. She talks about hunting in the woods; she tells of rude taxi drivers. Recipes range from omelette des Ursulines from her travels abroad to the soft-shell crab of her childhood. "Do your thing your way," she writes in the introduction. "I don't like to get in people's business."

ROBERT F. SMITH

(1962–PRESENT)

"The opportunity you access should be determined by the fierceness of your intellect, the courage in your creativity and the grit that allows you to overcome expectations that weren't set high enough."

Robert Smith drew widespread attention in 2019 when, during a commencement speech at Morehouse College, he promised to pay off the student loan debt of the entire graduating class that year. An article in the *Washington Post* reported: "It's hard to estimate the cost of Smith's gift to the 2019 graduates of the all-male, historically Black college, but it could be in the $10 million range, according to some estimates. There were 396 graduates in the class, and tuition, room and board, and other costs run about $48,000 per year. There's a saying, 'Put your money where your mouth is,'" and in this moment Smith did exactly that.

It was an extraordinary gesture by the businessman and philanthropist, who had recently signed a pledge to eventually donate most of his money to nonprofit causes.

Smith founded Vista Equity Partners in 2000, a private firm with a focus on investing in software companies. Enjoying more than $50 billion in assets and high-performing returns, the firm has a track record for success.

With an eye toward eventually working in Silicon Valley, the young Smith got his first internship at Bell Labs as an eager high school student, even though the positions were offered only to college students. Smith kept persistently calling the office in hopes they'd make an exception for him, given his excellent grades in advanced courses. They refused—until an intern was a no-show one day. Smith was in.

He studied chemical engineering at Cornell University and worked for companies like Goodyear and Kraft. After receiving his MBA from Columbia University, he entered the world of investment banking on Wall Street. He helped lead a division of Goldman Sachs that advised on business dealings in enterprise software and mergers and acquisitions from 1994 until he left to launch his own company in 2000.

An industry tracker found that one of Vista Equity Partners' funds returned, over a four-year period, more than two dollars for every dollar invested, a better record than those of other large funds between 2006 and 2010, the boom years for private equity. Smith is also known for adapting an IBM personality test as a tool to put together a diverse workforce and to better predict applicants' success. Black people and people of color fill many leadership roles throughout the firm and its respective companies. In 2016, Smith donated $20 million to the National Museum of African American History and Culture at the Smithsonian.

There are billionaires who never feel the need to help those less fortunate, but it's clear that Smith deeply believes the words he delivered in his Morehouse commencement address: "When Dr. King said that the 'arc of the moral universe bends toward justice,' he wasn't saying it bends on its own accord. It bends because we choose to put our shoulders into it together and push."

ANDRÉ LEON TALLEY

(1948–2022)

"Wearing clothes should be a personal narrative of emotion. I always respond to fashion in an emotional way."

Definitively recognizable in his flowing, dramatic caftans, standing six foot six, and with a voice that boomed across whatever runway show or fancy party he attended, André Leon Talley spent the last four decades of his life making certain that he was seen. A groundbreaking fashion journalist since his hiring at US *Vogue* in 1983, he served as the magazine's fashion news director, creative director, and then editor-at-large.

He presided in the front row of countless couture shows, often the lone Black figure in a sea of petite white women. At Condé Nast's premier fashion publication, he wrote features; commented on film, music, and events; and was the point person on path-paving photography sessions.

Talley grew up in Durham, North Carolina, raised by his grandmother, who worked as a domestic. His parents had left to seek work out of state. Bullied as a kid, Talley found solace watching Julia Child's cooking shows and making weekly trips to more affluent white neighborhoods, where he perused copies of *Vogue* and *Harper's Bazaar*. He attended North Carolina Central University and went on to Brown University, where he earned a master's degree in French literature.

While studying at Brown's Ivy League campus, he began, through social connections, to translate what he saw in those old fashion magazines into real-life experiences. He met Diana Vreeland, who mentored him in New York, worked at *Interview* magazine with Andy Warhol, went to Paris while on staff at *Women's Wear Daily*, and finally landed at *Vogue*.

Confident in his education and instincts, Talley quickly became a reliable figure in the story of fashion. He understood the origins of garment features and embellishments. He appreciated the legacy of a gloved lady's hand—think Michelle Obama at her husband's first inauguration. His stories about vacationing with royalty, jet-setting to Europe or Asia for shows or research, or watching historic moments emerge on the runways captured audiences for years.

In 1974 he began his role reporting on the Met Ball (now Met Gala), which began in 1946 as a fundraising event for the Metropolitan Museum of Art. The largest event for the fashion world, it connects invite-only figures from movies and Broadway, fashion, and music. Talley used his position not only to recognize the great aesthetic statements, but to highlight the creativity of Black personalities and the stories that Black people's experiences and reference points contribute to fashion: think Beyoncé, Rihanna, and Diana Ross, who once wore a dress made solely out of bird feathers.

The documentary *The Gospel According to André* captures his unique turns of phrase and personality. He is the author of two memoirs, *The Chiffon Trenches* and the earlier *A.L.T.*

ROBERT ROBINSON TAYLOR

(1868–1942)

"The institute has steadily advanced in power and influence.... Its educational policy has served as a model for numerous similar institutions in this country and abroad."

Robert Robinson Taylor was the first known Black student to graduate from MIT and the first accredited Black architect. He was recruited by Booker T. Washington to help develop the campus for the Tuskegee Institute, in Alabama. He eventually went to Tuskegee to teach; he spent a forty-year career as a professor and architect at the institute. In that role, he served as second-in-command to Washington.

Taylor's father, Henry, was the son of a Black enslaved mother and a white owner. Raised in a time when the one-drop rule reigned—meaning children from mixed families were considered fully Black—Henry nonetheless was able to build a career as a contractor; he was believed to have worked on many commercial and residential buildings in Wilmington, North Carolina, where Taylor was born.

Taylor enrolled at MIT in 1888 and graduated in 1892. It's believed he worked and traveled before taking up the invitation to head to Alabama. (Wash-ington was known to make recruiting trips to the Northeast.) Once at Tuskegee, Taylor helped to create the overall curriculum, modeled after that of MIT, and established a number of buildings that defined the campus for decades. These buildings included the chapel, completed in 1898 and later featured in Ralph Ellison's novel *Invisible Man*; Thrasher Hall, built in 1893; and the Oaks, the president's house, built in 1899, where Washington resided.

In 1942, Taylor died while attending services in the Tuskegee chapel, the building he thought to be his crowning achievement as an architect. MIT created an endowed chair in Taylor's honor in 1994. In 2011, the university created the Robert R. Taylor Fellowship in its School of Architecture and Planning. In 2015, the US Postal Service created a postage stamp using his likeness. Taylor is the great-grandfather of Valerie Jarrett, who served as an adviser to President Barack Obama.

MARY CHURCH TERRELL

(1863–1954)

"While most girls run away from home to marry, I ran away to teach."

Today, the murders of people like George Floyd, Breonna Taylor, and Michael Brown have been the catalyst igniting the political activism of many young Black leaders. For Mary Church Terrell, the daughter of a wealthy real estate agent in Memphis, Tennessee, the radicalizing event was the lynching of her childhood friend in 1892, when Terrell was almost thirty. Thomas Moss was killed by a white mob because his business was seen as too successful. The impact of that incident changed the course of Terrell's life, leading her on a path dedicated to seeking racial justice throughout the country. Along with her friend Ida B. Wells, Terrell took extraordinary risks to confront the terrorism that Black citizens faced as they sought to make sustainable lives for themselves in the decades following the end of chattel slavery, with no protection from the government.

Terrell was born to formerly enslaved parents, both of whom were mixed race. The family's fair skin allowed them social mobility and access denied to darker-skinned Black people, but Terrell understood that her life too was deeply constrained by racial prejudice. Among the first Black women to get a bachelor's and a master's degree from Oberlin College, she went on to teach Latin at Wilberforce University, a historically Black college. She spent some time in France, then moved to Washington, DC, and taught at a high school for Black youth. It was there that she met Robert Terrell, whom she married.

In the early 1890s, Terrell was among the first of her generation to merge the experiences of higher education and street protest with a focus on the collective power of Black women. She advocated in the nation's capital for equal access to education and pushed white suffragists like Susan B. Anthony to be more inclusive in their quest for women's right to vote, even while Terrell and other Black women were forced to march in coloreds-only sections at women's suffrage marches.

After *Plessy v. Ferguson* upheld racial segregation in 1896, Terrell cofounded the National Association of Colored Women, which connected Black women's social and political clubs, to encourage them to educate their members about their civil rights, discuss urgent local issues, and fight to end segregation.

Terrell coined the motto "Lifting as we climb." She saw that, although the US owed Black people an insurmountable debt, it was Black *women* who, in holding up their communities, were crucial to any political effort to address Jim Crow practices and white terrorism. A founding member of the National Association for the Advancement of Colored People, she protested lynchings and argued for Black people's civil rights. "I cannot help wondering what I might have become and might have done," she wrote, "if I lived in a country that had not circumscribed and handicapped me on account of my race but had allowed me to reach any heights I was able to attain."

SISTER ROSETTA THARPE

(1915–1973)

"Can't no man play like me."

Rock 'n' roll music owes a great debt to Sister Rosetta Tharpe, a Black woman who, in merging the sounds of juke joints and nightclubs with Sunday morning gospel music, forged a path that would change the course of American music. Born Rosetta Nubin in Arkansas to a family of cotton sharecroppers, she grew up surrounded by the songs and rhetoric of the Christian evangelism that accompanied the traveling church groups so popular in the 1920s. Tharpe was a musical prodigy. By the age of six she was playing the guitar for her mother's evangelical troupe.

One couldn't help but be struck by her style. She looked like a church lady—sensible pumps, a printed tea-length dress, her hair pressed and coifed. But her voice and her skill as a guitarist told a different story. She landed in Chicago in the 1930s and was inspired to fuse the sounds of New Orleans jazz with the Delta blues, which had made its way north from Mississippi with the thousands of Black Americans fleeing the South. A woman guitarist with a distinctly raspy voice wasn't common at the time, but, outfitted in a chic dress and wielding her instrument, she had a presence that captivated. She landed a gig as part of the Cotton Club Revue in New York City and cultivated a dedicated following in the United States and abroad that grew over four decades.

Her tune "Rock Me" planted its foot firmly on the evocative and sexual side of the emotion and urgency already present in gospel music. This sound, a crossover style that few women had been given the opportunity to capture so boldly, shocked and delighted audiences. Her rhythmic sensibility and style paved the way for Chuck Berry, Elvis Presley, Aretha Franklin, and Brittany Howard—who inducted Tharpe into the Rock & Roll Hall of Fame in 2018.

MICKALENE THOMAS

(1971–PRESENT)

"Here I am, the artist, the person, the black woman, and the stereotype. I'm using myself and it has nothing to do with my muses or other women. It has to do with me."

Born in New Jersey, raised by "Mama Bush," her six-foot-tall mother, Thomas was exposed to art at an early age. She and her brother attended an after-school art program at the Newark Museum. In the 1980s Thomas moved to Portland, Oregon, to attend school. She then returned east to receive a fine arts degree at Pratt and an MFA in painting from Yale University. From there, Thomas leaped into the art world, stunning audiences with provocative depictions of Black women (often herself) in intimate poses, sometimes in a cosplay of a pop culture icon such as, say, R&B singer Mary J. Blige or the 1970s model Naomi Sims.

Mickalene Thomas launched her own highly anticipated and celebrated show in 2012 at the Brooklyn Museum and the Santa Monica Museum of Art (now the Institute of Contemporary Art), an exhibition of large-scale vibrant collage paintings depicting Black women. Regrettably, the exhibit wasn't picked up by other institutions. The feedback she got was that audiences weren't "ready" for her work. One critic asked, "Has Thomas gone too far?" The exhibition, titled "Mickalene Thomas: Origin of the Universe," contained giant portraits of Black women amid mosaics of rhinestones and busy patterns, which lent a 1970s-era playfulness and hip-hop-era brashness to their femininity, boldness, and sensuality. It's interesting to consider what about this series—a collection of works that gaze affectionately upon Black women, done by a Black woman—was too much for certain museums and their perceived audiences.

But Thomas, with her patchwork approach to image making, doesn't appear to be concerned with anyone's readiness. Inspired by the works of Romare Bearden, Carrie Mae Weems, Jacob Lawrence, and a vast archive of Black media publications such as the beloved *Jet* magazine, Thomas uses her work to interrogate, honor, and expand on what we value in the Black American aesthetic. When asked what advice she would give to emerging queer Black artists, she answered in a way that revealed her fearlessness: "There are great opportunities, but I've said no to a lot of things. As a Black artist, you've got to know your worth, and we got to know when the opportunity is for them or for us. There's a great power saying no. Say to yourself when you're asked for material: is this a win win situation for both of you? If it's just a win for them, if you just want little increments of exposure, think about what you *really* have to gain. If they really want you, they will wait for the right opportunity. Don't be afraid to ask pressing, difficult and uncomfortable questions. Cut through all the B.S. As artists of color, we're at the top of the pyramid in the market. Without us, there is no market. Period."

Whether she's reflecting herself or channeling the influence of Édouard Manet or Henri Matisse, Thomas uses her work to engage with the Black female body and its historic narratives and possibilities.

VIVIEN THOMAS

(1910–1985)

"I had always taken my activity in life as a purely personal matter, yet now I began asking myself questions: Was my story worth the effort? Would others really be interested?"

Despite never having attended medical school, Vivien Thomas developed a stunning surgical technique while working as a lab assistant to Alfred Blalock, a white surgeon, at the height of segregation in the Jim Crow South. Thomas wasn't a doctor; he hadn't even graduated from college. But with Blalock, he pioneered the "blue baby" procedure, which corrected a cardiac defect in newborns in which the blood was misdirected. This surgery was considered groundbreaking for several reasons. First, until Blalock and Thomas, no one had ever performed heart surgery. And second, performing heart surgery on toddlers or babies required specialized tools. Thomas made this equipment in Blalock's laboratory.

Although he was born in New Iberia, Louisiana, Thomas grew up in Nashville, where his father, a carpenter, had relocated the family in 1912. He intended to pursue a medical degree, but the Great Depression impacted his ability to earn money for his tuition, and he was forced to postpone his education. In 1930, Thomas was referred to Blalock at Vanderbilt University, who needed an able and responsive assistant. They ultimately worked collaboratively together for more than thirty years.

It wasn't a simple dynamic. Early on, Thomas had to work relentlessly, studying textbooks and overseeing the lab experiments for little pay. In a segregated society, there was no demonstrated path toward promotion or tangible opportunity for a Black man. But Thomas persevered, becoming a senior research fellow within four years and reaching greater heights as his career evolved. When Blalock was invited to Johns Hopkins in 1940 as chief surgeon, he bucked tradition and made sure that Thomas was a part of the deal. Blalock described Thomas's hands as being more instrumental in the development of open-heart surgery than his own. Thomas became renowned not just for his dexterity, but for his ability to take large medical queries, distill them into simple actionable steps, and then actually execute those steps. The pair's advancements helped the medical community treat not only their patients in the United States but also shock-affected servicemen during World War II.

Thomas's status among cardiac surgeons is legendary. In the latter part of his career, he joined the medical school faculty at Johns Hopkins and was responsible for training many surgeons—without his ever having secured a degree in the field himself.

TONI TIPTON-MARTIN

(1959–PRESENT)

"I hope to disrupt the messaging about African American food traditions and have people simply accept, honor, and appreciate this work at its face value."

In 1991, early in her career, Toni Tipton-Martin became the first Black food editor at Cleveland's *Plain Dealer.* She then topped herself by being appointed editor-in-chief at *Cook's Country* magazine in 2020, the first person of color to lead an America's Test Kitchen publication. Her role makes her one of only a handful of Black editors to command a major American food publication (or a food section of a general publication) in US history.

A constant thread throughout Tipton-Martin's work has been the expansion of the story of Black food in the United States. Her contributions are in conversation with leading writers and culinary historians such as Jessica B. Harris, Frederick Douglass Opie, and Adrian Miller, whose collective work conveys a full, rich narrative of American food. To tell the story of Black food is ultimately to tell the true story of America.

Although the most optimistic interpretations of American cuisine acknowledge a wide-ranging cultural input, the story according to mainstream media has been that Black cooking authorship, when it exists, is ancillary to Eurocentric preferences and born of instinct and thoughtless rudimentary acts. Tipton-Martin noticed this biased narrative while working as a food writer at the *Los Angeles Times* in the 1980s. The test kitchen library was filled with both modern and early recipe collections, cookbooks that stretched across time and place. But Black cooks were absent, which she knew to be a misrepresentation of Black contributions to American cuisine. After all, it had been Black women, in a large number of cases, who had led white-owned kitchens throughout more than three hundred years of slavery and segregation.

Her interests resulted in a decades-long accumulation of Black-authored cookbooks, a collection that has grown to more than three hundred tomes today. That research yielded her important and beautiful book *The Jemima Code* (2015), which through vivid illustration, photography, and contextual essays records two centuries' worth of African American authorship. In telling the stories of these mostly women authors, Tipton-Martin confronts the visual manifestation of the domestic "mammy," Aunt Jemima, whose caricature was created to reinforce white-dominant narratives of Black inferiority during the rise of Black parity in the early 1900s. In making visible and timely so many long-forgotten pages, Tipton-Martin acknowledges the true authority, professionalism, and creativity of Black American cooks. Building on the award-winning scholarship of *The Jemima Code*, Tipton-Martin published *Jubilee: Recipes from Two Centuries of African American Cooking* in 2019, for which she won the James Beard Award for best American cookbook.

KWAME TURE

(1941–1998)

"['Black Power'] is a call for black people in this country to unite, to recognize their heritage, to build a sense of community. It is a call for black people to define their own goals, to lead their own organizations."

Kwame Ture, born Stokely Carmichael, was a civil rights leader best known for coining the term "Black Power" and for his leadership of the Student Nonviolent Coordinating Committee (SNCC). He changed his name in 1978 to pay homage to the African leaders who inspired him—Kwame Nkrumah, the Ghanaian revolutionary, and Ahmed Sékou Touré, who became the first president of Guinea.

Ture's path as a political leader began in Trinidad, where he was born, and landed him in the Bronx, where he spent part of his childhood. While working with SNCC in the early 1960s, Ture protested in the South and was repeatedly arrested in places like Greenwood, Mississippi. This was a town where the White Citizens' Council enforced sharecropping on Black residents in response to efforts to organize and vote. He was jailed alongside John Lewis in Mississippi, and he marched in Selma. He learned nonviolent resistance from SNCC founder Ella Baker, who'd also mentored Diane Nash, among many other young activists.

But after being arrested so many times—he said he lost count after thirty-two—and seeing so many people abused and killed as a result of government-sanctioned violence, Ture revised his thinking and expectations about what the United States could ever hope to offer Black people. His resulting "Black Power" represented a new approach to asserting Black political and cultural identity. Acting on his Black Power stance, Ture joined the Black Panther Party and later became its prime minister. His positions met with some resistance within the Black community: in the same way that the Black Lives Matter movement faced intentional misrepresentation, the words "Black Power" were perceived as too radical and off-putting by many Blacks—those who were inclined to follow the more accommodating path of the SNCC and the Southern Christian Leadership Conference. Despite qualified acceptance of his approach, the influence he wielded was vast; at almost every stage of his life people were staggered and swayed by his overwhelming charm and intellect.

In his influential 1967 book *Black Power: The Politics of Liberation*, which he wrote with Charles Hamilton, Ture spoke about the web of "institutional racism" that Black people were fighting to overcome. In an increasingly volatile political environment, his calls for Black Power were seen as approaching anarchy, even while he spoke of Black people uniting across the diaspora to join forces and organize. He lived in Guinea for the last decades of his life and continued to advocate for the All-African People's Revolutionary Party, which worked toward the liberation of all Black people.

MORRIE TURNER

(1923–2014)

"It has to be real. And funny. I don't think anybody would remember it unless it's funny. You make 'em laugh, then you make 'em think. They might even change their mind."

The comic strip *Wee Pals*, about a group of childhood playmates, made history when Morrie Turner first syndicated it in 1965. Very early in his career, Turner wondered why there were no Black people in cartoons. His mentor, *Peanuts* cartoonist Charles M. Schulz, encouraged him to create one. *Wee Pals* was the first comic to feature characters from different racial and ethnic backgrounds. That's all it took for the comic to be considered edgy. At the time, only a couple of newspapers carried it, even though the syndication service had hundreds of newspapers signed up. Then tragedy struck when Martin Luther King Jr. was assassinated in April 1968. Thousands of people in cities across the United States erupted in anger and despair, and the uprisings held the nation's attention. Suddenly, more newspapers began subscribing to Turner's comic strip for their local audiences. When he was interviewed by a TV reporter, he said of that shift, "Suddenly everybody was interested in me." Within a few months of King's death, the number of newspapers carrying *Wee Pals* went from a couple to more than a hundred.

Turner was born "Morris" in Oakland, California, but preferred to go by "Morrie." He was primarily raised by his mother, a nurse, while his father, a Pullman porter, traveled for work. Although he'd had an interest in drawing from childhood, he developed his craft as a journalist and illustrator for the Army Air Corps in World War II, working for the Tuskegee Airmen's newspaper. He went on to freelance for various publications, including *Ebony* and the *Saturday Evening Post*.

In *Wee Pals*, Turner set out to create the characters he didn't see portrayed elsewhere. His character Nipper was a Black boy who wore a Confederate baseball cap and had a dog named General Lee. In an interview late in his life, Turner said the cap represented "forgiveness" of the South. He realized years after creating the strip that he was Nipper. "I didn't know that at the beginning," he said.

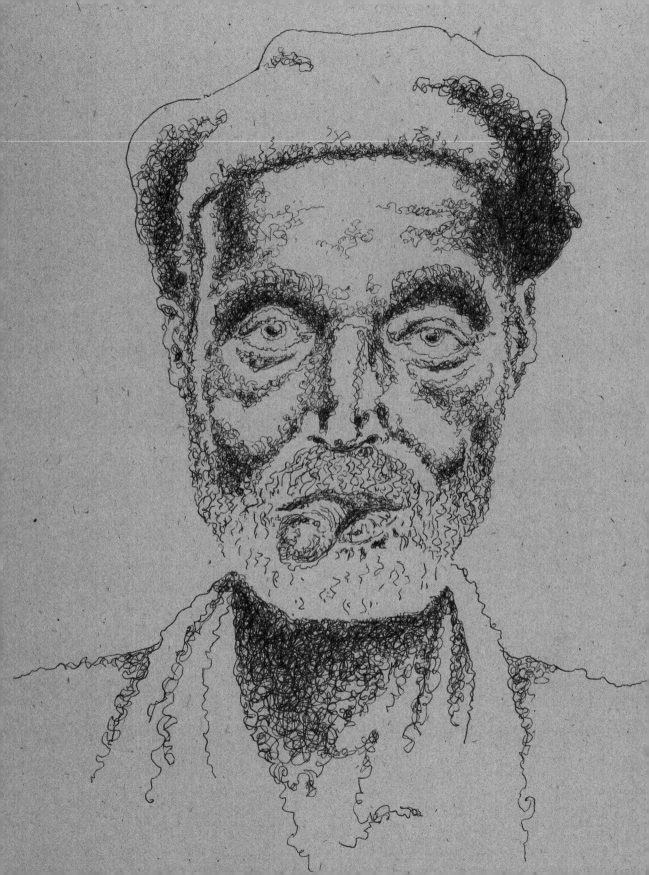

MELVIN VAN PEEBLES

(1932–2021)

"I don't consider myself a sociologist, I consider myself a filmmaker, among other things. Maybe an asshole but a filmmaker."

Best known for his work as a filmmaker in his self-produced 1971 Blaxploitation action thriller *Sweet Sweetback's Baadasssss Song*, Melvin Van Peebles has led the most unordinary life. A musician, writer, and pioneer of rap music, he made his art in his own way.

When I think about Van Peebles and his enormous footprint on American culture, I find myself thinking about language. There's language defined by white people and language defined by Black people. And of course, there's all the discourse in between. This language, these labels—what we call ourselves, what we call each other—are constantly shifting. I suspect that the word "Blaxploitation" will be one that shifts beneath our feet. Is it a word that's due for a narrative makeover? Will "Blaxploitation" become a word viewed through a Black lens and experience? We Black folks haven't had a discussion about our own reckoning of this moment in filmmaking, but we will. And who will lead the charge? I wouldn't be surprised if it were Van Peebles himself, the man whose films birthed the term, who ultimately acted as translator and guide.

Born in Chicago, Van Peebles grew up in Illinois. He studied at Ohio Wesleyan University, where he earned a degree in English literature in 1953 before joining the US Air Force. After serving, he lived abroad for several years, including in the Netherlands, Mexico, and France (where he took to writing novels in French), and then tried his hand at making short films.

In Hollywood, no one was interested in his early efforts at becoming a filmmaker. While he waited for his fortunes to turn, he wrote another French novel and then based his first film on that book, *La Permission*. His 1967 short *The Story of a Three-Day Pass* was Van Peebles's entry in the San Francisco Film Festival, submitted as a French national film. In the movie, Van Peebles explored the complications of life as a Black soldier in the US Army. The film was released in 1968 in the US, and Van Peebles began his work in Hollywood.

The revolutionary implications of *Sweet Sweetback's Baadasssss Song* are impossible to miss. On the run from the police after rescuing a Black Panther member in a bad situation, Sweet Sweetback emerges as the victor, a role not historically given to Black male actors on the screen. Produced, directed, written, and scored by Van Peebles, with a soundtrack featuring Earth, Wind & Fire, the movie defined the independent Black cinema of the "new wave." The film, funded by private investments, earned more than $10 million, forever changing the expectations of Black-led, Black-funded movies.

SARAH VAUGHAN

(1924–1990)

"I am not a special person. I am a regular person who does special things."

If the definition of bebop could be distilled to a single voice, the honor might go to Sarah Vaughan, one of the greatest singers the jazz form has ever seen. Known as "the Divine One" or "Sassy," Vaughan was regarded by iconic contemporaries including Billie Holiday and Ella Fitzgerald as possessing a singular gift. Vaughan consistently captivated audiences with her rich, warm tone throughout her fifty-year career, recording music or touring with the likes of Count Basie, Quincy Jones, Benny Carter, and Billy Eckstine.

Vaughan grew up singing in her church in Newark, New Jersey, where she also learned piano. She often traveled into New York City, and once she entered the Apollo Theater's Amateur Night contest in Harlem. She sang "Body and Soul" and won the evening. But the prize—ten dollars and a week's worth of performances—changed her life. She returned to the Apollo as an opening act for Ella Fitzgerald in November 1942.

While singing at the Apollo, Vaughan was introduced to bandleader and pianist Earl Hines. After a quick audition, Hines replaced his female singer with Vaughan. She joined Hines and Eckstine's band in 1944 and later went on to record solo. She famously collaborated with Charlie Parker and Dizzy Gillespie on her interpretation of Gillespie's hit "A Night in Tunisia." On her version of that tune, "Interlude," she sounds at once light and airy, with the deep soulfulness and sweeping loops that made her voice so beloved and identifiable throughout her career. She accomplished the rare feat of being able to lend her own style to popular standards with a far-reaching, operatic skill; at the same time, she could dig into straight-ahead jazz with improvisation, soaring tonal heights, and grooves equal to any other musician on the bandstand.

Sarah Vaughan was one of those rare singers whose voice soundtracks the first kiss, that third Valentine's dinner. You want it playing in the background when you not only say you're sorry but mean it. For me, Vaughan's music moves me to dance. Well, if I were a dancer. I'm not, but when I put her record on, I listen to her songs and imagine which one I would sway to. "Misty" springs to mind, but so does "Cheek to Cheek." Her voice braces a mood, deepens an emotion. I think of my feet as willing but awkward. "Embraceable You," "Lullaby of Birdland"— both songs hold a quiet laughter. I feel altogether shy. "Tenderly." No. For me, it's "Summertime." Every time I listen to Vaughan's rendition, I find myself feeling courageous. One of these days, I'm going to slip close to the man I love and dance.

MADAM C. J. WALKER

(1867–1919)

"I am not satisfied in making money for myself. I endeavor to provide employment for hundreds of the women of my race."

Born as Sarah Breedlove to formerly enslaved parents who became sharecroppers in Louisiana, Madam C. J. Walker was seemingly headed down the path toward domestic labor. She died in Irvington, New York, as one of the wealthiest businesswomen in history.

Her older siblings were enslaved by Robert W. Burney on his Louisiana plantation, but Walker was born into freedom in 1867, four years after the Emancipation Proclamation. In 1872, her mother died of cholera. Her father remarried, but then he too died a year later. She was orphaned at the age of seven. Walker moved to Vicksburg, Mississippi, at ten years old, where she lived with her sister. There, Walker worked as a maid. When asked about her life, Walker would often say, "I had little or no opportunity when I started out in life, having been left an orphan and being without mother or father since I was seven years of age." She received only three months of formal education. When Walker was a teenager, she worked as a sharecropper in cotton fields in Mississippi. She married and had a daughter soon after that. After her husband died in 1887, she relocated to St. Louis to join her brothers, who had settled there as barbers; she worked as a laundress. Her estate credits relationships with other Black women in the area, specifically those in the National Association of Colored Women, with helping her imagine new opportunities for herself.

Suffering from hair loss as a result of poor scalp health, Walker sought out products and home remedies. She was introduced to Annie Malone's hair-care line and later became an employee of Malone's, selling her products in Denver in 1905. Walker changed her name after marrying her third husband, Charles Joseph Walker, and launched her own business after that. She sold Madam Walker's Wonderful Hair Grower and kept a robust schedule traveling throughout the South, promoting her scalp treatments and using her own experiences as public testimony.

Walker's company was incredibly successful, eventually making her a millionaire. By 1910, she had a training school in Indianapolis, where she manufactured her product and trained sellers and hair-care professionals. Building on her success, Walker expanded her business into the Caribbean and Central America. As her company grew, Walker became known for her philanthropy, donating to the YMCA, educational scholarships for students, and the NAACP, among other causes. She moved to Harlem in 1913, and then to the Hudson Valley in 1918, where she lived at Villa Lewaro, a sprawling Italian-inspired estate designed by the Black architect Vertner Woodson Tandy. She died there at the age of fifty-one in 1919.

MAGGIE LENA WALKER

(1864–1934)

"Let us put our money together.... Let us have a bank that will ... turn [the nickels] into dollars."

Born in 1864 to Elizabeth Draper, a former slave, and Eccles Cuthbert, an Irish-born white Confederate soldier who some historians believed raped her mother, Walker grew up in Richmond, Virginia, helping her mother work as a laundress. She joined the Independent Order of St. Luke (IOSL), an African American mutual-aid society founded by Mary Prout, a free Black woman, in Baltimore. Like many organizations of its type, it worked communally to support Black families. After completing her studies at the Richmond Colored Normal School in 1883, she worked as a teacher. But she was forced to resign after marrying her husband, Armstead Walker, as married women were prohibited by the school from teaching.

Walker became more active in the IOSL, becoming the organization's leader in 1899. Seeing the impact that Black women had on their families and communities encouraged Walker to create programs and share resources in Richmond that could better support and develop these women. "Who is so helpless as the Negro woman?" she asked in a 1901 speech. "Who is so circumscribed and hemmed in, in the race of life, in the struggle for bread, meat, and clothing, as the Negro woman?"

In 1903, she founded the St. Luke Penny Savings Bank, which under her leadership grew, by the mid-1920s, to more than one hundred thousand members. Until the passage of the Civil Rights Act of 1964, it was legal for white-owned banks to refuse to lend money to Black customers. When those banks did accept business from Black people, it was often at higher rates, a practice that often drove Black borrowers to more predatory payday lenders and loan sharks. Those experiences made Black people deeply suspicious of banking practices.

Walker went as far as New Jersey to encourage Black depositors, even hiring young students to promote the bank door to door. She was successful, with assets reaching about $530,000 in 1920, which today would be about $7 million. Her clientele were primarily Black women. Walker moved the bank into the also-new St. Luke building in 1905, but white merchants boycotted any vendor that supplied the store. The Emporium was devastated, but Walker persevered.

The bank kept evening hours most of the week to ensure that working Black customers could handle their affairs. Walker used local references when assessing creditworthiness, rather than relying solely on financial assets. The bank made small loans, knowing that small gestures could be deeply meaningful to those rubbing pennies together. By the 1920s, Richmond had some of the highest levels of Black-owned homes in the country. Walker managed the bank through the Great Depression.

In her lifetime, Walker trained accountants, stenographers, journalists, and secretaries and was known to match her entrepreneurial efforts with a consistent philanthropic presence.

CARRIE MAE WEEMS

(1953–PRESENT)

"Art is the one place we all turn to for solace."

The Kitchen Table Series, Carrie Mae Weems's twenty-picture work from 1990, uses black-and-white photography and text to document the interior, deeply personal universe of a Black woman's kitchen. With herself as the central character, she shows a woman interacting with the friends and loved ones in her life. The series had an extraordinary impact when it was first shown, and it remains today an iconic and unmatched feat of exploring an artist's identity. Part of the reason Weems made the series is because she hadn't seen women, particularly Black women, engage as subjects with the camera in such a way.

The series confronts the idea of family, the constraints of monogamy, the responsibility of parenthood, and the limits of lovers. Various works from the series are now housed at the Los Angeles County Museum of Art, the National Gallery of Art in Washington, DC, the Library of Congress, and the Museum of Modern Art in New York, among others.

For decades, Weems has used photography to examine class, racial identity, and culture in the United States. Often relying on herself as subject or character, she is celebrated for her pivotal and challenging works on gender in both the mundane and extraordinary circumstances of life. In 2013, she was awarded a MacArthur "Genius" Fellowship for her contributions to the field. She became the first Black woman to have a retrospective at the Guggenheim, in 2014.

Weems grew up in Portland, Oregon, born to former sharecroppers who had migrated from Mississippi. She graduated from the California Institute of the Arts and the University of California, San Diego, and studied folklore at the University of California, Berkeley. Later, when she moved to New York, she was greatly influenced by the Kamoinge Workshop, an organization of Black photographers, and her friend and mentor photographer Dawoud Bey at the Studio Museum of Harlem. The works of Zora Neale Hurston inspired her, as did the collaborative work of Roy DeCarava and Langston Hughes in *The Sweet Flypaper of Life*.

Her work has always pushed against the political. In 1995, Weems used an archive of 1850 daguerreotypes of formerly enslaved Black women, initially commissioned by a Harvard scientist, to challenge their depiction as property, as objects. She reproduced the images to enhance the humanity of the subjects. At first Harvard threatened to sue Weems, seeming to miss both the irony of the role the institution had played in dehumanizing those Black women and the fact that violence over race had persisted, over one hundred years later, when Weems attempted to reclaim that history, that stolen narrative of Black womanhood. Later, the university acquired part of the series for its own collection.

Weems continues to make art and create space for others to develop and flourish, hosting workshops and creative "think tanks" where artists can mine the contradictions of this country as they ask their own questions.

IDA B. WELLS

(1862–1931)

"One had better die fighting against injustice than die like a dog or a rat in a trap."

In 1892, Ida B. Wells published a pamphlet called *Southern Horrors*, documenting the use of lynching as a terrorist tactic to intimidate and oppress Black people. In it, she recounted the genocidal efforts by white Americans to enforce notions of Black inferiority in society. An intrepid journalist, activist, and researcher, she made it her life's work to bring awareness to what Black people were enduring on the other side of so-called freedom.

Born into slavery in Holly Springs, Mississippi, in 1862, Wells was freed by the Emancipation Proclamation. When she was sixteen years old, both her parents and little brother died from yellow fever. She then went to work and, with her grandmother's help, took care of her remaining siblings.

She relocated to Memphis, where she worked as a newspaper editor for the *Memphis Free Speech and Headlight*, which she co-owned. In 1884, a train conductor ordered Wells to give up her seat in the first-class ladies' car (prejudice having survived where slavery couldn't). She refused the conductor, and two men dragged her out of the car. Wells sued the train company. She hired a Black lawyer to represent her, but he was paid off by the railroad.

She then hired a white attorney. Ultimately, she won her case.

In 1889, Thomas Henry Moss, owner of the People's Grocery, was murdered by a mob in Memphis, Tennessee. In her role as a journalist, she investigated the attack and began chronicling it and other incidents of white mob violence. Her writing was known to be incisive and courageous, openly criticizing the notion that Black men were lynched in response to attacks against white women. She had found through dogged investigation that these accusations were untrue. So compelling was her writing that Frederick Douglass, himself no slouch with a pen, wrote to her that his words paled in comparison to hers. Her articles were circulated overseas and in Black-owned publications throughout the United States.

Wells was eventually forced to leave Memphis after her writing angered white locals so deeply that they burned down her press. She moved to Chicago, but she continued to travel globally and was known to confront white women during their suffrage efforts with the realities of lynching and its impact on Black people back home.

CHARLES WHITE

(1918–1979)

"Art must be an integral part of the struggle. It can't simply mirror what's taking place. It must adapt itself to human needs. It must ally itself with the forces of liberation. The fact is, artists have always been propagandists. I have no use for artists who try to divorce themselves from the struggle."

The 1943 mural *The Contribution of the Negro to Democracy in America* by Charles White remains in an auditorium at Hampton University in Virginia. Employing a particularly Black American aesthetic of transposing historical periods, White painted Black Union soldiers on the march, George Washington Carver at work in his laboratory, and abolitionists and revolutionaries Frederick Douglass, Denmark Vesey, Harriet Tubman, and Nat Turner poised in action. The work is sweeping and almost sensational in the vast, Odyssean style White used to convey more than a century of Black history in one piece. White went on to create paintings, lithographs, and pencil drawings with other grand historical themes. At the time of his death, his work was being shown concurrently in forty-nine museums.

Born and raised in Chicago, White spent many childhood hours at the library, where his mother would often drop him off when she went to work; there he read about African American history. He took weekend classes at the Art Institute of Chicago and was later offered scholarships to study at the Frederic Mizen Academy of Art. Both academies refused to officially admit him once they learned he was Black, however. He went on to become a staff artist for the National Negro Congress, an organization that, from the mid-1930s, worked to establish civil rights and force New Deal policies to include Black people.

White's style of art focused on representational figures, even while many other artists moved into more abstract forms. He would eventually call his works "images of dignity." In *Hope for the Future*, a mother holding a child in front of a window looks upon a desolate view outside—a noose dangles from a tree in the background. With softness, White manages to highlight the harshness of the lived experience of Black people in their daily lives. He never resided in the South but visited relatives there. In fifteen years, his family experienced five lynchings: three of his uncles and two cousins.

White moved to Southern California after losing a lung to tuberculosis, which he'd contracted while serving in World War II. On the West Coast he became friends with photographer Gordon Parks, painter Jacob Lawrence, and actor Sidney Poitier, whom he'd met in New York. Harry Belafonte was also a friend and supporter. In the foreword of White's 1967 book *Images of Dignity: The Drawings of Charles White*, Belafonte wrote, "His lines are clear, his people are alive with a zest for life and the story of living manifest in their faces and their bodies."

White taught in the LA area, joining the faculty at the Otis Art Institute in Pasadena in 1965. His students included David Hammons and Kerry James Marshall.

MAURICE WHITE

(1941–2016)

"I have learned that music helps a lot of people survive, and they want songs that can give them something—I guess you could call it hope."

An innovative band that drew from jazz, R&B, funk, and Latin traditions to define its own unique sound, Earth, Wind & Fire was cofounded by Memphis drummer and singer Maurice White and his half brother, Verdine, in 1969; they were later joined by fellow lead vocalist Philip Bailey. The band broke new ground with infectious songs that captured the groove and high energy of the 1970s and continue to inspire younger generations.

White was born in Memphis, Tennessee, where he lived with his grandmother in the projects. While attending Booker T. Washington High School, he started a band with childhood friends. He also made frequent trips to Chicago to visit his mother, Edna, before moving there. Maurice White attended a Chicago music conservatory before playing with artists like Muddy Waters and Ramsey Lewis. He also became a studio musician at Chess Records in Chicago. He played with artists such as Etta James, Chuck Berry, the Impressions, and Buddy Guy.

When White launched Earth, Wind & Fire, he drew inspiration from a core of jazz and blues standards but sought also to cultivate a unique type of energy through an uplifting lifestyle—eating well, honoring one's spirituality, practicing self-education, and generating meaningful connections in life—that could be felt in the music. White's vision gave birth to one of the most influential funk bands in American music, with its high-octane live performances that evoked an acrobatic circus, and visual imagery full of African religious and mythological symbols. White sang of fantasies, getaways, and soaring through dreams. His music was like science fiction; it created worlds to explore. In a masterful career that lasted decades, he helped articulate a vision of Black life that felt approachable and real even as it was divined only in his imagination.

CLARENCE "CAP" WIGINGTON

(1883–1967)

"Most of his buildings are still in use today—a testimony not only to the beauty and grace of form but also the functionality."

—David V. Taylor, historian

The city of St. Paul, Minnesota, lays claim to being the site of sixty municipal buildings designed by Clarence "Cap" Wigington, the first Black architect registered in the state and the first Black American to serve as the senior architectural designer on any project. More than fifty years after his death, his output remains among the highest of Black architects in modern history—a stunning commentary on both his talent during a pre–Civil Rights Act era and the architecture industry's long-criticized failure to nurture and support Black talent.

Wigington served the city of St. Paul from 1915 to 1947, during which time he designed park buildings, schools, fire stations, and recreational spaces. Several of his works are featured in the National Register of Historic Places: the Highland Park Water Tower (1928); the Clarence W. Wigington Pavilion (1941; renamed from the Harriet Island Pavilion in 1998); and the Holman Field Administration Building (1939). His work, often featuring clean lines, unobstructed facades, and classical references, showcases a muted approach to modern design.

Born in Lawrence, Kansas, and eventually landing with his family in Omaha, Nebraska, Wigington graduated from high school in 1898. A few years later he took a clerk job with Thomas Kimball, a nationally celebrated architect. He was later promoted to draftsman, a technical role that required him to make sketches of works in development and include calculations for their eventual construction, from materials to weight restrictions. Ten years after getting his high-school diploma, he left Kimball's company to form his own practice.

In 1914 Wigington moved to St. Paul, contributing to the growing population that was turning the city into a boom town. After taking a civil service exam, he was hired as a municipal architect. Although he was eventually promoted to senior architect, he never made the lead role of city architect, which would have been a political appointment. An artist at heart, Wigington, like many other Black artists, sought creative outlets for his talent: he was renowned for designing massive ice castles for the annual St. Paul Winter Carnival in the late 1930s and the 1940s. In 1941, in Como Park, 270 WPA workers executed Wigington's ice palace, which used 22,000 ice blocks from McCarrons Lake. It came in at an impressive 80 feet high and 123 feet wide.

Wigington cofounded the Sterling Club, a social group for railroad porters and other male service workers. He's credited with founding the Home Guards of Minnesota, a militia for Black men, which he created after the Minnesota National Guard denied him entry. In the Home Guards, he held the rank of captain. The nickname "Cap" followed him ever after.

RAVEN WILKINSON

(1935–2018)

"People were curious because they had a certain idea . . . of what African American people were like . . . and they didn't believe my mother and I were African American."

When five-year-old Raven Wilkinson attended a 1940 performance of *Coppélia* by the Ballet Russe de Monte Carlo in her home city of New York, she was so taken with the theatric sensibility of the orchestra and the lights that she cried. Fifteen years later, she emerged as a pivotal dancer in that same company, the first Black woman to tour with a classical ballet company.

Wilkinson began taking classes at the age of nine in Manhattan. Her father was a dentist and her mother a homemaker; it was she who had taken Wilkinson to see that first, influential performance. The family lived in Harlem, in the Dunbar Apartments, known at various periods to be home to such figures as W. E. B. Du Bois, Paul Robeson, and Bill "Bojangles" Robinson. She was the only Black girl in her class. Her fair skin often allowed people to project onto her their own interpretation of her background. In 2006 interview, Wilkinson recounted, "People always thought we were something; they never dreamed we were what we were."

In 1951, the dance school at which Wilkinson studied was sold to Sergei Denham, the director of Ballet Russe. Wilkinson soon began studying at Columbia while continuing her dance education, and she set her sights on dancing professionally. In 1955, at age twenty, she was accepted by Ballet Russe and admitted to its corps de ballet. She began touring in its ensemble. Wilkinson's first solo role came during her second season, a waltz in *Les Sylphides*.

Wilkinson's love of dance coincided with a stunningly violent period for Black people in the United States, which meant that her willingness to tour in the segregated South put her at constant risk. She recalled arriving in Montgomery, Alabama, in November 1956: "As we drove into the town the streets were covered in sheets and hoods. . . . It was a Klan rally." Later on in that same trip, she observed in a hotel dining room dozens of white parties eating at their respective tables. They appeared to her as normal, average people. Then, as she went to sit down, she noticed a pile of white sheets and hoods folded on a chair in the corner. She suddenly realized that many of the folks eating around her were the same people who had marched down the street in celebration of white-supremacist ideals. It was a crystallizing moment, one that she never forgot. Experiences like that, combined with intimidation, as when two Ku Klux Klan members stormed the stage during a performance in an Alabama theater, weighed heavily.

Wilkinson died in 2018 at the age of eighty-three. Her influence can be seen in the groundbreaking choreography and dance of Debbie Allen, who has transformed ideas of what classical dance should look like. And Wilkinson's trailblazing was clearly part of Misty Copeland's historic achievement: in 2015 Copeland became the first Black woman promoted to principal dancer in the American Ballet Theatre.

GEORGE WASHINGTON WILLIAMS

(1849–1891)

"Let Ohio speak for human rights, for universal manhood suffrage, for fair and honest elections, for economy and purity in public affairs, for honest money and stable government."

In his brief forty-two years of life, George Washington Williams published three exhaustive tomes on the Black experience in the United States—the two-volume *History of the Negro Race in America from 1619 to 1880: Negroes as Slaves, as Soldiers, and as Citizens* and *A History of the Negro Troops in the War of the Rebellion*, published in the late 1880s. In addition to his work as a historian, he was a soldier and minister.

Born in Bedford Springs, Pennsylvania, in 1849, Williams ran away at the age of fourteen to join the Union Army. After serving in the Civil War, he went to Mexico in support of the troops that fought Maximilian, the Austrian archduke who reigned during the Second Mexican Empire. Williams returned to enlist in the 10th Cavalry, an all-Black unit of the US Army. After a medical discharge in 1868, he studied to become a minister and worked at churches in Boston and Cincinnati. Pursuing an interest in the welfare of Black peoples elsewhere, in 1890 Williams visited the Congo Free State, where he famously wrote an open letter to King Leopold II enumerating the ways he was "disenchanted, disappointed, and disheartened" by the treatment of native Africans at the hands of the king's men.

The historian John Hope Franklin noted in his biography of Williams that he came across correspondence between Williams and many contemporaries of the day, including Frederick Douglass; Robert Terrell, the first Black judge of Washington, DC; and Congressman John Mercer Langston, the first Black person to serve in the Virginia House of Representatives.

Williams is celebrated for his combined use of oral history and print archives in documenting Black stories. For his work on the Black Civil War troops, for example, he gathered extensive oral histories and used accounts from newspapers. His work is studied in academic circles that usually privilege Eurocentric traditions and forms of passing on knowledge over the forms found among people in the African diaspora. Williams is acknowledged by academics and historians for writing objective rather than biased accounts of Black history.

Williams became ill in Egypt and traveled to London, en route home. He died in England in 1891, from tuberculosis and pleurisy. In 1975 a tombstone was placed at his gravesite, memorializing Williams as an "Afro-American historian."

MARIE SELIKA WILLIAMS

(CA. 1849–1937)

"The Paris Figaro *said the soprano sang with perfect ease from C to C and had trills like a 'feathered songster.' The* Figaro *continued saying her 'Echo Song' could not be surpassed. 'It was beyond any criticism. It was an artistic triumph.'"*

—Sonya R. Gable-Wilson, professor

Marie Selika Williams was the first Black opera singer to perform at the White House, where she sang for President Rutherford Hayes and his wife in 1878. A wealthy benefactor's interest had allowed her to study music in Cincinnati, Ohio, where her family had moved after leaving Natchez, Mississippi. Williams performed in the White House Green Room with a repertoire that included "Ernani, Involami" and "The Last Rose of Summer." She toured nationally, in the Caribbean, and in Europe, where she sang for Queen Victoria.

Before there was Marian Anderson, before Kathleen Battle, there was Marie Selika Williams. Her life is filled with accomplishments. It is for that reason I am constantly stunned that she is not better remembered. Who honors this woman? Who marvels at her gift? I found two video examples that in a strange way explicate Black excellence in America. The first is a young Black girl from Natchez, Mississippi, giving a school presentation about Williams. It perfectly captures a moment when some young person realizes, "Once, in my small town, where no one I know got very far, there was a Marie Selika Williams. And she was so undeniably talented, she sang for the president of the United States. She traveled all over the world. She sang for kings and queens." The second video also extols Williams's virtues, but its agenda is clear: Williams is a Black opera singer who sang for a Republican president, which means that the Republican party is a friend of Black people, even today. While championing Williams's accomplishments, this argument robs Marie Selika Williams of her humanity. It's sadder still when you realize for most of her life, Williams wanted to be a brilliant musician, first and foremost.

Opportunities to entertain as a Black classical vocalist were sorely limited for Williams at a time when minstrelsy dominated live performances. Williams taught at the Martin-Smith Music School in New York in the latter part of her life. She died in New York at the age of eighty-seven.

PAUL REVERE WILLIAMS

(1894–1980)

"Without having the wish to 'show them,' I developed a fierce desire to 'show myself.' I wanted to vindicate every ability I had. I wanted to acquire new abilities. I wanted to prove that I, as an individual, deserved a place in the world."

Los Angeles is often defined by its climate, its geography, and the mark of the entertainment industry, but it's the portfolio of architect Paul Revere Williams, a native of the city, that for many best captures the spirit of Southern California.

Williams became known for his residential work—he designed more than two thousand private homes, often with a nod toward midcentury modern panache—including for celebrities such as Frank Sinatra, Lucille Ball and Desi Arnaz, Bill "Bojangles" Robinson, and Cary Grant. But his commercial work is just as impressive. He renovated the Polo Lounge at the Beverly Hills Hotel, designed the MCA Building in Beverly Hills, and contributed to the design of the 1961 Theme Building at the Los Angeles airport. Many iconic LA design elements—think curving staircases, the color combo of pastel pink and green, and outdoor spaces that blend seamlessly with indoors—can be attributed to Williams's aesthetic.

When looking at Williams's achievements, one can't help but notice what he had to do in order to become a successful architect. Williams developed an interesting skill when dealing with his moneyed white clientele: he taught himself how to draw upside down. In this way, his clients were able to sit across from him (and feel comfortable), rather than having to sit side by side with a Black man. When he was on a construction site, he often walked the grounds with his hands behind his back so that his white workers wouldn't be tempted to shake his hand. He wasn't worried about his construction team being racist; rather, a white passerby who saw such an exchange might cause problems. Like so many Black professionals before and since, Williams pursued a career where it wasn't enough to be brilliant; he had to soothe racist fears as well. That he learned how to operate successfully in such compromised situations is evidenced by the fact that he was certified as a building contractor in 1915, became a licensed architect in California in 1921, and went on to become the first Black member of the American Institute of Architects in 1923.

BRADFORD YOUNG

(1977–PRESENT)

"This is not a competition, this is life ... it's not a game. Take every opportunity to do your best. Don't be distracted nor persuaded by somebody else's opinion of what is and what isn't. You are the only person who can determine what is and what isn't."

Most people watch movies for the actors or the story line. And then there are people, far fewer, who watch movies to see where the light is sourced from. Though light is what allows a movie to exist, it's a factor often overlooked by passive viewers. When the lighting is wrong, a movie may become lifeless. But when it's right, it makes the story sing. Bradford Young, a celebrated cinematographer and director of photography, is a master of capturing light. His definitive style is apparent in films such as *When They See Us*, *Selma*, *A Most Violent Year*, *Solo: A Star Wars Story*, and *Arrival*, for which, in 2017, he was the first Black person to earn an Academy Award nomination in cinematography.

Young is known for his ability to use natural light, his style of creating richness in skin tone by nurturing underexposed light, and his willingness to allow the camera lens to remain intimately close to its subject, as was so painfully evident in *When They See Us*, the Ava DuVernay multipart film that chronicled the devastating story of five Black boys who were falsely accused and ultimately exonerated of attacking a white woman in New York's Central Park in 1989.

A native of Louisville, Kentucky, Young lived in Chicago later in his childhood before moving to Washington, DC, to attend Howard University, where he studied film and was inspired by artists including Jacob Lawrence, Aaron Douglas, and Romare Bearden. An eternal student of the form, even as he has become someone others hope to emulate, he constantly references the films that precede his work and publicly celebrates the mentors and colleagues on whom he relies for guidance and inspiration. Those figures include Ava DuVernay, Boots Riley, Malik Sayeed, Ryan Coogler, Johnny Simmons, and Ethiopian filmmaker Haile Gerima, who became Young's mentor at Howard. Watching Spike Lee's *School Daze* was pivotal for Young, who beforehand hadn't seen Black people reflected in cinema in a way that felt real for him. It's from this experience—seeing the film and seeing how Black audiences in theaters reacted to a film made for them—that he understood he wished to become someone who could also make stories come alive onscreen.

Young's work as a director of photography can also be seen in films such as *Pariah*, *Middle of Nowhere*, *Ain't Them Bodies Saints*, and *Mother of George*.

NOV -- 2022

KAREEM ABDUL-JABBAR JOURDON ANDERSON AMY ASHWOOD GARVEY 1936 BERLIN OLYMPI CS ATHLETES MARY MCLEOD BETHUNE TERRI LYNE CARRINGTON LEAH KAT CHE CELIA CRUZ

CATO ALEXANDER MAYA ANGELOU JAMES BALDWIN ED DWIGHT J. MAX BOND JR. HANNAH CRAFTS ROY DECARAVA ALTHEA G

BLACK LIVES MATTER CO FOUNDERS TARANA BURKE

LEBRONN P. BROOKS STEVE CANNON DICK GREGORY BE HA THA HAR GRA

CLAUDETTE COLVIN ABBY FISHER BILL T. JONES JO LE

JULIE DASH LYLA EASON LEAH PENNIMAN EMORY DOUGLAS

TONI MORRISON EVA JEFFERSON PATERSON HARRIET PO M

SATCHEL PAIGE PAUL ROBESON PATRICK RUSH SOS

DAVID RUGGLES AUGUSTA SAVAGE NINA SIMONE CARRIE MAE MA WEEMS

GIL SCOTT-HERON MADAM C.J. WALKER SARAH VAUGHAN CHARLES WHITE RAVEN MAURIE W WILKINS